PICKING
UP THE
CLYDE COLVIN
BESSON
PIECES

*Comments from some who have attended a **Picking Up The Pieces** seminar:*

"I was surprised to find myself so taken by your seminar. I am a Catholic and a former Trappist monk, so I consider myself fairly well grounded in the scriptures. Your extremely Christian approach to the problems faced by a divorced person was the best I have ever heard. Your seminar transcends the denominational aspects and gets to the heart of the matter. Your simple, honest and down to earth style is marvelous." — J.P.M.

"This was the most helpful seminar I have ever attended." — G.P.

"My only regret is that I didn't hear you a year ago . . . thanks so much for caring." — B.R.

"I thank you particularly for your ideas on 'Red Beans and Rice' (giving thanks to God in all circumstances and asking Him to provide red beans and rice when steak is out of the question for now)."
— C.L.C.

"Your thoughts have provided more personal relief and more constructive insight into my life than I have been yet able to find." — F.R.M.

"Thank you for helping so many with these lectures. Three years ago my marriage of thirty years fell to pieces. You have helped me find a way to pick up those pieces." — E.S.

Clyde C. Besson, founder and director of Christian Growth Ministries of Houston, Texas, is a graduate of Louisiana College and New Orleans Baptist Theological Seminary. He has had two decades of experience in pastorates and pastoral counseling (including extensive marriage and family counseling and work in the areas of drug and alcohol abuse), and is a professional adviser to Parents Without Partners, an organization which uses him frequently as a speaker. Besson is a widely traveled speaker and seminar leader, conducting his "Picking Up The Pieces," "Growing Together," "Keys to Success," and various other seminars and retreats aimed at providing resources assisting people to grow as whole persons.

PICKING
UP THE
CLYDE COLVIN
BESSON
PIECES

MOTT
MEDIA

PICKING UP THE PIECES: SUCCESSFUL SINGLE
LIVING FOR THE FORMERLY MARRIED

Leonard George Goss, Editor

Designed by Kurt Dietsch
Cover Photo by Tim Bieber
Manuscript edited by Leonard G. Goss and Joyce A. Hovelsrud

Manufactured in the United States of America

ISBN 0-915134-83-7

TABLE OF CONTENTS

1094

Preface

A man who had gone through a divorce told me that it was not only his marriage that fell apart but HIS WHOLE LIFE! As I reflected upon this statement, I thought of the desire of Jesus to help people pick up the pieces of their lives. With an inner urging to share His burden, I became concerned for the needs of the formerly married. I feld that the church was failing to meet these people where they were. Pious platitudes about the sacredness of marriage were of little help to those whose marriage had ended. In their pain, they were crying for practical help. I listened to these questions and began the search for viable answers.

I became involved in singles organizations within and without the church, teaching a Bible study on Sunday and speaking for different organizations, like Parents Without Partners. One Sunday several of these singles asked if I would be interested in doing a series of units to help the formerly married. I acknowledged that I was working on some ideas to provide practical Christian answers to the real questions being asked. However, I knew that I needed help to organize and promote the seminar. Several volunteered to assist, so PICKING UP THE PIECES was born. In July, 1975, I began the first series, presenting one unit a week for ten weeks. Since then, we have conducted seminars sponsored by Baptist, Methodist, Catholic, Church of God, Presbyterian and other churches, along with organizations such as Parents Without Partners.

People from areas outside Houston learned of the seminars and expressed a desire that we find some way to conduct the series in their areas. Thus, the weekend format evolved, utilizing Friday night and all day Saturday. We are excited about this new area of ministry with seminars either already conducted or presently being planned in many different states.

The publishing of this book fulfills the dream of many who wanted to see these ideas shared with those who could never at-

tend the seminar. Some gave their time and money for the tapes
of the sessions to be transcribed, as the first step toward publication. Our hope is that this book will help its readers as much as
the seminar has helped so many of its hearers.

I want to express my heartfelt gratitude to those who have
assisted in special ways. Barbara Baker Anderson provided the
organizational and promotional skills to get the first seminar
from the dream stage to reality. Jim and Loretta Thomas are due
mention for their dream and impetus to raise the money for
transcribing the tapes. Words cannot express my feelings for
Lana Gould, who transcribed the lecture tapes for subsequent
editing by the Mott Media staff. Lana, having profited from the
seminar, shared my dream and transformed PICKING UP THE
PIECES from spoken to written form. Without her assistance,
this book would still be a dream.

I am indebted to Jimmy Patterson for providing an office
for Christian Growth Ministries, and to W.D. Broadway, pastor
of the First Baptist Church of the Woodlands, for his
understanding and encouragement during the most difficult time
of my life.

To my former wife Joann and my children Cathy, Keith and
Janet, I express my love and thanks for sharing their time with
me as I developed the concepts presented in PICKING UP THE
PIECES.

I am thankful to Kevin and Chris Reagin for their
understanding during the times my wife travels with me as I conduct seminars. To my wife Cathy, my ultimate thanks for believing in me, sharing my dream and walking with me in this
ministry.

It is to the singles all over this nation that this book is
dedicated.

Chapter One

Making the Most
of a Difficult Situation

Many formerly marrieds have had very painful experiences. Some, after having been married for a number of years, have experienced the death of their mate. That is a painful experience. Others have been deserted by their mates, perhaps for another woman or another man. That is a painful experience. Some may have walked out on the other person after many years of frustration. That, too, is a painful experience. Whatever the reason for singleness, many problems and frustrations arise. Being single is not all it's cracked up to be.

To make the most of a difficult situation, you must first realize that you cannot give way to hopelessness. Since suicide is the natural culmination of hopelessness, it's a dangerous state in which to be. However, the person who feels the best years of his life are behind him because his mate has died, or because he's been divorced, has committed emotional suicide. That, too, is a dangerous state. Fortunately, that kind of suicide is not irrevocable.

Many of you are at the point of saying, "The best years of

my life are over; I might as well just roll up and die!'' Well, I want you to know your best years are not necessarily behind you. They can unquestionably be before you if you can comprehend some simple truths and put them into action.

There is an axiom which states that the bird with a broken wing will never again fly as high. One day a couple came to me for counseling. Both said they has been involved in extramarital relationships, had many other problems and that their lives were in a mess. They had reached the point of hopelessness.

I thought to myself, ''If that is true—if the broken wing will keep them from reaching the heights—then they might as well take a gun and shoot themselves.'' Fortunately, however, that axiom is not true, and it certainly did not hold true for this couple. They put their lives and their relationship back together, and now they have an excellent marriage. That is one side of the coin.

On the other side, I have seen others for whom the experience of divorce became one of the best things that ever happened to them. No one likes divorce, but it can begin a growth process that builds a better life than could have been experienced within the framework of the destructive relationship from which it came. To illustrate: I recall one woman who came to me for counseling. She had not finished high school and had married an aeronautical engineer. She had enmeshed herself so totally in her husband's personality she had no identity of her own, no self-confidence. She went through a divorce; and because she was kicked out of the nest, she was forced to go back to school, get an education, find a trade and make something of herself. She had to become a person in her own right. In so doing, though she didn't like the way it happened, she could look back and say, ''It was good. It was the best thing that ever happened to me because it caused me to become a whole person.''

There are several biblical reasons why I can say that the best is yet to come. One is stated in Romans 8:28, which says that God works in all things for good to them that love the Lord. I had seen this principle work, and still it was difficult for me to accept—especially when a trying personal experience had been caused by things which were evil. Later, while doing a study of that verse, I was directed to the 50th chapter of Genesis. There, Joseph's brothers came to him saying they feared that since their father had died, Joseph would get even with them for selling him into slavery. Joseph looked at them and said, "Why do you fear, seeing that I sit in the place of God? You meant it for evil, but God meant it for good to save much people alive." Here is proof that God can take evil and use it for good.

Often I have thought about David in that light. David, a man who had committed adultery and then committed murder to cover it up, was referred to by Jesus as a man after God's own heart. In addition, although the child born from the adulterous affair died, the second child born to that relationship became king after David. God used evil for good in that situation, and He can take the evil that we do and use it for good also. So don't give way to despair. I have news for you. The best years of your life can be ahead of you if you want them to be.

How are you going to assure that? First of all, you must determine to grow. Let's face it—that which has happened to you can cause you to do one of three things: stagnate, become bitter, or grow.

An illustration of stagnation can be found in the situation which often occurs when one loses a mate by death. The surviving spouse determines there is no reason for him to go on, especially if he was married for a good number of years. So he says, "What's the use?" He stagnates; and within six months or a year, he's dead. This is a tragic waste.

An equally tragic waste is present when the surviving mate tends to deify the deceased. Nobody is perfect! One must recognize the marriage is over and admit there was good *and* bad in the person who is gone. Only then will the survivor be able to accept the death and go on to a full life of growth.

A second reaction is to say, "I'm bitter." A person may not state that in so many words, but he lives in bitterness. He goes through a divorce and becomes resentful and bitter toward the former mate, bitter toward God, and bitter toward friends. These persons merely become grouches. They're critical; they gripe about everything from sunshine to rain; they're resentful toward life and everyone with whom they come in contact.

The third alternative is to say, "I'm going to learn something from this." A wise choice, obviously, since the only wasted moment or experience in life is that from which we learn nothing.

I'm a little hardheaded, and some experiences in my life have cost me dearly because God had to gain my attention with a baseball bat. Now, an experiece may have cost me dearly; but if I have learned something from it, I have emerged the winner.

If you will say, "Okay, death of my mate (or divorce) has happened to me. . . I don't like it, but I am determined to make something out of this situation so that the best years of my life are before me," then I can promise you that although the working through may not be painless, ultimately you'll be able to look back and be thankful for what happened. It is your decision. You can stagnate, you can become bitter or you can grow.

The Need For Accepting The Situation

Once you have determined to grow from your experience, you must then accept the reality of the death of the marriage. That acceptance is relatively easy for those of you who have lost mates by death. You can go to the cemetery where you can see the resting place and say, "There lies my former mate."

Accepting the fact physically is only one part, however. You must also accept the death emotionally. If this is your situation, you must come to grips with a hard truth, difficult though it may be. That truth? The Bible teaches there is no giving and receiving of marriage in heaven. In heaven we will all be brothers and sisters. If you are still saying, "I can't date because it would be disrespectful to this one I loved so much," then you are still married emotionally.

The kind of love you had for the deceased must be exchanged for the kind of love you would have toward a brother or sister, as in the heavenly relationship. That relationship will be even better than the husband/wife relationship on this earth. The failure to make such an exchange ties one to the casket and is no less cruel than the ancient custom of burning the widow on the funeral pyre along with the dead husband (as was done in India in past years).

I once went to a Christian bookstore and overheard the owner of the store and another lady criticize a man because he had remarried about a year after his wife's death. I knew the owner of the store. After her friend left, I turned to her and said, "Why were you so critical of the man?" I shared the biblical principle that death ended the marriage.

She said, "I don't want my husband to marry too quickly because I don't want him to forget me."

"In other words," I said, "even though remarriage would be best for him and your children, you'd selfishly cheat him. I thought you loved him."

We talked on a while, and I pointed out that she was actually saying, "Hey, that's my place!" I reminded her that it was her place as long as she lived. "Once you die," I said, "it's no longer your place."

We discussed the matter a few minutes and I left. The next time I came into the store, she said, "Clyde, thank you." She had faced the fact that death ends the marriage. She had realized that when one dies, the marriage, which is of this earth only, dies with it. The heavenly relationship of brother and sister is going to be sweeter and more intimate than the best husband-wife relationship here on earth. (When I bring up this point in my seminars, someone usually quips, "I certainly hope so!")

Those who have lost mates by divorce find it more difficult to accept the death of the marriage than do those whose mates have died. For one reason, you can't bury the person (though you may say you'd like to!). The process you must work through is more complicated.

Perhaps you have been in a marriage from which your mate

walked out, but you still have an abundant love for this person. Don't let go of the love. The opposite of love is hate, and any hate that you have automatically decreases your capacity to love. One's capacity to love is diminished by the sum total of all bitterness or hatred that one retains. If you hate, you are cheating yourself. You must accept, however, that at that point when one person says, "I no longer want to be married," the divorce takes place. The law courts of our land never create a divorce. Marriage unites two people in spirit and mind and body to become one, to make each other better. It is two individuals coming together for the purpose of increasing—not decreasing—the ultimate fulfillment of each other. When one or the other says that he is no longer committed to that relationship—to making better the persons and the union—at that point, divorce takes place. All the judge does is the same thing the doctor does when he signs the death cerificate. He gives legal verification of that which has already transpired. The tragedy is that many divorces take place fifteen years before they ever go to court, and for those fifteen years someone has been dragging a corpse. I do not like divorce. I do not like death. But I must accept the reality of both.

When is divorce justifiable? Someone has written, "Divorce is right when the marriage makes one bitter rather than better." Now, I know that no one can make me bitter. If I am bitter, it is because I choose to be so. But with that idea, divorce must become justifiable when the relationship becomes destructive.

I served as a police chaplain in Texas for three and one-half years. When I started riding with the officers, I had to make a decision about what I would do if someone opened fire on us. I made my decision. Although I did not want to kill anyone, I trained myself so that if a person took the first shot, he would not get many chances for a second or third before I would be ready to fire back. It was not a choice I desired, but one which I had to be prepared to make.

Similarly, if you saw a woman whose husband was feeding her arsenic every day, would you tell her to stay with the man and take the arsenic? Of course not.

There is emotional arsenic as deadly as any physical arsenic that can be administered. When a relationship becomes destructive and there is no reconciliation because one person refuses to attempt to change to make the relationship good, the marriage is justifiably ended. At that point you must learn to say, "It's dead. It's over." When it is ended, you bury the marriage, not the person. (I will elaborate on the theology of divorce in the chapter on preparation for remarriage.) In examining the reality of the death of a marriage, there must come a time when the emotional justification for divorce is accepted and the fact of divorce is acknowledged.

I have some friends who experienced a great deal of difficulty in burying their former marriage. I suggested they put their marriage certificate in a nice cigar box and offered to accompany them to the cemetery where we'd conduct a funeral for the marriage.

The point that suggestion illustrates is that you must have an emotional cutting and literally say, "It's over." As long as you carry that corpse around, you will not be able to live effectively. How many people can carry an extra 150 or 200 pounds of weight and not be tired out? Bury it and say, "Okay, Lord. With your help, now I'm going to grow."

The Need for Cutting Ties That Restrict

After you have accepted the death of the marriage, you must cut the ties that would restrict you. There are some people with whom you may have to cut emotional ties. Some of you may have to cut the umbilical cords with parents. Frequently parents are so uptight about the divorce they will put pressures on you to go back into the relationship no matter what the cost.

Church friends may be among those with whom you must cut ties. Some of them may put pressure on you to make the marriage work even if it's not workable.

Some of you even may have to talk very strongly with your

children. You may have lost a mate by death and may have older children, perhaps grown children, who are almost paranoid at the idea of your dating. The reason may be a neurotic need on their part, such as some unresolved guilt toward their deceased parent which has rendered them unable to accept his or her death. Perhaps they fear that if you start dating, you'll find somebody else to "take Daddy's place." Remember, no one can take Daddy's place because Daddy is gone. You may have to "sit on" some children and say to them, "Thanks, but no thanks, Friend. I'm responsible for my life, and I must go on living. I loved your father, but I was not buried with him."

You must say to those friends or family members who would restrict you, "Hey! I've got a life. I still have to live. I must find myself and be myself and move forward."

A similar problem is experienced by some people in their thirties and forties who have been married fifteen or twenty years, have divorced, and have gone through a period of relating primarily to other couples. Some of these couples still tie you to the marriage. Others do not relate to you at all, especially if you are a divorcee, because they fear their husbands may think the grass is greener on the other side of the fence and start chasing you. You are experiencing a lack of previous feelings of friendship and of warmth that you want. I hate to tell you, but you will find yourself forced to go out and make some new friends. You must leave old relationships behind. You don't have to ignore old friends and never relate to them again, but you must make new acquaintances. Other people must become your primary friends. One of the things I like most about working in a church Bible study program for singles is the fact that people have a chance to meet new friends to whom they can relate as brothers and sisters in Christ and for whom a friendship and comradeship develop. You must cut some old ties and make new friends.

The Need for Accepting Responsibility

The third step in making the most of a difficult situation is to determine to accept responsibility for yourself. I've got news for some of you. No one person other than yourself is responsible for your happiness. Any time you try to make anyone else responsible for your happiness, you have put an impossible demand on that person. You are responsible; you are in charge. You are influenced by everything that has happened in your life, even those things in which you were not personally involved, from your birth and childhood forward. Your past has had a tremendous bearing upon your life, but you are still in charge. You are responsible for what happens, for what you do with *you*.

I would love to blame my parents for my imperfections. They were not perfect, and I am not perfect. Many things which I share have been learned by personal experience. But I cannot blame my father or my mother for what has happened to me. I cannot blame them for who I am today because I am responsible. I have assumed that responsibility.

This point is very important to comprehend. Some of you may have a tendency to blame what you are today on your parents or your former mates. What they have done has hurt you and has influenced you; but you are in charge, and you can do something about your present and your future. You are responsible. I have determined to accept responsibility for Clyde. You must accept responsibility for yourself.

The Need for Identifying Emotions

Having taken the first three steps toward learning to grow, you must now identify the emotions and feelings you are experiencing. To use a current phrase, you must get in touch with "where I am." Each person is in a different stage in his journey through relationships. Now, if you are going somewhere, you must first know where you are. People have called me and said, "How do I get to where you are?"

I always ask, "Where are *you*?"

Sometimes they reply, "What does it matter where I am?"

Until they tell me where they are, I can't tell them how to get where I am. Similarly, until you get in touch with where you are emotionally, there's no way you can get where you want to go. Have you ever been too proud to admit you were lost and refused to ask for directions? (You drove a long way in the wrong direction, didn't you?) To keep you from wasting valuable time and energy going in the wrong direction emotionally, I want to help you to identify the emotions you have experienced or are now feeling, so that you will know "where you are" and can progress from that point with directions to where you want to go.

Failure

The first thing most people feel when they experience the breaking up of their marriage is failure. Many widowed people often admit feeling they have failed because they couldn't keep a mate alive. "Why couldn't I have done this, or why couldn't I have done that, to enable him to take better care of himself?" The feeling of failure is especially common for the one whose mate has died of a heart attack, in an accident or from some other cause over which the survivor imagines the ability to control. It is also common for the person who does not want a divorce but is forced into one. And it is common for the person who made the decision to get a divorce after many years in a dead relationship in which there was no communication. In either case, that person finds himself saying, "What was I lacking? Where did I go wrong?" If the mate has left for another, the injured party may ask, "What does that person have that I don't have? Where did I fail?"

Anger

Following failure, the next emotion people experience is anger. Perhaps you have experienced it. Perhaps you are experiencing it now. First, you are angry with yourself. You give yourself a good tongue lashing. Soon, however, your self-defense mechanism begins to go into action. You have been attacked, and so you defend yourself by becoming angry with the former mate. Even those who are widowed experience this anger. The problem here is that such an emotion is confusing to the person, and he seldom has the courage to admit it. He thinks, "Why did you leave me? That doesn't fit my plans. My plans were that we live until sixty-five or seventy, then I was to die rather quickly. You were to live long enough to bury me and see that I had a good funeral. Then before you had a chance to chase anyone else, you'd die. Now you're gone and that doesn't fit my plans." So you become angry with the former mate.

Frequently the next anger is with society in general, and then your family. You become particularly angry with your family because they don't understand what's going on. They seem to turn against you, and you want to say, "Hey, get off my back!" You then find yourself angry with God. The feelings of anger are very real; but, fortunately, they will pass.

Rejection

Accompanying the feeling of anger is the feeling of rejection. You start thinking of all these little things that happened and look upon them as rejections. How can a man reject his wife in death? You and I know that's not rejection. How can a person feel rejection in death? I'll give you an example. Suppose a man died of a heart attack. His wife had been trying to get him to lose weight and take care of himself. She feels, "You didn't care about me. You rejected me." Or perhaps he had a bad habit of driving too fast, or of driving while he was drinking. He wouldn't stop that habit, and he died in a car wreck. His former mate will want to say, "You didn't care enough; you rejected me."

It is very easy to understand how a person can feel rejected in divorce, expecially if he is the person who has been deserted. Perhaps the husband has gone to live with another woman. That's a real blow. Maybe you are a man whose former wife rejected you for another man. In my counseling experiences I have observed that although a woman hurts very deeply if she has been rejected for another woman, a man's reaction when he has been left for another man is much more devastating. The male ego is more fragile at this point, and it seems almost to wipe him out, at least for a time.

The rejection feeling comes even if you are the person who left. You may be the one who actually filed for the divorce, but you look back over the marriage and want to say, "Hey, why didn't you talk to me? Why didn't you communicate?" Perhaps he was too busy playing golf, or too busy with his job, or with a hobby. You feel it wasn't in the divorce that the rejection took place. It took place twenty years before, or ten years before, and you want to say, "I was rejected."

Bitterness

Then comes the feeling of bitterness. You say, "I'll get even with you. God, just give me a chance!"

I know what that feeling of revenge is like. Several years ago I was serving in the pastorate and the church burned twice. The second time was arson; and my study, about $8000 worth of uninsured furnishings — including my books, my recording equipment, and many items which could never be replaced — went up in smoke. Although we were unable to prove it, we believed we knew who had set the blaze. A friend of mine said, "Clyde, if God would just let me get in a room with him for about thirty minutes, I'd have a book of matches and I'd get my revenge."

You know that feeling of revenge. It runs all the way from the feeling a woman has when her man comes home late and she thinks, "Man, you ain't gonna touch me tonight," to the extreme form where you say, "God, I wouldn't really kill him, but if he were to die in a car wreck, I would praise Your name."

Bitterness. Revenge. "If I could just get revenge! I certainly can't let God have the revenge, because He is too patient and too merciful. I know better what to do." Have you ever lain awake at night thinking of things you would like to do? You may have at least half a dozen things you know you *could* do, and you could probably get away with some of them. It surely is a temptation once in a while just to act on that revenge drive.

If you have difficulty identifying bitterness within yourself, or if you don't believe you're a victim of it, you may find it helpful to make a bitterness list. (An example is given at the end of this chapter.) Such a list can aid you in identifying and weeding out this destructive emotion.

Guilt

The emotion which follows bitterness is guilt. Guilt is experienced in two ways: real guilt and misdirected guilt. Many people feel guilty for the wrong thing. Bitterness is wrong. But instead of feeling guilty about the bitterness, we feel guilty about the divorce. That's misdirected guilt. Let me give some examples. One of the most difficult things to deal with in the death of a mate or a loved one is unresolved bitterness. Perhaps that person did something that hurt you. You knew you needed to make it right, but you never did. When he died, you thought, "Now it's too late. I can't do anything about it."

There are few couples who have not experienced this type of feeling. Houston pastor and T.V. personality John Bisagno expressed the anger which can be felt like this: "Divorce? No. Murder? A thousand times."

Perhaps a person is experiencing difficulties with his mate; and though he would never consider divorce, he becomes so angry that just for a moment he thinks, "Oh, God, if that person were just dead and out of my life, I wouldn't have to worry about her." Then the mate dies, and the guilt sets in.

Perhaps one feels guilty because he thinks, "If only I had made her go to the doctor. I should have made her (or him) take care of herself." The real reason for the feeling of guilt, however, is not that you did not make your mate go to the doctor. The real problem is the bitterness, the feeling of resentment and murder that you've had in your heart. In divorce, it is not the divorce itself that causes the guilt. It is all your feelings of bitterness that make you feel so guilty.

What happens, then, when you feel guilty? You run from the ones who can help you the most. You flee from where you need to go. Sad to say, the result of your fleeing and running is loneliness, a state which can be defined as not having anyone with whom to share in a very personal, intimate way. Unfortunately, there is no instant remedy for loneliness. If it were synonymous with laziness, then the remedy would be "busyness." But loneliness and laziness are not the same. Nor are loneliness and "aloneness" the same, for we all need some time to be alone. Loneliness is not having anyone with whom you can share your inner feelings; and if you have run from friends who really care, you may find yourself among others who always sympathize with you, always agree with you. Sometimes that can be far worse than being with friends who will be frank with you. A real friend is one who will tell you you need *Scope*. The person who always agrees with you is not your friend. He or she may say, "I love you, bad breath and all," and that's fine; but always agreeing with you is not real friendship.

In examining the emotions experienced at the end of a marriage, you may find it helpful to ask, "Where am I?" Many of you may find yourself dealing with three or four of these attitudes at the same time. You vacillate. One moment you're here, one moment you're there. One moment you're filled with despair. One moment you're on top of the world. Another moment you hate everybody. The next moment you love everybody. You wonder what in the world is going on. You say, "Man, will I ever get my head straight?" Yes, you will. I have news for you, especially for those of you who are just beginning the process. I find that it takes at least six months to get your head on straight. The average person who works at it can get himself together in about six months to a year; but if you don't work at it, you can spend the rest of your life with the pieces lying all over the floor, and griping at everybody around you because things are not going right.

The Need for Avoiding Self-Pity

One final observation must be shared on the steps to make the most of a difficult situation. You must get off the "pity-pot." I know of no other way to put it. Many people sit around and feel sorry for themselves, and they may run home to Mama or to Daddy or to whoever will listen to them while they spew forth their woes. All the while they are pitying themselves, they are dying. In my personal counseling I will permit a person to use the pity-pot for about three sessions. After that, I make sure I'm wearing my cowboy boots with the needle toes, and I apply them at the right place to get them off the thing. Those who want to stay there are going to have trouble because I'll keep needling them until they do get off.

If you are off and running — if you're ready to make the most of a difficult situation — I'm with you all the way. I really believe you can come out of this experience a better person. Six months from now you can say, "Hey, man! This is the best thing that's ever happened to me." I hope that is where you are going.

EXAMPLE OF THE BITTERNESS LIST

NAME OF PERSON I AM BITTER TOWARD

ACTIONS THAT HURT ME   MY RESPONSE

	RETALIATION RESPONSE
"My mate came home drunk."	"He will not get any lovin' from me tonight!"
	WITHDRAWAL RESPONSE
"My mate forgot my birthday."	"I suffered in silence. I decided I would not share my feelings."
"My mate did not give me approval."	"I determined that I would not try anymore to please my mate."

Chapter Two

Developing a Healthy
Self-Love

A healthy self-love is the foundation on which all healthy relationships are built. It is *the* most important aspect of life. Image of self, or self-love, determines to a great extent how the individual responds to life. It determines largely his academic achievements, vocational fulfillment and marital happiness. The ability to love others exists in direct proportion to the ability to love self. How important it is, then, that every individual develop a healthy image of himself—a healthy love for himself.

Through my counseling experiences, however, I have become increasingly aware that this vital area of life is the one with which many people have the most difficulty. I have come to recognize that there are some universal truths which cause man to have difficulty in learning to love himself. It is important that those causes be identified, for then, and only then, can we learn to appropriate solutions which can bring about a healthy self-love.

Some interesting research was conducted in a California elementary school recently, the results strongly supporting the importance of a healthy self-image. Students were given a test, and from the scores achieved, researchers selected the top students for each grade. A teacher was assigned to each "chosen group" and at the end of the year, the students were retested. As was expected, those in each chosen group had learned and improved far more than those in other groups. It was then the researchers disclosed that the so-called chosen ones were not the best students at all, but were in fact the average students. Those average students had accomplished far more than others because they, their parents, and their teachers *believed* they were an accelerated group. This is but one of countless illustrations of the tremendous effect attitude can have on achievement. The one who believes he can accomplish something most often can. And that, of course, is good reason for developing a healthy self-image.

Another important reason is this: No one can love another person more than he loves himself. Jesus said, "Love your neighbor as yourself." Many people have told me, "I love my children (or my husband or my wife) more than I love myself." I want to tell those people, flatly, that is impossible. A battery cannot give what it does not have. You cannot love another person more than you love yourself. You can love that person to the maximum of your ability, but your ability to love is regulated by the amount of love you have for yourself.

If self-love is so important, why then is there such a problem with appropriating it?

In his book *I'm Okay, You're Okay,* Thomas Harris states that the problem has roots in childhood. The child, who is two feet tall, feels he can never measure up to Daddy, who is six feet tall; and so he grows up believing he will never do anything right. As I considered this theory, I realized that Harris is simply stating Freud's ideas in different terms. I was still troubled. I did not believe their answers to be complete. There still seemed to be some vital aspect missing from their solutions.

It dawned on me that the root of the problem lies in the

problem of original sin. The Bible states that God visits the iniquity of the parents to the third and fourth generations. That statement had always troubled me. I could not understand how a just God could hold me responsible or accountable for what my parents did. Then I realized the Bible does not say that I am *held accountable* for what my parents did. It says that I am *influenced* or *affected* by it.

There are many areas in which our self-love is influenced or affected by the curse of original sin. The church is one of these areas. In emphasizing the sinfulness of man, the statement is often made that man is no good. I once heard a preacher say, "Man is garbage. Why should we have so much trouble giving our lives to Christ? Why should we have so much trouble surrendering ourselves to His lordship? We're garbage."

That idea didn't sit well with me. The Bible says we are fearfully and wonderfully made in the image of God. It does not say we are garbage. In his desire to address the sinfulness of sin, that mininster went a step too far. Unfortunately, many other Christians do the same.

For every good thing God made, the devil created two perversions, believing we'd find one; and in our horror of it, we would then literally back ourselves into the other. This principle could be illustrated by the ditches on either side of a highway. It matters not which ditch you get into—if you're in a ditch, you're in a ditch. It is true that people are sinful, but we are not garbage.

Another area in which church attitude has adversely affected our self-love is its confusion of issues regarding the old nature and the ego. They are not the same. Ego is not the heart of sin, yet the church often speaks about dying to self as if we must annihilate the person. That is a misconception. Jesus Christ was a person and had a personality. God created me and gave me a personality; He never intended that my personality become nothingness.

For a period in my life I adopted the attitude of the church and thought, "Okay, I'm going to be nothing. I have some unique things about me, but I must smother them." And so I chose to do so. What happened? I became miserable and everybody around me was miserable until finally I saw a beautiful truth. When I was born again, my old nature was taken away, but my ego remained intact. Granted, that old nature can still have an influence on me, but I am not to mistake that influence for ego. I am me. I am a unique creation. The fact that I died to self and took up my cross to follow Jesus did not mean I died to Clyde's being Clyde. My personality did not die. My ego did not die.

The last words of Jesus were, "Father, into thy hands I commend my spirit." To take up one's cross means to yield control of one's life. It does not mean to denounce one's life. This difference is very important. You are still a person. You still have a spirit about you. You still have uniqueness. You still have a personality. When you are born again, you simply yield that unique, wonderful personality and person to the control of God. He becomes Lord of your life.

Another area in which misconceptions regarding the curse of original sin can harm our capacity for self-love is in the equating of self-love and selfishness. They are not the same. When I mention self-love, people frequently say something like this: "Don't talk to me about self-love. I've lived with the most selfish person that ever set foot on earth."

I tell them, "Wait a minute. Selfishness and self-love are not the same."

Selfishness is actually a form of self-hate. It says, "I don't like myself; therefore I don't believe you could like me. Because you don't like me, you would never give me anything; therefore, if I'm ever going to have anything, I must take it away from you." Selfishness, then, is predicated upon hatred of self.

It is easy to see how attitudes regarding the curse of original sin can affect so many people since they sometimes receive improper teaching on that subject from the church. It is also easy to see that confusing self-love and selfishnesss can cause many people to think that striving for a healthy self-love is undesirable. But wrong attitudes regarding the curse of original sin are not found just in the church or among individuals. The attitudes of society as a whole have been affected, and sociological and racial prejudice are a direct result.

An incident from my own high school days in Louisiana illustrates society's attitudes. I attended Istrouma High, which was located in the north section of Baton Rouge. It was the less affluent section of the city—the "kicker" hangout division. Our arch rival was Baton Rouge High. On the Tuesday before the game, a local disc jockey asked a Baton Rouge student, "By the way, which school are you playing this week?"

The student stumbled as if he couldn't remember the name, then finally said, "Oh, you know, that school across the tracks."

Now, just because we lived on the other side of the tracks did not mean we were not of the same status, but that was the prevailing attitude. (By the way, that comment became the rally cry, and Istrouma won the game. Needless to say, the Baton Rouge team was mighty sorry that student make the remark he did!)

Society, you see, more or less implies that your worth is determined by where you were born or what you have achieved. The truth, however, is that worth—which is synonymous with the ability to love self—is not determined by *what we do,* but rather by *who we are.* It is a gift. Society says you're worthy if you achieve; therefore, man strives always to achieve. But no matter how hard he works at it, he never feels comfortable because he always wonders, "What if I fail tomorrow?"

The Bible says: You're worthy—therefore, go achieve. Your worth comes first. Your achievement comes out of your worth, not just the opposite as the world would have you believe.

The greatest adverse effect of the curse has been on the family. It evolves from our misunderstanding of the concept of authority. One must understand what authority is and what it is not, for the ability to surrender to it is an aid to developing self-love.

To the degree that my parents did not have a healthy self-love, they did not do a good job in exercising authority. That is, they were more concerned with the authority itself than they were with what was taking place. The parent with a weak self-image will consider any child's challenge to his authority as an affront to his character, as a disregard for his position.

Suppose, for example, a child asks, "Why can't I do this?" and is told, "Because I said so."

The response "Because I said so" is a weak excuse of a weak ego. You see, a reasonable God has a reasonable answer. I may not agree with His answer or His reason, I may not understand it, but He can give me the reason at the appropriate time. If God, as supreme authority, recognizes man's need to understand His reason, then parents must recognize the child's need to understand their reasons. If the child is to develop a healthy attitude about authority, that is.

Now, I believe that when a parent says "Jump," those kids ought to jump; but I also believe they should be given the reason for it later.

For example, if my son were standing in the street and I saw a car half a block away doing seventy miles per hour, I'd shout, "Keith, jump!" and expect him to jump. If however, I'd say, "Now, Keith, it would behoove you to remove your body from the street...," bam! He's dead.

But there needs to be the freedom for the child to ask why. Parents who do not have a healthy self-love, however, become more concerned about their authority than about their children's growth. A parent's dogmatic imposition of authority will undermine his child's feeling of worthiness—his self-love.

In understanding man's difficulty in learning to love himself, then, we must understand that the root problem lies in the curse of origianl sin. Closely related to that problem, and the second important influence on our capacity for self-love, is the degree to which we receive fulfillment of two very basic needs: *approval* and *acceptance*.

To the degree that my needs for approval and acceptance are not met, my personality and my self-love are going to suffer. To the degree that my parents cannot accept themselves or feel good about themselves, they will have difficulty giving me acceptance and approval. This problem is very subtle most of the time. To understand it we must examine our upbringing. My purpose is not to blame anyone. It is not to put blame on parents, but rather to help them get in touch with the areas of their deficiencies, so that they can know how to appropriate God's truths to meet those deficiencies.

One subtle "little" thing in the area of non-approval is kidding; it can be very harmful. You see, my brain is a computer. Everything that happens to me is stored in the memory bank of my brain. Scientific research has found that every cell of my brain stores just one incident—one "byte" of information, to use computer talk. It is stored there permanently. Eighty-five percent of that information is in the subconscious. I don't even think about it, but it affects everything I do.

If a child falls as he is learning to walk, and Daddy says, "You're clumsy," that statement is stored upon that child's computer tape for life.

The child thinks, "Daddy's kidding," but the next time he falls, perhaps later when he's learning to skate, he recalls that tape, "You're clumsy...you're clumsy." After a while the child may become so scarred by this idea that he is afraid to try anything requiring coordination.

Perhaps the child is told he's the ugly duckling of the family. That child may grow up believing he's ugly, and everything he does will be affected by that belief.

Then there's the statement, "You're dumb." That is one of the most vicious of all. Many a child goes to school thinking, "I'm dumb," and because he believes it, he does not produce. The teacher assumes he is dumb. It is just a kidding tape, but it has a deadly influence on everything that child does.

Comparison is another subtle form of non-approval. If you are adversely influenced by this sort of thinking, it would be well to remember two things: One, you will always find someone who is better at a given thing than you are. Two, one of the worst phrases in the English language is "the best." Anytime you try to become "the best," you are in competition with everybody else in that area. To the degree that you are in competition with anybody, you are that person's enemy. God never intended for you to be *the* best. He intended only for you to become *your* best. When being *your* best, you are trying to achieve what you are capable of achieving—nothing more, nothing less. But to be *the best* is always destructive because you are always striving to be number one. Ultimately it will destroy you.

One area where comparison is frequently harmful is in sibling rivalry. Often we see children squabbling, trying to be the best. The second child of the same sex, without an intervening child of the opposite sex — especially if the children involved are only one or two years apart — is especially vulnerable to comparison. That child often has a great deal of difficulty in attaining a healthy self-love. It is natural for the younger of the two to want to do what the older child is doing. The older child is granted more privileges, and the younger begins to feel inadequate because he cannot have the same privileges.

The parent complicates the matter further by saying, "Why can't you be like your brother?"

Then the child enters school, and the first thing he hears is, "Oh, you're so-and-so's brother," or 'You're so-and-so's sister." The child feels as if he must live up to an image, yet he is a different person with different abilities.

At one time I was counseling three teenage girls from three families. All three had drug problems. Each of the girls had older sisters who were the "church angels," the little "straight" ones. These girls had gone the opposite way to say, "Hey! I'm me! Why can't you love me for me? Let me be myself!" They had fallen into the opposite ditch in the process.

If one has been the brunt of comparison, he has received a subtle form of non-approval which can be very harmful to his capacity for self-love.

Often non-approval is stated. When such is the case, those statements are expressed in three ways.

The first way is statement by griping. The person who gripes about what others do (or do not do) is expressing non-approval. Even though the griper may be simply showing a lack of self-love by being a perpetual malcontent and scapegoating others, the person who receives griping interprets it as non-approval.

Another way of indicating non-approval is statement by silence. One wife with whom I was counseling complained that she felt no approval from her husband because he rarely commented on anything she did. His reply was, "It's not that I don't approve. If I'm not saying anything, everything's okay!"

Men, I want to give you some important advice. One of the things wives need is approval. Often the reason women go to work is not to make money, but to receive the approval they do not get at home. There is an awesome danger in that. When the wife is out in the working world and the boss or another man starts giving some attention or approval, she may find herself becoming emotionally attached to that other person whether she intended to do so or not. She may never have an affair or take action on her feeling, but she will find that person to be meeting an emotional need that the husband is not meeting. That is one of the reasons why many marriages in the 15-20 year category are falling apart.

Another illustration comes to mind in a situation I observed with a young man and his father. A group from the church had gone roller skating. This young man had paid for skates for himself and his date. The attendant gave him change, but charged him for only one rental. The young man called the error to attention and paid the correct amount. I complimented the young man for his honesty. Later, when I mentioned the incident to the father and asked why he had not praised his son, he replied, "Honesty is to be expected. I don't see any reason why I should praise him for doing something which is expected." The father did not realize that by saying nothing, he was giving a subtle form of non-approval to his son.

The third, and probably most vicious way of expressing non-approval is statement by negation. For example, "Honey, that's good, *but*. . ." You've heard it. Mary comes home with a 90 on her paper, and Mama says, "Honey, that's good, but if you had worked harder, you could have made a 95."

What does *but* do? It negates everything that precedes it. When one says, "That's good, but. . .," the *but* stops everything that has been said before. All the person hears is, "but you didn't do enough." The result of this sort of treatment is sad. The child reaches out to take the gift offering; and just as he gets his hands on it, it is taken away. After a while the child stops reaching out. Have you ever met a person who couldn't accept a compliment? Most often that person has had this kind of parent. The person grew up afraid to accept a compliment because it was always taken away before it was actually received.

Receiving approval, then, is important if one is to develop a healthy self-love. But perhaps even more important than approval is acceptance. And just as there are subtle ways to express non-approval, there are subtle ways to express non-acceptance, which is another term for rejection.

Prenatal rejection is a form of non-acceptance which is often not recognized. I had difficulty recognizing it myself in the case of adopted children, for example. I noted they seemed to have greater problems with self-love than natural children had, and that concerned me for years. I wondered why.

In exploring recent studies, I was shown that all communication — including rejection — can be communicated nonverbally. We have all experienced this in a person's attitude or look. It has even been determined that a child can feel his mother's rejection before he is born. Most adopted children, I realized, come from a situation where the mother did not want to get pregnant. These children experience that rejection even in the womb! Others receiving this form of rejection are those children of unplanned pregnancies whose mothers say, "Oh, boy, what a crimp this puts in my plans!" Although the parent overcomes the feeling of rejection and accepts the infant before he is born, the child has experienced it nonetheless, and he must deal with it later in his life.

Another very real form of rejection is that of being the "wrong sex." You know — Daddy wanted a girl and you were a boy, or vice-versa. I did not know until I was an adult that my father had wanted a girl when I was born. A year later Mother gave birth to a girl, and she became his favorite child. Throughout my childhood I had a vague feeling that Daddy didn't want me, and that really hurt me at times. I knew he wanted a girl. I couldn't rationalize it, but I could feel it. Now that I understand the situation, I can look back and comprehend what I was feeling. I can overcome that childhood tape of rejection and can forgive my father's actions by saying, "Okay, Daddy. I accept that you did not intentionally reject me. I accept that you were not perfect." Now I can deal with the problem and erase that bad tape.

Parental anger is another area in which a child can experience rejection. I can discipline my child in a healthy manner, or I can totally explode upon my child. When I explode, that anger comes across to the child as the feeling, "Hey, Kid, you're in my way." That feeling is especially strong if the parent disciplines a child because the child is interrupting something the parent is doing, like watching television. The child says to himself, "You're not interested in me. You're concerned about yourself and that ball game or that TV program." The child feels that the expression of anger is unjustified and he comprehends it to mean, "You don't want me. You don't care about me. I am rejected."

A child can experience rejection in the premature death of a parent or in the divorce of his parents. One thing I frequently question in counseling is whether either parent died early, or whether there was a divorce in the family in the early years of the person's life. Although the divorce is a result of the parents' difficulties between themselves, the child nonetheless feels rejected.

In the death of a parent, a child may intellectually deal with it by accepting that God has taken the parent home, yet emotionally he still feels rejected. He asks the silent question, "What about me and my needs?"

One lady with whom I counseled expressed it this way: "Not only did I feel rejected because of my daddy, but I also felt rejected by God for taking my daddy. Often in my early years my friends received bicycles or skates that my mother couldn't afford, or they went somewhere I couldn't afford to go. In such instances I was angry because I didn't have a daddy to take care of me." She felt rejected in that her parent was not there to love and accept her. She felt she was being forced to become what she was not, that she was being rejected by life as a whole. Such feelings are not uncommon for those who have lost parents by early death.

One lethal form of rejection is the imposition of the impossible demand. I coached little league baseball for years, and I could have enjoyed it much more if I could have eliminated the daddies. The problem was the men who never made it as athletic stars. They were pushing their sons to be stars so that they could say, "There's my son!"

Ladies often impose the impossible demand through music, tap dance, ballet and school. When I was pastoring, a lady made arrangements to use our gym two hours each day during the summer so that her daughter could practice baton twirling. One day I walked into the gym and saw the daughter crying as she twirled the baton. Mama was sitting at the side of the gym, sewing sequins on the little costume and changing the record on the record player. I learned later that the girl had been practicing for five hours because she hadn't gotten it right. Mama was pushing this nine-year-old girl to be an excellent baton twirler so that the daugher could twirl the baton on the sidelines at the Oiler game. Then Mom could sit in the stands and say, "That's my daughter." She was living her own weak ego through her daughter. The child was feeling totally frustrated and rejected as a person.

Often children who are pushed come to hate piano, guitar, sports or whatever the parents forced them into. The imposition of the impossible demand can be very damaging to the child's image of himself.

A closely related form of rejection is pushing a child into a line of work for which he or she has no desire. This tendency is frequently seen in the professions. Medicine, for example. There are many doctors who are miserable because they were forced into the profession by a parent. "Granddaddy was a doctor. Daddy was a doctor. You've got to be one, too." That sort of thing.

Law and ministry are other such professions. In Houston, Texas, there is a man whose grandfather and father were both lawyers. His family would not be content until he had finished law school and was admitted to the Bar. He deferred to their wishes, then did what *he* wanted to do. His diplomas now hang on the wall of the service station he owns and manages.

The word *educate* means to lead forth. Unfortunately, however, many parents do not lead. They push. And those who are forcing their children to be what *they* want them to be, rather than enabling and encouraging those children to be what *God* wants them to be, are transmitting a very real form of rejection to them.

To this point we have been dealing with how one's background and upbringing can adversely affect one's self love. Another time in life which frequently has a negative effect on one's self-image is often called mid-life crisis. As the term implies, these feelings begin in the 35-50 age bracket, although some may have such feelings as early as thirty.

The male who is often affected by this malady is one who has climbed the ladder as high as he can in his chosen occupation or profession, and has been a success. Frequently he has become "married" to his job, while his wife has wrapped herself completely in the children. He climbs the ladder until he reaches the apex, and then he is promoted one step beyond his level of competency — the so-called "Peter Principle." He is then pigeonholed. What happens? The man's ego is shot. He tries various changes. He may change jobs or totally change careers at this point. He may suddenly start trying to become a sports pro. In other words, this golfer who was just a golfer may begin coming home in the evening and practicing out in the back yard. He may turn to the bottle. This is a critical age for alcoholism among executives. He may start chasing other women because he has lost both his job satisfaction and his relationship with his wife. When a warm, interesting female gives him the attention he craves, it will be very difficult for him to go back home.

What happens to the woman in mid-life crisis? Her problem is just as unsettling, but from a different cause. Women have a tendency to believe that men are more concerned about beauty than about anything else. (That may be true in the eyes of a 20-year-old male, but she doesn't realize that it is not so important to the 40-year-old.) When she reaches the age where she is not quite as trim and attractive as she once was, and when the wrinkles and gray hairs start appearing, she begins to doubt herself. Many women at this age must have a hysterectomy or may go through the normal biological change of life. I am more convinced every day that the problems many women face in the after-effects of a hysterectomy are not merely physiological. The woman begins to think, "I'm not all woman any more," and this psychological attitude creates many physiological problems. She begins to think, "I'm not as attractive as I was." To add to the problem, the children she has been nurturing are starting to move away from the nest. No longer feeling needed by her children, and perhaps failing to receive the approval or strokes she needs from her husband, she goes out to find fulfillment in a career. She then begins to get the strokes she needs through her career, and she finds herself being pulled away from the family.

It is easy to understand what is happening to the family unit during the mid-life crisis. In my counseling I often encounter an average of one new case per week involving problems related to this crisis. If you have not yet reached the age where this tendency applies to you, please take note of its dangers nevertheless.

Perhaps you can avoid becoming its victim through awareness of the potential problem.

We have seen, then, that the problem of the difficulty of achieving self-love is deeply rooted in many individuals and is overwhelmingly prevalent in our society. Few people are fortunate enough to totally escape the damaging influences which adversely affect our abilities to love ourselves. Having examined and defined the problem, our next step is to determine what we are going to do about it.

Thomas Harris proposes that one simply has to accept his worth. While I respect his concept, this solution seems to be an over-simplification. How can a person who has doubted his worth and has had inadequate self-love for thirty years suddenly say, "It's okay to love myself"?

I believe that most people would likely say, "I'm from Missouri — show me!"

Again using the comparison of man's mind to a computer, let me point out that a computer is logical. It must have an input to compute. It cannot produce that for which it has not been programmed. I want to give you a computer tape that you can store in your mental computer so that at any time circumstances cause you to feel you are no good, or not okay, or unlovable, you can turn on this tape and play it loud and clear. I want to program your computer to say, "God says I'm a beautiful person."

Seven Needs for Self-Love

Acceptance

There are seven basic needs upon which we must build our self-love. The first one is this: I need to know that I am loved, and love means acceptance.

It is important that we understand the basic difference between two closely related words: like and love. *Love* equals acceptance; *like* equals approval. Perhaps I cannot always expect *approval*, even from myself, because I am imperfect. It is imperative, however, that I know I am loved.

The Bible says, "For God so loved the world that He gave His only begotten Son, that whosoever believeth in Him might not perish, but have everlasting life." It goes on to say, "But God commended His love towards us, in that while we were yet sinners, Christ died for us." Almost twenty years ago I read an article in *Redbook Magazine* entitled "Seven Things You Ought Not to Tell Your Child about God." I have forgotten six, but the one that stuck in my mind was that you ought not tell your child, "If you do that, God won't love you." There is nothing you or I can do that will ever cause God to stop loving us. God loves us just as we are. He *accepts* (loves) us even when He does not *approve* of (like) what we are doing.

One of the members of a singles' class I once taught came to me saying, "Clyde, you've got a problem." When I inquired as to the nature of it, she continued, "You know 'So-and-so' in the class?"

Aware of what she was getting at, I replied, "Yes, I know her."

"Well," she continued testily, "don't you know that she is having an affair?"

I'll never forget her look of surprise and confusion when I explained that not only was I aware of the situation, I also knew the man's name.

"Well," she said, "you're inviting her to be a part of the Sunday school class. Isn't that approving?"

I explained to her, "No, I am not *approving* of what she is doing. I am *accepting* her as God accepts her. When I come to church every Sunday morning I come as a sinner. She comes as a sinner also, seeking help from God. With God, sin is sin. In His eyes there are no big sins or little sins."

Often I use an illustration which I first communicated in a sermon entitled "To Kiss a Frog." (As a result, the frog has become a sort of trademark for me; and both friends and family members have helped me accumulate quite an assortment of frog and toad replicas over the years.) Most people have heard the fable of the wicked witch who put a curse on the handsome prince and turned him into a warty frog. He could be turned back into the prince only by the kiss of a beautiful princess. The analogy is that the responsibility of the church is to go around kissing frogs because Satan has put a curse on mankind and has turned us into warty frogs. Although Christ has turned us back into handsome princes and beautiful princesses, we still have a few *warts*—hang-ups, imperfections. The important thing I must realize is that God loves me and accepts me just as I am. The Bible says that when we shall see Him, we shall be perfect; but God knows that I am not going to be perfect until He comes or until I die, whichever comes first. He does not expect me to be perfect. God accepts and loves me, warts and all.

Forgiveness

The second basic need upon which one must build his self-love is a sense of forgiveness. To understand how to fulfill that need, we must explore four aspects of our relationship with God: guilt, punishment, confession and judgment.

God's purpose in causing man to feel guilt is to tell him something is malfunctioning so that he will take it to the Master Mechanic to get it fixed. I can do three things with guilt: ignore it, punish myself, or take it to the Mechanic. Further, there are two types of guilt: real guilt and pseudo guilt, or misdirected guilt.

If I get uptight because I see a state trooper while I'm driving down the highway at ninety miles an hour, that's real guilt. But if I get uptight seeing a state trooper when I am driving down the highway obeying all the speed limits, that's misdirected guilt. Why do I feel guilty? Because I know about the times I exceeded the speed limit and *didn't* get caught. In other words, I'm feeling guilty for something other than what I'm doing at the time.

Several years ago I was driving through the swamps of Louisiana where for miles there were no houses or any sign of civilization. My oil light came on, indicating some problem in the system. Upon investigation, I discovered the oil pan plug had come out and I'd lost my oil. I signaled to a friend who was ahead of me, and he came back to help. We found a makeshift plug, filled the car with oil, and I drove home and got the car repaired.

That incident is a perfect illustration of God's purpose for guilt in our lives, and of our alternatives in dealing with that guilt. I could have ignored the warning light and continued driving. If I had done so, I'd have seriously damaged the engine and repairs would have been costly. I could have punished myself by blaming myself and saying, "You stupid idiot, why didn't you check that oil plug?" Or I could have done both. That is, I could have driven until I ruined the engine *and* then blamed myself by saying, "You dummy. Not only did you not check the drain plug, you kept driving until you ruined your engine. Now you're in a real pickle. Can't you do anything right?"

The obvious and most practical solution, however, was to do what I did: acknowledge the warning light, examine the car, find the problem, get assistance and take the car to a mechanic. When we understand the purpose for guilt and take the problem to God for repairs, we have the help of the Master Mechanic, whose work is always faultless.

If God's purpose for guilt is to motivate man to seek help for his problems, why is it so difficult for many people to take that guilt to God? Because man is afraid of punishment. He has adopted what I like to call the "gotcha" concept—the idea that God is waiting for the chance to say, "Aha! You goofed and I gotcha!"

The fact of the matter, however, is this: God does not desire to punish you. Because God loves you, Jesus Christ paid at Calvary for all of your sins—past, present and future. Everything you ever will do wrong, God has already made provision to forgive.

Confession is the means by which we may take advantage of God's provision for forgiveness. 1 John 1:9 says, "If we confess our sins, He is faithful and just to forgive." Confess means to speak with or to agree with God that our action is sin. God is just. He abides by the rules. When we confess our sin, God forgives us by looking at Jesus. Seeing that His blood had already paid the price, He no longer holds us accountable.

Supposing I borrowed a hundred dollars from the bank and had trouble paying the note. If a friend were to pay the note for me, the bank could never again hold me accountable for that debt. It was not I who paid, but my friend. So it is with Jesus' death on the cross. He paid it all. When Jesus cried out, "It is finished," He used a term which in bookkeeping means, "Paid in full." At the moment I received Christ as my Savior, I said, "God, I'm taking your payment for my sins." At that point God deposited in the bank of heaven sufficient payment for all my sins. I am no longer accountable for them.

Let me give another illustration, for it is vital that this point be understood. Whenever there is a problem in a relationship, it's as if a drawbridge has been raised. For the relationship to be restored, both sides of the bridge must be let down. The one who was hurt must do his part on his side by forgiving, and the one who caused the hurt must let down his half of the bridge by confessing or apologizing. At Calvary, God let down His side. For me to have a right relationship with God and to have fellowship restored, I must confess. When I do not confess, my side of the bridge remains elevated, and I have separated myself from fellowship with God. But God stands ready to forgive me. I don't have to beg for forgiveness. All I must do is confess.

Let me illustrate just what happens in forgiveness. The Bible says that when we are forgiven, our sins are buried in the deepest ocean, remembered no more, removed as far as east is from the west, and covered by the blood of Christ. Typists know what Liquid Paper is. You make a mistake; you cover it. The most effective and beautiful covering in the world is the blood of Jesus Christ.

What about the judgment? I met my judgment at Calvary.

44

When I die and meet the Lord, I'm going to give a video account of my life. But here's an interesting thing. Whenever one of my sins passes by, it will be covered by Christ's blood. Not only that, but the sound will be bleeped on my videotape—the whole picture will be bleeped. That portion of my tape will be blood red. I may hate to see it, but there will be a lot of blood red on my tape. I imagine that will be the case for every Christian on that day.

The other thing the Bible says in 1 John 1:9 is that He forgives and cleanses me. The word *cleanses* comes from the word *justify*. A good way to understand the meaning of "justify" is to sound the word out, syllable by syllable: *just-as-if-I*. . . God looks upon me just as if I'd never sinned.

The first two needs, then, which must be fulfilled to achieve a healthy self-love, are love and forgiveness.

Belonging

The third need is a sense of belonging. The Bible says, "To as many as received Him, to them gave He the right to become sons of God." I am a child of God. You are a child of God. We belong to the family of God. Receiving Him meets the need for belonging.

Worth

Man's fourth basic need is a sense of worth. If we are children of God, the Bible says we are joint heirs with Jesus Christ. Have you ever *really* thought about the meaning of that statement? If I am a joint heir with Jesus Christ, then I don't have to feel that anyone is superior to me. Jesus is the most respected person I know, and I am an equal heir with Him. I have worth—not because of my achievement, but because of the gift of God through faith in Jesus. Worth is my free gift, received by faith.

Not only do I not feel inferior to anyone, but I cannot feel superior to anyone because others have that same worth. That equal worth is the most loving attitude I know. I cannot look up to, or down on, you. We have equal worth as joint heirs with Jesus Christ. Frequently people try to address me with a title before my name. When that happens, I ask that they simply call me Clyde. We are brothers and sisters in Christ, and the greatest privilege you can grant me is to call me by my name.

Purpose

A sense of purpose or accomplishment is man's fifth basic need. In Ephesians 2 Paul states that we are God's workmanship, created unto good works which God has before ordained, that we should walk in them. God has intended that we should do good works. Those works are not just moral "duties." God has a purpose for your life and mine. That purpose is something great. The greatest thing anyone can do is that which God wants him to do, whether it is to be an engineer, a garbage collector or a preacher.

Confidence

Sixth, man must have a sense of confidence if he is to achieve a healthy self-love. We're told in Philippians 4:13, "I can do all things through Christ who strengthens me." Not only that, but we are also assured, "My God shall supply all my needs according to His riches..." What better confidence can man achieve than to know God's power is available to help him accomplish not only all that he *needs* to accomplish, but far more than he is aware he is *able* to accomplish!

Security

Man's seventh basic need is a sense of security. That need is closely related to confidence, yet is perhaps even more important. Confidence is knowing you can walk a tight rope; security is knowing there's a net to catch you if you fall. Romans 8:28-29 gives us that security. "And we know that all things work together for good to them that love God, to them who are called according to His purpose. For whom He did foreknow, He also did predestinate to be conformed to the image of His Son, that he might be the firstborn among many brethren." We can have security, knowing that no matter what happens in our lives, no matter what hardships we may face or what mistakes we may take, God can work all things together for our good.

There is a simple exercise which I give to anyone who is having difficulty zeroing in on his self-love. I have that person write these words on a card: "God says I'm a beautiful person." I then ask him to look at that card three times a day for twenty-one days and memorize those words. He can then recall them when someone attacks his sense of acceptance. You may wish to try such an exercise. It's effective. (Other exercises for developing self-love appear at the end of this chapter.)

Once you understand the problem of the difficulty in achieving self-love and the needs which must be fulfilled to achieve it, you must then learn to love yourself. How do you go about that?

The first thing you must learn is to accept yourself.

Accept Your Physical Self

Some people are tall and some are short. Some are skinny; some are not. You must accept the fact that you cannot change your basic physical nature.

When I was young I wanted to play end for Baylor University. I dreamed of being 6'6" and weighing 225 pounds. I was playing football at 130 pounds, standing 6'2". Needless to say, my nickname was "birdlegs." I tried everything I could to grow. Finally I got up to 170 pounds. Within six months after I was married, I had gained thirty-five pounds—but in the wrong places. I have had to learn to accept my basic physical self. I have a friend who plays professional football. He stands 6'5" and weights 245 and can work out at a health club for a month and have a 50-inch chest. I've been working out for three years and cannot do better than a 42-inch chest. I've simply had to accept my basic physical nature. I can make sure I'm in good condition, but I can't change my basic nature.

Accept Your Mental Ability

I'm smart in some subjects and not so sharp in others. Math? That's a breeze. English? That's another story. Whenever I must put anything in writing, I find an English major to help me. I have accepted that. One must accept that there are some things he can do well mentally and others that he can't.

Accept Your Personality

Your temperament, or basic personality, is another thing which you must learn to accept about yourself. You cannot change your basic personality. You can temper it somewhat, but you cannot completely change it. For example, I am an extrovert. You may be an introvert. For you to try to become an extrovert or for me to try to become an introvert would be impossible. I may learn to sit back at times and let others take the lead, or you may learn to be more outgoing; but we cannot change our basic natures. Organization is not my strong point. By considerable time and effort I have improved in that area, but I know that I will never be the most organized person in the world. I have learned to accept that.

Accept Your Imperfections

One of the most difficult things for people to learn to accept is their imperfections—their "warts." Some people I have counseled have a great deal of difficulty in accepting themselves just as they are. They're always putting pressure on themselves, constantly trying to be better, better, better. I remind them, "God loves you, warts and all." Then I give them a simple exercise. The Bible says in all things give thanks. Make a list of your strengths. Then make a list of your weaknesses, your "warts." When you wake up in the morning, say, "Good morning, Lord." Then say, "Now, Lord, I want to thank you for loving me just as I am; and in order that I may love myself as you love me, I'm going to give thanks for my warts. I thank you for my temper, I thank you for my lack of organization, I thank you for..." right on down the list. "Thank you, Lord. Now today help me to learn to love myself just as You love me."

That sounds almost crazy, doesn't it? Yet love is being accepted, and you must accept yourself totally. Only as you learn to accept yourself can you really grow.

Your next step in learning to love yourself is to make some commitments to yourself.

The first thing I must commit myself to is accepting responsibility for myself. I could blame my dad and mother for all the things that happened in my childhood. I could blame my wife for any problems in our relationship. I could blame the deacons for any conflict in my ministry. But I must realize something. Whom does God hold accountable for Clyde? Clyde. I have learned to say that Clyde is responsible for Clyde.

Second, I must commit myself to making the most of every situation. Not every situation is good. There is rain as well as sunshine, but I have learned to make the most of every situation. Have you noticed, for example, that thriving businesses aren't the ones that sit around and complain when times are bad? They make the most of the situation, spending what they can to advertise, changing policies when necessary, keeping on going; and when times are better they continue to grow. The businesses that sit around and gripe when things are bad are the ones that fold.

I am determined with God's help to make the most of every

situation. Further, I have determined that no matter how far I fall—even if I hit bottom—I will look up and say, "God, forgive me," and I will pick up and go forward.

The Bible says that David was a man after God's own heart. Yet David had committed murder and adultery. David did not throw in the towel and say, "God, I can't." He faced his failure, confessed his sins, said, "God, thank you," and went forward.

Many people relate God's treatment of man to the childhood game of "red light." Basically, the rules are that the person who's "it" turns his back, counts to ten, turns abruptly, and if he catches someone moving, that person has to go all the way back to the beginning point. God doesn't make us go back to the beginning point. When we fall, we pick ourselves up and say, "God, forgive me," and go on from there. I have made a commitment to myself that no matter what happens, I am going to get up and keep going forward.

In addition to accepting myself and making commitments to myself, I must also give to myself.

I have learned to give myself certain physical and material things. There was a time when I felt guilty about buying anything for myself. I meet many divorced people who have a real problem with this. I have observed that women, especially mothers, frequently have problems in this area. Some, of course, may get into the opposite ditch and buy more than they need. But I have learned that to love myself, I must give myself certain material needs. I have also given myself the right for certain physical needs. Food is obviously a necessity, but what about rest and recreation? I have learned to give myself that time. There are times when I deliberately disappear because I must have time for myself. Jesus had times of retreat. If he needed that time, why should I feel guilty about it?

More importantly, I have learned to give myself several emotional needs. The first of these I give myself is the right to be me.

Romans 13:8 tells us, "Owe no man but to love him." That verse originally was intended in the area of money, and credit buying is not in God's plan. One day, however, I realized that the verse implied much more than money. Whenever the term "people pleaser" or "men pleaser" is used in the Bible, it always has a negative connotation. I am to *please God* and *love people,* but most people get it in the reverse. Any time I do anything merely to please another person, the ultimate result is resentment. If I am doing something merely to please you, I have a hook in that action that says, "Give me approval." If you don't give me approval, I will immediately resent you. If you give me approval, I will resent you later because I'll feel that you don't love me for myself, but rather the "me" that I become to gain your approval. Children go through a phase of testing to find out if their parents love them for themselves, or love them because they are good. I have learned that I am to love people, but that the only one to whom I am responsible—the only one I have to please—is God.

I remember a specific circumstance which taught me that truth. A number of years ago I decided to grow a mustache. My in-laws were visiting, and they told my parents about the mustache. My mother wrote a letter saying that Daddy would not come to visit as long as I had the mustache. I thought she was kidding. Six weeks later, however, I received another letter with news about a trip they had taken to see my sister. Mother closed the letter by mentioning that she would have to ride the bus to see me because Daddy would not visit me unless I shaved my mustache. I was scheduled to have lunch with them three days later on my way to a seminary meeting in New Orleans. I immediately sent them a special delivery letter in which I said, "I wish you could love me even if I were doing something immoral, but especially when I'm doing something you don't agree with even though no morals are involved. If that's the way you feel, I'll not even stop for lunch."

Mother called the day she received the letter, saying,

"Clyde, Daddy feels that way but I don't. Will you please stop by for my sake?"

I did stop by for lunch. Later I shaved the mustache—not because of Daddy's disapproval but because I was tired of it.

Some time later, I decided to grow a full beard. Just as it had reached a full size, I got a call that my mother was in the hospital. My wife asked, "Are you going to shave your beard?"

I said, "No, because if I shave it just to please them, I will resent them."

Owe no man but to love him. Please God, love people—not the reverse. I give myself that right.

Another right I give myself is to be assertive without being aggressive. That's taking the middle of the road. I could choose one ditch on that road and be so passive that I'd become a doormat; I could choose the other ditch and be so aggressive that I'd trample the rights of others. My choice, however, is assertiveness without aggression.

Often people who have been very passive and have allowed others to take advantage of them overcompensate by becoming aggressive. This frequently happens when a passive wife is divorced. Her attitude is, "Nobody's going to tell *me* what to do anymore. I'm free. I'm independent. Don't you dare get in my way, or I'll run over you jut to prove it."

When I assert myself in proper ways, I am giving myself the right to tell you what I think, what I feel and what I believe. I do not give myself the right to force you to agree with me because that is aggression. Telling you what I think and feel and believe is a right God has given to everyone, and marriages or even friendships need that kind of communication. If one spouse is not telling the other what he feels and thinks and believes, the marriage is a sick one. The self-love of the person who does not communicate is low. On the other hand, if one person tries to force the other to agree with him, normally the aggressor's self-love is low. That's the reason he feels compelled to use force. I give myself the right to be assertive. I give myself the right to say "no" as well as "yes."

Self-approval is another right I give myself. I need approval. Now I could pat myself on the back so much that I break my arm. That would be extreme—that's one ditch. Yet I have learned that if I do a job well, there's nothing wrong with looking at myself and saying, "Clyde, that's good." There are days you can comb your hair and it looks right. Other days it doesn't. If it looks good I think you should give yourself the right to say, "Hey! That looks great! You look sharp!" I'm serious about that.

Several years ago I had the privilege of speaking about self-love to students in the Bellaire High School homemaking courses. I spoke to classes four times during the day and then spoke on the same topic at a "Picking Up the Pieces" seminar that evening. Each time my talk was slightly different because it was never perfect. Even so, I felt each talk was good. Afterwards I said to myself, "Clyde, that was pretty good." I patted myself on the back because I had done a job well.

One final comment on achieving self-love. In learning to love myself, I must learn to forgive myself. The failure to forgive myself is just as big a sin as any other sin. That point should be underscored on everybody's mental tape because it's an important one.

How do I forgive myself? I must look at how God forgives me. God looks to the cross, sees the blood of Jesus Christ, says that Jesus paid the debt, and therefore he cannot hold Clyde accountable. How do I forgive Clyde? I look at the cross, see the blood of Jesus Christ, say Jesus has paid the debt, and therefore I no longer have the right to hold Clyde accountable. I forgive myself even as God forgives me—by looking at the cross.

When I make that statement, invariably someone says, "I know God has forgiven me, but I can't forgive myself. I expect more of myself than that."

"In other words, you're more righteous than God?" I'll ask.

"But I've got to pay for it," they continue.

"You mean to say the death of Jesus Christ wasn't sufficient?"

It's important to understand the point here. First, Jesus' death was sufficient. Second, if I have an excuse for what I do, I don't need forgiveness. Forgiveness is necessary only when there is no excuse. When I sin, when I fail to live up to God's laws and to my own expectations, I must learn to say, "I did it. No excuse possible. Thank you, God, for forgiving me."

Now when God forgives me, I have no right not to forgive myself. Failure to do so is itself a sin. There are many people today who are suffering from guilt trips because they have never learned how to forgive themselves, not realizing that their lack of forgiveness is just as serious a sin as any other sin—as serious as the one for which they cannot forgive themselves.

EXCERISE PROJECTS FOR DEVELOPING SELF-LOVE

1. Put the "Seven Bricks in the Foundation of a Healthy Self-Love" on 3 x 5 cards to read at least three times daily.

A SENSE OF BEING LOVED
"For God so loved the world, that He gave His only begotten Son, that whosoever believeth in Him should not perish, but have everlasting life."

John 3:16

"But God commendeth His love toward us, in that, while we were yet sinners, Christ died for us."

Romans 5:8

A SENSE OF FORGIVENESS
"If we confess our sins, He is faithful and just to forgive us our sins, and to cleanse us from all unrighteousness."

1 John 1:9

A SENSE OF BELONGING
"But as many as received Him, to them gave He power to become the sons of God, even to them that believe on His name."

John 1:2

A SENSE OF WORTH
"So God created Man in His own image, in the image of God created He him; male and female created He them."

Genesis 1:27

"For thou has possessed my reins; thou has covered me in my mother's womb. I will praise Thee, for I am fearfully and wonderfully made; marvelous are Thy works, and that my soul knoweth right well."

Psalms 139:13-14

"The Spirit itself beareth witness with our spirit, that we are the children of God; and if children, then heirs—heirs of God, and joint-heirs with Christ; if so be that we suffer with Him, that we may also be glorified together."

Romans 8:16-17

A SENSE OF PURPOSE
"For we are His workmanship, created in Christ Jesus unto good works, which God hath before ordained that we should walk in them."

Ephesians 2:10

A SENSE OF CONFIDENCE

"I can do all things through Christ which strengtheneth me."

Phillippians 4:13

A SENSE OF SECURITY
"And we know that all things work together for good to them that love God, to them who are the called according to His purpose. For whom He did foreknow, He also did predestinate to be conformed to the image of His Son, that He might be the firstborn among many brethren."

Romans 8:28-29

2. Make a list of qualities that you like about yourself and give God thanks for them daily.

3. Add to your list new strengths as you discover them.

4. Keep an Approval Diary by making note of the compliments received during each day. At the close of the day, read and give thanks for each one. In times of despair, go back and read pages from earlier days.
5. Make use of any of the following statements that meet your need.

I am God's child. Since He loves me and wants me to enjoy His abundance, I face each day with the expectancy that something beautiful will happen to me.

God knows the limitations of my being, so he commanded me to rest. Therefore, I give myself permission to rest and to play.

My worth is a gift from God. I do not have to earn it or prove it, just enjoy it.

Only God is perfect. Since I am human, I give myself permission to make mistakes. When I do, I will claim God's forgiveness, forgive myself and go forward just as if it never happened.

God made me unique! Therefore, I give myself permission to be different!

God made me, me; therefore, I give myself permission to be me, whoever that may be!

I am God's child and a joint heir with my brother, Jesus Christ.

Chapter Three

How To Trust
After Being Burned

How do we trust after being burned? If you've ever been too hasty in removing the cap from an overheated radiator—as I once was—you know the answer to that question. "Very carefully." Let's examine the problem in learning to trust after a relationship has been severed.

Since previous hurts are stored in our memory, they cannot simply be done away with. Scientific research has found that each cell of our brain stores a separate memory. Nothing that happens to us is ever forgotten. About eighty-five percent of our memory is in the subconscious; and even though we are not consciously aware of it, it affects everything we do. Our brains are like computers. Each separate cell has a separate byte of information. One's every past experience is stored on a tape. Each time one of these subconscious tapes plays a message saying, "You've been hurt—you'd best be careful," the individual is leery of what is happening around him. He finds himself withdrawing.

Further complicating the problem of trusting is the basic attitude people have toward the world. Most of us have a fatalistic concept of it—an attitude the church has promoted by teaching that the world will become worse and worse until Jesus comes again. So the idea is planted in the memory. "If the world is only going to get worse, there is no reason to trust anybody." Or, as the cliché goes, "Do unto others before they do unto you."

In addition to individual hurts and the climate of the world as a whole, we also must deal with a society in which misrepresentations occur repeatedly. For example, many buyers of used cars have been burned, so to speak, because the product was misrepresented to them. Frequently those who respond to an advertised sale find the store "out" of the advertised item although it "just happens" to have a slightly more expensive item in stock. The truth in advertising laws being legislated are a result of people's taking advantage of the weakness or ignorance of others.

In learning to trust, it is not difficult to see those problems which stem from past experiences that have made us skeptical. But not so obvious are the problems which stem from our basic concept of God—a concept I refer to as the "gotcha" concept.

To illustrate: Prior to a golf game, the pro asked the preacher how many strokes he wanted. "None," the preacher replied, "just three gotchas." "Now really," the pro said, "how many strokes?" Again, the preacher insisted on three gotchas. Despite confusion over the term, the pro consented. He understood what he'd agreed to upon teeing off, however; for just as he reached the top of his backswing, the preacher poked him in the rib cage, exclaiming gleefully, "Gotcha!"

Those who live in fear that God will get them for making mistakes can never really relax and enjoy life because they never know when the next "gotcha" is going to come.

Thus our past experiences, coupled with our concept of God, make us afraid to trust. Yet trust is essential to any meaningful relationship. If one cannot trust others, then he must be defensive. When he is defensive, he is closed to receiving anything from anyone.

When I speak before a group of people, I notice their body language. I can tell whether or not they are receptive by the positions of their bodies. As the book *BODY LANGUAGE* by Julius Fast describes, the sign of defensiveness is a closed position — arms folded, legs crossed at the knees. Someone who sits in this manner is saying, "Who is this idiot up here trying to tell me how to trust? He hasn't been burned like I have."

One day I realized that the body in its most open position, arms outstretched, pictures the cross. That position signifies total openness, complete vulnerability.

Without trust there can be no real intimacy, and therefore there can be no meaningful relationship. How does one trust after being burned? First, let's consider a theological foundation and then the practical aspects of it.

The foundation upon which to build trust is this: The Bible says that God works in all things for good to them that love the Lord. It says that nothing can happen to me without God's permission.

The book of Job illustrates this point. The first and third chapters relate that Satan came meandering up and down the earth and was asked by God what he had been doing. He replied that he had been looking at people. God then asked if he had observed Job and had noticed how much Job loved Him. Satan's reply, in effect, was, "He wouldn't love you so much if he were deprived of his wealth."

When God permitted Satan to take Job's possessions, Job still praised God. Satan was then permitted to make Job physically uncomfortable so long as he did not kill him. To Satan's chagrin, Job continued to love God through it all.

It's important to note that nothing could happen to Job without God's permission. In the end, God restored to Job everything he'd lost and more, making him far more blessed than he'd been before his suffering.

God will not keep us from experiencing hurt or pain. He does, however, promise that the pain will be limited to something that He can use for ultimate good.

Another important thing to realize about God is that He is a God of love. The Bible describes many aspects of the nature of God, but it states only one thing that God *is*: love. Love is a concern for the one who is loved. It causes the lover to do whatever is best for the loved. Because God really loves me, He is concerned about what is best for me. He wants me to have the best. He wants me to have life abundantly. Because of His love, he is honestly concerned to give me those things which will assure abundant living.

Many people, however, have difficulty believing that God wants them to have the best because they have a guilt complex. Psychiatrists say that probably the biggest problem in mental illness today is guilt. When one realizes God's love and forgiveness, however, he can eliminate that complex. God says if we will give the problem to Him, He will forgive; and once *He* forgives, it's done with forever. Not only that, but because we are spotless and blameless in the forgiveness of His love, nothing, absolutely nothing, can happen around us without God's first approving it as being something He can use for our good.

He does not promise to keep us from pain, however. There are two important reasons for that. The first is that in order to grow, there must be pain. That principle is as true in emotional growth as it is in physical growth. When an individual sets out to develop physical muscles, he cannot avoid experiencing pain. Muscles will be stiff and sore until the person's in shape. And even then muscles can be sore after an especially intense workout.

So it is with developing emotional stamina. To grow emotionally, one is certain to experience pain. Many people do not like counseling because they do not like the pain associated with growth. Yet God desires that we grow. He does not want to keep us in an incubator all our lives. He doesn't want us to remain emotional infants. And so He pushes us out into the world where pain and hurt exist, for He knows it is through problems we will grow. Problems may hurt us, but the hurt will not destroy us if we

permit God to help us work through the pain. Paul describes the pain he experienced as being knocked down but not out. We experience pain, but we are not annihilated.

The second reason God does not shelter us from pain is that He must allow evil if He is a God of love. That sounds like a contradiction; but if God is going to let me be a free moral agent, then He must allow evil to exist in order to give me a choice. If He were to manipulate me — if He were to take away my right to free choice — He would have to take away my right of personhood.

Some time ago a lady asked my advice on how to explain a situation to her child. She and her husband had been separated for six or seven months, and just that week they had decided to go ahead and finalize the divorce. Their 13-year-old son said, "Mama, I don't like God. God didn't answer my prayer. Ever since Daddy moved out, I've been praying that God would work out the situation. And Daddy is not coming back. God didn't answer my prayer."

I told her to say to her child simply this: "God in His love heard you. But in His love He would not force your daddy to come back home unless he wanted to do so. If God forced him to come home, He would take from him the right to choose." A God of love must allow evil.

So here we have established the means by which we can have the courage to trust. When we come to recognize that God in His love is working all things for our good, that He promises to put a limit around us so that we will not be destroyed by evil — then we can recognize that we may be hurt, but not destroyed. We may experience pain, but we will not be annihilated. And any pain we experience will be the kind which can enable us to become the persons God intended us to be. We will be able to say, "I trust you because I know that ultimately God is taking care of me."

Once such a firm theological foundation has been established, there are practical suggestions we may employ to help us put faith into action.

The first is to remove the garbage from the computer. Any time I have garbage — negative input — in my computer, it does not matter what else I put into it, the output will be garbage. The garbage I must destroy is bitterness. I believe the reason many people are afraid to trust each other is that they believe God will "get them," not for things over which they are actually guilty, but for misdirected guilt — for bitterness, which is the failure to forgive.

Bitterness is the opposite of love and is therefore a form of hate. There is no middle ground. One may love and hate simultaneously, but there is no emotion which links the two. One either loves or he hates.

How can you determine if you have any bitterness? Women, if you can go to the wedding of your former mate and be happy for him — even if he is marrying the most beautiful young woman in town — you don't have any bitterness. Wait, we're not finished yet. If you're happy when they leave for a honeymoon in Acapulco — a place you've always wanted to go but never had the chance — your bitterness is gone. And you'll *really* know it's gone when you're actually rejoicing because you know that "ex" hit it rich when the oil well came in on the property *he* got in the divorce settlement! (Men, the principle here applies to you, too.)

In other words, you can know all bitterness is gone when you can be happy every time you hear of something good happening to the person who has hurt you. Since bitterness is the opposite of love, and love is wanting the best for the person loved, only when you can actually desire good for that person can you know bitterness is gone.

The reason bitterness must be eliminated if you are to trust after being burned is that bitterness does not destroy the person you resent; it destroys you and the ones you love, and the destruction is both physical and emotional.

For a number of years medical doctors have recognized that one of the primary causes of stomach problems — ulcers, spastic colons and the like — is unresolved bitterness, or repressed hostility. It is also a major contributor to heart attacks. I have maintained for years that one of the major contributors to cancer is unresolved bitterness; and according to a Canadian doctor whose research on the subject was reported in the *New England Journal of Medicine* recently, it is indeed a contributing factor. I believe the reason two people can work around the same chemical, one contracting cancer, the other not, may well be that the one who becomes ill has bitterness.

Bitterness is destructive emotionally in three significant ways: 1.) As long as you have any resentment toward a person, you are negatively tied to that person. The relationship can be compared to a bank account. A bank closes out an account when the computer reads zero balance. If there is a plus balance, the account is open. If there is a negative balance, the account is still open. When the account gets to zero, it will be closed. Many people harbor resentment toward a mate who has walked out on them, and that resentment keeps them as tied to that mate as if he or she were strapped around their necks with a chain. The resentment keeps the account open with a negative balance. It keeps them from being able to start a new life.

One man I know kept an open account of resentment toward his father, and it literally drained his pocketbook. For years, he had gone from job to job without having much success at any of them. As a child, this man had been in a serious accident resulting in a lawsuit and settlement out of court. Two weeks before he was to become of age and receive the money, his father took off with all of it — about $250,000.

I pointed out this man's unresolved bitterness was costing him a sizable sum in unearned income and, unless he changed his ways, that would amount to a loss far exceeding that which was taken by the father. As the man thought about the matter, he realized he would be cheating himself. He then decided he'd kept a negative balance long enough, got rid of his resentment, went out to get the job he really wanted and began a new direction toward success.

2.) One's capacity to love is diminished by the sum total of all his bitterness. It is not possible to measure love; but for the sake of illustration, let's suppose we could. Suppose you could love with a capacity of one hundred units. You also have twenty-five units of bitterness — five to this person, three to that person, and so forth. The result is that the person whom you desire to love perfectly could receive only seventy-five units of love.

3.) All bitterness is always transferred to those whom you love. Any unresolved bitterness toward your parents will be transferred to your mate. Ladies, has your husband ever said to you, "Yes, Mama?" If so, I can guarantee you two things: one, you were doing something like his Mama that he didn't like; two, you probably were in the mama role instead of the wife role. When he made that statement, most likely he was expressing hidden, negative feelings left over from childhood.

Bitterness toward a former mate will be subconsciously transferred to others, including a future marriage partner. For example, consider a woman who was married to a man who ran around on her. She was the last person to find out, and the marriage ended in divorce. Subsequently, she married a man who wouldn't run around on his wife if he were paid to do so. Her first husband had used the excuse that he was working late. One night the new husband called to tell her he had to work late. Intellectually she accepted the fact. However, the moment he walked into the house, she unconsciously checked him over for any foreign scent of perfume, a stray hair on his coat or a smudge of make-up on his collar. Although she did not say a word, she sent out subconscious waves which her husband picked up, and a wall was built between them.

Children can also be hurt by transferred bitterness. I was called one day by the Pasadena police department and asked to go to the juvenile detention center to talk to a teenage boy. The young man had run away from home. Rather than detain him for a first offense, the police had tried to persuade him to go home, but he had refused. When they learned from him that I had been counseling with the family situation, they called me. As the young man shared with me, I quickly picked up on the problem. His parents had split up their marriage because the father was one of those people who would lie even when it was to his advantage to tell the truth. Mama, without realizing consciously what she was doing, had determined that there was going to be at least one decent male in this world; and whenever this young man would tell a lie, she would whip him unmercifully, releasing all the feelings of bitterness she still retained toward her "ex." The boy preferred to stay at the juvenile detention home rather than go home with his mother. She was hurting that boy by transferring her bitterness to him.

I could cite dozens of examples to illustrate how bitterness affects those we love. It is even the direct cause of attempted suicide among teenagers. Take my word for it, *bitterness destroys you.* I am convinced that the number one problem in early marriages — that is, people who marry between fifteen and twenty years of age — is not "immaturity"; it is unresolved bitterness toward parents. And the number one problem in second marriages is unresolved bitterness toward a former mate. Oh, people may say their problems are caused by their children, but those problems are nothing more than the external manifestation of the unresolved bitterness.

For that reason, I want to stress this point to men and women: If you are dating someone who puts all the blame on an ex-mate, run — don't walk — to the nearest exit! I will guarantee you, from a dozen-plus years of extensive work in this area, if you marry that person who places the total responsibility for the breakup of the marriage on the other peron, within two years you will be the next one that person is blaming.

If getting rid of bitterness is so vital to learning to trust, why do so many people hold onto their bitterness? Two reasons. They think the person who caused their pain deserves to be punished, and they think God is too loving to "get even" with people.

Often we spend hours of time in the fantasy of a revenge wish toward someone who has caused us pain. We hold onto the bitterness for the sheer pleasure of imagining outrageous forms of retaliation. Often we do not realize that God has made provision for all things, including the easing of our pain, if we will allow Him to do it His way. But we don't want to give God a chance. We know that God is a loving and forgiving God, and we're afraid He will be merciful rather than punish those who have hurt us. But that is God's job, for He says, "Vengeance is mine; I will repay." If you and I have bitterness, it does not hurt the other person. In holding onto bitterness, we only hurt ourselves. It is our responsibility to get rid of our bitterness.

How do we go about ridding ourselves of this destructive emotion? I recommend the following "prescription" for those who attend my seminars. It has proved an effective treatment.

Draw a vertical line down the center of a sheet of paper. At the top of the page, write the name of the person with whom you are dealing. (You can work with only one person at a time although you are likely to find there are many people with whom you must complete this exercise — a former mate, another male or female who was involved in the split, your parents, "friends," and even God.) On the left side of the paper, write down what that person did to hurt you. Perhaps it was something s/he failed to do. If he forgot an anniversary, for instance, that hurt you. List everything you can remember which caused you pain. (A word of warning here. When you begin to make the list, you will remember some things long forgotten. That is healthy because if you have forgotten the incident, you have not dealt with it; you have suppressed it. You have merely put scar tissue over it so that it comes out in misdirected ways. Time does not heal bitterness.)

On the right side of the paper, write your response to the action. Write what you did or what you wanted to do. Don't just list that you cried, or that you walked out of the house. After you finished crying, or after you walked out, then what did you do? Perhaps you didn't do what you wanted to do for fear of retaliation. Perhaps you are a woman who would liked to have "beaten the devil out of him," but you were afraid to attempt it because he was bigger than you. Perhaps you are a man who refrained from the violence you wanted to do only because you do not believe in hitting a woman. List what you did, what you felt, or what you thought. Do not write on the back of the paper, and don't be upset if you use two or three pages.

When you have completed your list, cut the paper on the line. Look at that right-hand side, your responses. You will find they fall into one of three categories: retaliation, withdrawal, or forgiveness.

Retaliation is the thought or action which says, "No matter what it takes, I'll get even with you." These responses may vary from the attitude of the lady who nonverbally communicates to her drunken husband, "Honey, you ain't gonna touch me tonight — forget it," to the action of another lady in the same circumstance who throws something at him. (One lady with whom I counseled said she was so annoyed by her husband's constant complaining about the food, she removed his dinner from the table one night and flushed it down the toilet.)

Your reaction may be something like the thought, "God, I wouldn't kill him, but if he were to die in a car wreck tonight, I surely would be thankful." I have learned through counseling that this wish is a prevalent one. I have become convinced that one of the primary problems which must be dealt with in the death of a mate is the guilt the survivor feels from having, at least once in the marriage, wished that mate dead.

The second response is withdrawal — moving away. You may not physically withdraw; it may be emotionally. You may actually move out and leave the person. Or you may build an emotional wall round you, not allowing that person to touch you emotionally. Both reactions are forms of withdrawal.

The third reaction is to lovingly forgive and do something nice. I believe that God gives us a revenge drive. This is not a vengeance drive — it is a revenge drive. Whenever God gives us a drive, He also gives us a way to deal with that drive. If we deal with that drive any way other than in the manner He has prescribed, our action becomes a sin. In Romans 13 Paul describes God's direction for our revenge drive. He says that if your enemy is hungry, you are to feed him. If he is thirsty, you are to give him a drink of water. In so doing, you will heap coals of fire upon his head. God's way of getting revenge is to lovingly forgive and do something nice for that person. (Ladies, that means to bake a cake and leave out the arsenic.)

Now, look at the response side of your list. Next, realize that any time you have done anything other than lovingly forgive, you have sinned. Confess your action as a sin, knowing that with God sin is sin. (Two wrongs do not make a right.) Know that God forgives you when you confess. Take a red marker and cross out that item on your list. Remember your sins, once confessed, are covered by the blood. Go on down the list, acknowledging, confessing, and covering with the red symbol of Christ's blood, each action which was contrary to God's instruction for forgiveness. When you have completed the list, take that portion of the paper and destroy it. Either flush it down the toilet or burn it, or both.

My telling you to flush or burn the list may sound strange, but I am serious about it. One person who was dealing with this exercise one night didn't want to wake the family by flushing the toilet, so he just tore up his list and threw it in the garbage can. He went to bed but he couldn't sleep. He got up, retrieved the list, burned each little piece until he scorched his fingers, dropped the ashes in the toilet and flushed them away. He then went back to bed and slept like a baby. There is a psychological advantage in creating the picture of actually getting rid of the list. Remember — your mind is like a computer, and you must complete the program for it really to take effect.

Now it is time to deal with the left-hand portion of the list. God says that if we are to experience forgiveness, we must forgive. So what are you going to do? You guessed it. Take that list of the hurts, and one by one mark them out, saying, "Okay, God, with your help, just as you have forgiven me, I forgive him for this," and "God, I forgive her for that." You may come to one of those items on the list and think, "No way." You'll swallow a couple of times and say, "God, you still work miracles, don't you? Will you work one now? Okay, God, with your help, I forgive him (or her) for this, too." When you have completed each item on the list, destroy that portion in the same manner you destroyed the other.

There is one last step. Remember — the computer in your

brain says you must do all the steps before the program is complete. The Bible also says that one must make restitution whenever possible, and ask forgiveness, for the wrongdoing. Ask God to help you write out an apology which you will personally communicate to the individual involved (unless God stops you from that communication). Don't go into all the gory details — you've flushed those away. They're gone. All you are doing is communicating your request for forgiveness. You are saying you know there were situations in which you felt hurt, that you became very bitter toward that person, and that you want forgiveness.

Often when I give this final step, people will say they are afraid. They don't know what will happen when they talk to that person. I don't know either. Someone may call his or her "ex" to apologize and be told, "You sorry so-and-so, I'm glad you finally realize it wasn't all my fault." Perhaps some "ex" who never paid child support will be so shocked he dies of a heart attack and the women will collect social security.

Seriously, there is no way to predict what the response of the other person may be. But take the risk and follow through. Remember this: You have already asked God to help you in this matter, and you can rest assured He will respond to your prayer. He's in the business of forgiveness.

Some people have trouble forgiving because they confuse the concept of forgiveness with forgetting. Forgiveness does not mean to forget, for this is an impossibility. The brain stores forever that which happens to an individual. Forgiveness is declaring the debt paid in full. When a bank note is paid off, the bank does not destroy the note; it stamps it PAID IN FULL and files it in the official records.

However, the bank can never again hold one accountable for the debt. Thus, when one forgives, though one does not forget what happened, one no longer holds the debtor accountable.

After dealing with bitterness on your way to learning how to trust after being burned, you must accept the fact that no one is perfect. You and I both make mistakes. A person will give me a message, and I will forget it. I may promise to do something and then forget the promise. I am not perfect. Neither is anyone else. If you are going to trust anyone, you must trust within the framework of recognizing that people are not perfect. Expect perfection and you expect the impossible. Further, those who harbor such unrealistic expectations will find it difficult to enter into new relationships.

Now then, if you want to develop a relationship — and only after you have dealt with bitterness and accepted the fact that no one is perfect will you be ready — you must learn to develop that relationship slowly. How do you trust after being burned? Very carefully. Very slowly.

There are levels of emotional intimacy. For sake of illustration, let's suppose there are ten such levels. Level one is the least amount of communication; level ten is complete openness. Never go more than one level deeper with a person than that person is willing to go with you. In other words, if you are attempting to form a relationship with a person and s/he goes through a level two, do not go below a level three. If you do, that person may panic. He will realize that if he is to maintain the relationship, he must go on to a deeper level of communication of intimacy. If he is not ready for that level, he must run. If he does not run, he may be embarrassed or uncomfortable and may lash out at you. I repeat: Never go more than one level deeper than the person has gone with you!

An illustration comes to mind of a lady with whom I was counseling. She had been a "church angel"; but after having gone through a divorce, she felt very insecure. To prove her desirability, she went through a period of "bed hopping" and had all kinds of relationships about which she felt very guilty. Then she met a man whom she really liked; but because of her punishment concept, she felt it necessary to tell him about all her garbage on the first date. She wondered why he never called again. She did not realize that some things need never be told. When she bared herself to that extent, he felt pressured to bare himself to the same degree. He was not ready to do so; therefore he ran.

I have counseled many people in similar situations. All have a similar story to tell. They shared too deeply; the other party rapidly headed for the first exit. If you are ever tempted to say too much, stop. THINK. Remember, never more than one step deeper. . .

Another important step in learning to build relationships is to learn to listen. All people have some hang-ups. In building a relationship you must learn to listen to what the other person is saying. If a person is constantly finding fault with others or griping and complaining, then that person is not someone with whom you should attempt to form a relationship.

A healthy relationship must be formed by healthy people; and if someone is constantly finding fault with others, I can know that if I attempt to form a friendship with him, he'll only begin to gripe or complain about me next. Most everyone has some areas where they are less tolerant, or about which they may complain. By listening, I can determine in which areas a person is tolerant; and to avoid rejection by that person, I can simply avoid discussing areas subject to criticism. My desire is to find friends who can accept everything about me; but until I find those people, I can avoid rejection by listening to others and then selectively sharing only those portions of my nature which they can accept.

I recall an example of this principle when I was a pastor at a church in Port Arthur. Two of my deacons had selected areas of prejudice. One man had no racial prejudice whatsoever, but he detested divorced people; the other had love and compassion for divorced people, but his racial prejudice bordered on violence. I learned very quickly that if I wanted to talk about my ministry to the divorced, I did not go to the man who resented divorced people. I discussed that part of Clyde with the racially-prejudiced man who was very supportive of my ministry to previously married singles. On the other hand, I could not discuss with this man the need for ministry to the blacks who resided in our district. To get support for that ministry, I had to talk to the man who was prejudiced against previously married singles, but who could accept the principle of integration.

To minimize your vulnerability to hurt when forming relationships, then, you must learn to listen. You'll hear "where people are," and then you can share with them who you are (to that point which will not be destructive to you). You can also hold back at those points of destruction. Listen. Find those people who are critical and avoid them. That's biblical, by the way. Paul says to mark out the cantankerous persons and avoid them.

Let's do a review of learning to trust up to this point. We have seen that the reasons we fear trusting stem from our past experiences of hurt and rejection by others — both by individuals and by society as a whole — experiences which are stored on a "computer tape" in our brains. We also have seen that another problem is our "gotcha" concept of God. We have learned that trust is a vital part of forming relationships. To learn to trust, we must realize that God is a God of love, that nothing can happen to us without His permission, and that He has promised to use everything that happens in our lives for our ultimate good. In recognizing God's love and power, we can know there is nothing another person can do to us in a relationship that God has not permitted and that He cannot use to our ultimate good.

Once we have decided we can afford to learn to trust, then we must remove the garbage from our computers — get rid of our bitterness and resentment. Then we must accept that people are imperfect and learn to trust them within the framework of their imperfections. As we begin to build relationships, we must do so slowly, being careful not to rush the other person into a deeper level of sharing than he or she is ready to accept. We can further avoid placing ourselves in situations which will create hurt if we learn to listen, if we seek as friends those people who are open and accepting, and if we learn to select the information we share with people based on their areas of acceptance and prejudice.

A key principle in learning to trust and to build relationships is that we must learn to develop multiple relationships. There are several important reasons why multiple relationships are healthy and necessary. First of all, few people can hear and accept everything. As we seek to find someone who can accept us totally, we can find in the process one person who can accept one part of our nature, and another person who can accept another part and so on. Then we can experience acceptance of all parts of us by someone in our circle of friends.

Second, as I get into relationships, I may find that one person whom I love is not ready for a deep relationship. He or she may get down to a level three, and that's where the communication stops. Since I want to find a level ten, I keep building more relationships because I cannot force that person to a level with which he or she is not prepared to cope.

One of the things that concerns me about singles is that frequently when they get out of a marriage, the first thing they want to do is to "go steady." They latch onto one person and do not develop multiple relationships. That is very dangerous because if *that* relationship falls apart — which it frequently does with newly single people — they are left alone, having to cope all over again with the rejection they experienced at the end of their marriage.

Another reason why multiple relationships are important is that through those relationships, our capacity to trust grows. If you will build brother-sister, sister-sister, or brother-brother relationships, then you can grow in your ability to trust and to relate to others; and eventually you will become ready for a husband-wife relationship.

As I think back over my friendships, numerous examples of learning to trust through brother-sister relationships come to mind. One in particular stands out in my memory. I was counseling with a lady who had gone through a tremendously painful divorce. She had come to a point where she was afraid to trust men. She and I began to relate, first from my being her pastor, then her counselor, and finally her brother in Christ. Out of our brother-sister relationship she learned to trust men again. Even-

74

tually she was able to trust a young man whom she married. An amusing sidelight of that story is that six months or so after their wedding, the young man was sharing his feelings during a lay witness campaign in our church. He said at first it really bothered him that I seemed closer to his wife than he was. I seemed to know more about her, and she could share more with me than she could with her husband. He said he had come to understand, however, that my relationship with his wife had been the basis on which she had learned to trust; and as their relationship had matured, he no longer felt threatened. That brought an immense sigh of relief from me because he was the guy with the 50-inch chest I mentioned earlier, and I certainly didn't want him to get upset with me!

A fourth reason for building multiple relationships is that a person can have only one ten, but he can have many sevens and eights. A person who has one ten is a millionnaire. But if you can have several sevens and eights, and something happens to your ten, you are not destroyed. Knowing that you have these friendships can give you the courage necessary to give your ten the freedom to be himself, and thus keep you from destroying the relationship by smothering him. It's like the golfer who approaches a water hole. If he has only one golf ball, he knows he's out of the game if it goes in the water. He will be uptight, and chances are he will make a poor shot. On the other hand, if he has a dozen new Titleists in his bag, he can swing freely and make a more beautiful shot because he is not uptight about his game.

As a sideline here, I want to mention something that has troubled me. I find that when many people marry, they become so jealous and possessive of their mate they never relate with other people. That jealousy will ultimately destroy the relationship. For that reason, I have changed the vows I use in a wedding ceremony. I no longer use the phrase, "leaving all others to cleave to you only." I use the phrase, "to give myself without reserve to you."

It is important, then, to learn to develop many relationships at a light level. Out of these friendships you will begin to develop some deeper relationships in which you can share who you are and what you are feeling at a given moment. As you learn to share, you'll find you *can* trust again. As you learn to share with members of the same sex, then you can break from that to members of the opposite sex. Soon you will find that you have many friends; and it is not so painful to run the risk of developing a deeper relationship because if it should fall apart, you still have friends with whom you can share.

Yes, it *is* possible to learn to trust again after being burned; and if you employ the principles discussed in this chapter, there will come a day when you'll suddenly realize you are able to trust far more than you ever thought you could. There will come a day your world will smile again.

Chapter Four

The Nature of Love

My purpose as a counselor is to enable people to find happiness. My goal is to help each person remove any and all obstacles to valid relationships. The Bible clearly teaches that God made us to be in relationship, one with another. When we are not in meaningful relationships, we're miserable. We're discontented — unhappy. It is through establishing meaningful relationships that we can find happiness. One does not have to be married to be happy; but one must be in meaningful relationships to be happy.

The foundation for all meaningful relationships is love. The foundation for all negative relationships is hate or resentment. If you are to pick up the pieces and be happy in your life, you must work back to involvement in meaningful relationships. To do so, you must build upon love.

But what is love? We talk about it all the time, but what *is* it? There are three words used in the Bible which mean love: *eros, phileo* and *agape.* These words have been described as the three kinds of love. I prefer to designate them as the three *levels* of love.

The Three Levels of Love

The first level is a selfish love. It is *eros*. Many people define *eros* as sexual love. Actually, *eros* denotes a selfish type of love. If you will notice, the pervading thought in erotic literature is, "Meet my needs." This expression or level of love is the one with which a baby is born. A baby cries, "Whaa!" (I'm hungry! Feed me!) "Whaa!" (I'm dirty — change me.) In other words — meet my needs. Everyone enters life at that level of love, but hopefully we progress beyond it. Sadly, however, many people stagnate right there. I believe one of the reasons for the high divorce rate among Hollywood stars is that so many of the "prima donnas" are selfishly saying, "Meet my needs."

Hopefully, however, we then progress to *phileo* love. *Phileo* love has been defined as brotherly love. I like to describe it as "swap love." At the *phileo* level of love, one communicates, "I love you, if. . ." It is a conditional love. You see, I need to be loved well as to love. Because I have a fear that you may not love me, it is easy to "swap" love — "I'll love you if you love me." "I'll love you as long as you care for me." "I'll love you as long as I believe that ultimately you will care for me or love me in return." *Phileo* love is the highest form of purely human love.

The highest form of love is *agape* — gift love. With *agape* love, there is no condition. It does not say, "I'll love you, if. . ." Gift love says, "I love you; therefore I give. I give you what I can provide to meet your needs as long as I have the ability to give it." *Agape* love is giving without conditions. If *phileo* love is the highest form of purely human love, how do we progress to *agape* love? By establishing a personal relationship with God, believing that God will meet our needs. Without that relationship with God, a person will fear gift love. One will fear giving with no conditions because the gift may not be returned. There is that fear that over a period of time, one would have nothing left to give. Swapping love can be much more comfortable than giving love if a person does not have that faith in God's ultimately meeting his needs.

Kinds vs. Levels of Love

The reason I refer to the three biblical words for love as being levels, rather than kinds of love, is that there are many kinds of love. There is parental love, romantic love, puppy love. These *kinds* of love are relationships. A relationship can take on any one of the three levels of love; thus one *kind* of love can have three different *levels*.

For example, a parent-child relationship can be very selfish. Perhaps you have heard a parent say, "My child owes me such-and-such because of what I gave to that child. Twenty years of giving. The child owes me." A parent with such an attitude has, at best, swapped love. There was no gift involved. So you see the relationship of parental love may be on a selfish, swap or gift level.

What about romantic love? Romantic love is also a relationship which can take on the attitude of one of three levels. The quality which separates romantic love relationships from family or brother-sister love relationships is that in romantic love, there is a complementation. A person will be romantically involved or interested in someone who would complement him or her. Complement means to make whole. In the chapter entitled "Preparation for Remarriage," we shall examine in depth the complementary nature of romantic love relationships. For now, let me briefly say that a person will be romantically attracted to that person who meets him at his point of weakness — his point of need. There are some women I love dearly; yet if something were to happen to my wife, I would never have any desire to be romantically involved with them. I would keep on loving them. These are beautiful, great ladies. But they do not complement me. The key is that in a romantic relationship, there are complementary needs which, when fulfilled by each other, make a completion.

The Qualities of *Agape* Love

Agape love — gift love. If that is the ultimate love—the love to which we aspire — then how do we achieve it? What is it? How do you define it? At one time I tried to define love, but I had to give up. I began instead to search for terms that would describe it. I found in I Corinthians 13, eleven terms that describe gift love.

Love Is Patient. . .

The first quality of *agape* love is that it is patient. I want to give you two observations on that word *patient*.

First, patience accepts others just as they are, as equals. We have previously established that acceptance and approval are not synonymous. A person may do something of which I do not approve, yet I can still accept him as my equal. I often observe tragedies caused by the lack of that acceptance. Pardon me, ladies, but this is one area of feminine weakness. A lady will meet a man and think, "You know, he's a diamond in the rough. He's got this fault and that fault, but let me be married to him six months or a year, and I'll take off all the rough edges. He'll be the most beautiful diamond God ever created!" The moment she puts her thoughts into action, she changes from a mate relationship to a parent-child relationship. The relationship disintegrates, and the lady wonders why she feels so unloved and unaccepted. I believe this trait to be predominately feminine due to its evolving from the maternal instinct. Acceptance says, "I count on you as my equal even though I do not always agree with you or approve of you."

Secondly, that word *patience* involves not only the word *acceptance,* but also the idea of "I am willing to bear with you." This is an area in which I, as a counselor, must be very careful. My work is helping people to grow. In that process I often must be very understanding and patient, because if I move too fast I can destroy the person. Did you, as a child, ever plant carrots or radishes and as soon as you saw the greenery, pull it up to see what was there? You put it back in the ground and wondered why it died. By harvest time you had pulled up half your crop!

Love is patient—that is, it bears with others, giving them the freedom and opportunity to grow to become what they were intended to be.

Love Is Kind. . .

The second quality of love is that it is kind. I sometimes wonder what happened to common courtesy. Being kind is thinking about the other person — trying to help that person. It is not demeaning to be kind. Kindness can be something as simple as sending a card or picking up the phone just to say, "I was thinking about you." Kindness is consideration of the other person's needs, of the other's moods. You know, some days I'm in a great mood. There are other days when, very honestly, I'm down in the valley. Kindness is being sensitive to the other person's mood, accepting that person in whatever state he may be. Love is kind. It is thoughtful of the other person.

Love Is Not Jealous. . .

The third word I find describing love in that passage is very intriguing. Love is not jealous. I'm glad God said that rather than I, because I know so many people who want their loved one to be more jealous! But jealousy is not a thought about the other person. Jealousy is a selfish attempt to possess another and is based upon one's own personal insecurity.

Jealousy is a term that requires close examination. Many people are confused about the term because in Exodus, God is described as a jealous God. Some people rationalize that if we are made in God's image, and God is jealous, then we are created to be jealous. The argument sounds logical, but it is incorrect. In the first place, a more accurate translation would read "zealous." God is very concerned about His people. But for the sake of argument, leaving the term as translated, there is a valid reason for God's jealousy that is not valid for man. You see, man is God's creation. As creator, God has the right to possess man and thus to be jealous of man's worship of other gods. On the other hand, no one has the right to possess another person. People cannot be our possessions. I cannot possess you; you are my equal. You are a person. I can possess a thing. If I become possessive of you, I am treating you as a possession — a thing, rather than as a person. No, love is not jealous.

Frequently I am asked, "What is the cause of jealousy?"

Jealousy has its roots in two things: personal insecurity and lack of faith. When a person is insecure — when he lacks a healthy self-love — he thinks that because he sees himself as unlovable, no one could really love him. Therefore, he fears rejection to the point that he literally attempts to put his loved one in a cage. He thinks that by locking that other person away and preventing his or her relating to anyone else, he can hold onto that person's love. When a person lacks faith in God's willingness and ability to meet his needs, then this lack of faith will reflect in his relationships with his loved ones. There is no one in the world more miserable than the person who is jealous. If you are jealous, the person you love cannot walk out the door without your fearing he will not return. How can you enjoy life with such an attitude?

Love Is Not Arrogant. . .

The next description of love is that it is not arrogant. The best way to describe arrogance is this: "It's *my* way or no way! We will do what *I* want; I'm the dictator." Love, on the other hand, acknowledges the intelligence and competence of the other person; thus there is freedom to share. One of the things we'll examine in the chapter "The Battle Between the Sexes" is the way to have a good argument. Good marriages have good arguments; bad marriages have no arguments or bad arguments, one or the other. The secret to a good argument is that there is no loser. If one person wins and insists that he is right and the other wrong, he may think he has won just because he won the argument, when in effect they have both lost. They are both losers because the relationship has been undermined. No, love is not arrogant. It is not boasting about how good I am and putting you down. It is consideration of the other person, esteeming him as an equal.

There are two movements in our society today about which I am very concerned: the manpower and womanpower movements. You see, any time men and women get into competition as to who is stronger, more worthy, or more beautiful, they ultimately destroy one another. In God's sight, we're equal. Different, yes — but equal. Love is not arrogant.

Love Does Not Manipulate. . .

The fifth description of love is that it does not manipulate. There are many ways of manipulating. There is that obvious, bossy way of insisting that the other do one's will. There is also much more subtle manipulation. Ladies, have you ever manipulated a man by his stomach? You know—you want a new dress, and you know that his favorite meal is sauce *picante,* and so you cook up a good *roux*? How about a gumbo? Men, have you ever wanted a new fishing boat and manipulated your lady with a night on the town and a bouquet of roses? Love does not manipulate.

Did you ever stop to wonder why God said that love does not manipulate? One of the worst books ever written, in my opinion, was written by a man whom I respect, John Drakeford. The book is entitled *How to Manipulate Your Mate.* The concept is atrocious because it assumes that you know what is good for your mate, so you simply manipulate him or her into becoming what you know that mate should be. I couldn't disagree more. There is only one Being who knows what's best for me: God. And not even God will manipulate me. To manipulate me would be to take away my freedom of choice; and if God were to take away my freedom of choice, he would destroy my personhood.

If God, who is omnipotent, who really knows what is best for me, will not manipulate me, then what gives a person who loves me, and who *thinks* he knows what is best for me, the right to manipulate me? That person may *think* he knows what is best for me; but when that person becomes *certain* he knows what is best for me, then he has usurped the place of God.

Now, ladies, if you think you know what is best for that man, you've usurped the place of God. And men, if you think you know what's best for that woman you've been seeing, and you start trying to manipulate her, you are trying to play God in her life. You may think you're the best thing that ever hit this earth and she ought to know it. But you may not be. If you manipulate her, I'll guarantee you one thing — down the road she'll resent you for it. And women, vice versa. Love does not manipulate.

Love Does Not Keep a Record of Wrongs Suffered. . .

Sixth, love does not keep a record of wrongs suffered. Remember the description from the last chapter of the garbage bag? That is the best description I know of keeping a record of wrongs suffered. The proper treatment of a garbage bag is to put it in the refuse heap so that the garbage man may dispose of it forever. Love keeps no record — it forgives; and like that garbage which has been carried away, the wrong is gone forever. If you get into an argument with your loved one, and you bring up something from two or three previous arguments, you haven't taken out the garbage. If you keep bringing up the same old debris, you have not dealt with your bitterness. In counseling I frequently see couples play a little game with this record of wrongs. I call it "one upmanship." It goes like this: "You wronged me — therefore I have a wrong coming. Now, I let this one ride, but you wronged me again. I've accumulated two little ones — so instead of taking two little ones, I'll take one big one." Each person wonders why he or she feels so uncomfortable. It's no wonder. Each is afraid the other has the next "gotcha" coming. They're on a merry-go-round of retaliation and keeping score. I wonder, where is the love? Where is the relationship? No, love does not keep a record of wrongs suffered. As God forgives us, burying our wrongs under the blood of Jesus Christ, so we are commanded to forgive one another, burying each other's wrongs beneath that same blood.

Love Bears All Things. . .

The seventh quality of love is that love bears all things. The word translated "bears all things" is an interesting word. From the same word is translated the meaning "to cover"—like the roof of a building. It is true that a person must accept responsibility for his or her life, for his or her actions; but in love one must not share another's dirty linen with the outside world deliberately. There are two areas in which this lack of love is commonly apparent.

The first failure in this area is the old "put-down." I don't even like humor of this kind. My Irish temper really wants to come unleashed when I hear a man put a woman down in public, and I have to squash the impulse to put my fist down his throat. On the other hand, some of the most vicious cutting I have heard in my life has come from the lips of women. Put-downs are obnoxious.

But as vicious as the put-down may be, there is a companion action just as lacking in love, and that is gossip. Love doesn't go around sharing the dirt about others. Years ago when I was in the pastoral ministry, one of my first statements to a new church was this: "Don't any of you come to me with gossip about anybody. If you have a legitimate, honest concern for the welfare of that person, and you want to fall upon your knees in my presence and pray about and for this person, fine. But if you're coming to tell me gossip about somebody, I don't want to hear it. I am not their judge; only God is." I have little patience with gossip. I believe it to be one of the most atrocious, obnoxious and reprobate of sins.

Love bears all things. Love covers all things under the umbrella of love.

Love Is Loyal. . .

Another description is that love is loyal. Love believes in the beloved. Love relates to another with loyalty, a genuine concern for the welfare of the other.

We have all heard that old statement, "All's fair in love and war." I dislike that statement because it encourages one of the actions which becomes a roadblock to the development of meaningful relationships among singles. Have you ever been stabbed in the back, so to speak, by a trusted friend? Ladies, have you ever shared a secret with a lady friend, only to have her use that information against you when you find yourselves in competition for the same man? It is that type of behavior which causes one to fear developing meaningful relationships. Love is loyal — love is supportive. It believes in a person.

Another saying which concerns me is, "Where there's smoke there must be fire." All a person has to do to instigate a belief in fire is to throw a smoke grenade now and then. You know — the little insinuation, the innuendo. People look for reasons to doubt one another. Frequently singles are afraid to relate to others because of what "someone might say," knowing that their friends are not supportive. That is not love. Love believes in, is loyal to and supportive of the beloved.

Love Is Optimistic. . .

Love hopes all things. That is optimism. That is the belief that all things will work out for the good. I tire very quickly of hearing murmuring, griping, complaining that life is bad, or that people are bad. A study of the Old Testament will disclose that God chastised the children of Israel because of their murmuring, negative attitude. Love is not pessimistic — it is optimistic!

The Christian lifestyle should be like a fountain of youth.

People are old when they have more to look back on than they have to look forward to. If a twenty-six-year-old feels he or she has more to look back on than forward to, that person's old. A person may be ninety-five and young. If I believe in eternity, then I should always remain young.

There is a yardstick by which one may measure maturity. A person is immature when he can dream dreams but cannot accept the realities of life. A person is old when he can accept the realities of life, but cannot dream dreams. The mature person, then, is the one who can both dream and accept reality. Love is an attitude which says that there are going to be rough moments, but that those who love can overcome the problems together. Love is an attitude of optimism.

Love Never Ends. . .

The last quality of love is perhaps the best: Love never ends. Someone has said that whenever love has an ending, it is puppy love. This observation may be valid, but there is more to it than that. What is the opposite of love? Hate—also known as bitterness or resentment. We have previously established that any bitterness or resentment held toward another automatically diminishes one's ability to love. Now, here is something which is difficult for many to comprehend. If you stop loving your former mate, you are diminishing your capacity to love in the present. I can anticipate a puzzled frown from many a reader at this point. You may say, "Clyde, that man walked out on me and doesn't give a hoot whether I live or die. What am I to do?"

What you must *not* do is change the love you had for that person into bitterness or hate. You must change it into another kind of love. The marriage is dead, and so you bury the marriage. But you learn to love the person as a brother or a sister because your failure to do so diminishes your capacity to love now. True love goes on without end.

Learning *Agape* Love

How does one learn to love with an *agape* love? A gift love, no strings attached? First, let me clarify one thing. I do not believe anyone can love this type of love in perfection. But I know we can grow in that love as we relate to God. It is through my having a basic faith in God that He is going to meet my love need, that I can have the courage to love others without demanding or expecting anything in return. I can allow God's love to flow through me to others.

Chapter Five

Coping With Loneliness

"How do I cope with loneliness?" is the common cry of those singles who are picking up the pieces following the death of a marriage. The question is an important one, for loneliness must be dealt with if the single is to become "whole in one" again.

Let us examine the meaning of loneliness and its causes before we discuss solutions to this universal problem. As I said in the first chapter, loneliness and aloneness are not the same. Busy-ness is not an antonym for loneliness. Loneliness is not having anyone with whom you can share your feelings. One can be lonely in the midst of a crowd. If you doubt that statement, go to any singles' bar and really study the faces of the people you find there.

Sometimes leaders are the loneliest people in the world. Ministers, for example, are frequently lonely. Many of them have difficulty being really close or sharing with anyone. The minister who shares with any particular individual in his congregation is often accused of playing favorites. If he shares with anybody outside the congregation, he is condemned for being disloyal to his members. That is the reason so many ministers find it difficult to develop really meaningful relationships.

One is lonely when he has no one with whom he can share in

an intimate way. Loneliness is having no one with whom you have such a rapport and sense of belonging that you know you can express anything you feel, yet not be rejected if your feelings are negative.

The Causes of Loneliness

Fear of rejection is one of the causes of loneliness. The Bible clearly teaches that God made man to be in relationship. In his book *Games People Play,* Eric Bern stressed the fact that our deepest need is relationships. Bern stresses the word *intimacy,* referring to emotional rather than physical intimacy. Yet as John Powell, author of *Why Am I Afraid to Tell You Who I Am?,* explains, the thing which one needs most is also that which one fears most. "I am afraid to tell you who I am because if I tell you who I am, you may not like who I am, and it's all that I have."

Everyone suffers to a greater or lesser extent from fear of rejection. One reason for this fear is the criticism expressed by others. You see, if I hear you putting someone down for a fault, yet I know that I have the same imperfection, then I know if I shared with you who I really am and what I really am feeling, you would condemn me as well. I'm afraid because I don't like rejection. Fear of rejection causes one to play games. The party involved will seek companions who share his faults so that he can have a semblance of relationship without becoming totally vulnerable.

Competition is another cause of loneliness. We are in a competitive society. Our basic drive is to be the best. But, as Paul Tournier has said, "To that degree that I am in competition with another, that person is my enemy." If I am competing with you in some area, then I am afraid to tell you who I really am because one day you may use it against me.

People frequently find themselves in competition for relationships. For instance, if I want to be your best friend—if I want you to love me better than you love anybody else—then every other friend you have is a threat to me. I desire a closeness;

and yet I am afraid to share with you my innermost secrets, fearing that some day you may use that information against me, or you may use it to compete with me for the friendship of another.

Ladies, have you ever feared to tell a lady friend some your "warts" because you were afraid that some day the two of you might be competing for the affections of the same gentleman? Afraid she might "accidentally" let slip this knowledge in order to shoot you out of the saddle? Some people who have been burned by such treatment will build a shell in self defense, thus not allowing anyone to know what they are feeling or thinking.

So you see, when I am afraid to share with you who I am because I'm afraid of the competition, I find myself being a very lonely person.

A number of years ago a friend pointed out my own competitive nature. The friend's husband and I played on the same church basketball team. He was a coach and was five years younger than I. Yet, without realizing it, I was trying to be a better basketball player than he. I would have a tendency to try to make a difficult shot, rather than to pass the ball to him when he was wide open. Subconsciously I knew if he scored more points than I, he would be considered the better player.

Have you ever watched competition at work around you? Perhaps you're in an office, and you want to be the best secretary there. You want to receive more praise than any other secretary—or at least your share plus. So you find yourself comparing notes as to how many compliments you get compared to the secretary at the next desk. Without realizing it, you have become involved in a competitive rat race with everybody around you. Since the competition makes them your enemies, you start building a little wall around yourself. It is behind that wall that loneliness sets in.

A third cause of loneliness is the fear of what a relationship will cost. One closes others out because he does not like to have to pay the price. What is the price of friendship? One price can be measured in pain. Everyone has been hurt by others; some have been burned badly. When one has experienced a great deal of pain, his tendency is to protect himself against any pain. But the only way one can be totally isolated from pain is to shut oneself inside a wall. Any time one is in a vital, meaningful relationship with another, he will rejoice with that person's joys—but he will also hurt with that person's pain. Even lasting friendships contain an element of pain.

A second cost of friendship can be measured in time. To be a true friend, you must be available when your friend needs you. Friends don't always have needs when it is convenient. What if your friend calls you at two in the morning and says, "I need you?" Are you willing to crawl out of that warm bed to get out on a cold, wet February morning to help a friend in pain? Are you willing to pay the price?

In my counseling ministry I often tell people to feel free to call me at two in the morning if they really need me. Yet frequently people have been in desperate need, but would not call. Finally I realized the reason for that: They themselves would not be willing to be someone's friend at that hour in the morning. They hesitated to take advantage of my offer because they were unwilling to pay the price of friendship. They were afraid of the hook.

Yes, love costs. Love is a free gift, but the cost of providing the gift is expensive. There is nothing worthwhile that does not cost someone something. Yet the cost of friendship cannot possibly be as much as the cost of loneliness. The cost of friendship is borne jointly by you and your friend; the cost of loneliness is paid alone.

Overcoming Loneliness

How does one overcome loneliness? First, let me say that loneliness will never be overcome by busy-ness. As I said earlier, if loneliness and laziness were synonymous, then busy-ness would be the answer. In most articles I have read on loneliness, the very first thing stated is, "Get involved. Do something." I recognize the need to do something and the need to get out of one's shell, but I want you to know something. Just doing a hobby, just being involved in an organization, or just participating in something does not mean you will automatically overcome the problem of loneliness. Loneliness and laziness are not synonymous. Loneliness is not having anyone with whom you can share in an intimate relationship. Therefore, the only answer to loneliness is forming meaningful relationships. That is the only answer. If you are lonely there's only one answer, and I'll give it to you very bluntly: *Make some friends.*

How does one make friends?

Risk Vulnerability. . .

Step number one: *Accept the risk of vulnerability.* Risk is to relationship and love what the wick is to the candle—the very center of it. You cannot have a candle burning without a wick. You cannot have relationships without risk. There are ways, and we will discuss them, to minimize that risk. But there is no way to guarantee that you will never be hurt again if you get into a relationship. There will be times that others will hurt you accidentally; other times they may hurt you purposely. But I have observed from many years of counseling that staying in one's shell is ultimately more painful than finding meaningful relationships.

In working with singles' groups, I do a lot of people-watching. I can easily spot those people who are in a shell. They come into the group, and they stand to one side, or they sit down. There will be several of them, each seeking friendship, yet each waitng for the other to break the barrier and say, "Let's be friends." Why? They are afraid of the risks. Each thinks thoughts such as these: "They may not like me. They may think I'm crazy. They may think I'm silly. They may think I'm stupid. I may say something foolish."

Let me say again—you may be hurt in attempting to form relationships; but the pain of no relationship—loneliness—is worse than any pain you'll suffer in trying to establish relationships. Accept the risk and trust God to take care of the pain.

I am so glad that the Bible says God will not allow me to experience or endure more pain than I'm capable of enduring. Now, I will say one thing about that verse: Sometimes I think God has goofed, but I have always found that He knew I could take more pain than I thought I could.

Several years ago I was trying to build some muscle tone by working out. About once a week my instructor would force me to do more than I thought I could do. I would do my regular work-out, thinking I had really done well. I had really torn it up, doing ten repetitions of one exercise. He would say, "Okay give me five more." I would look at him as if he were crazy, but I'd do five more. Then he would say, "All right, now give me five more." At this point I *knew* he was crazy—but there was something inside me that wouldn't let me give up in the face of a challenge, and I was determined to do those five more even if I collapsed to the floor. Again, "Five more." Again, "Five more." Again, the determination to meet the challenge. Suddenly I realized I had done not ten, but twenty more. I had done three times as much as I thought I could do! I was capable of doing more—I just didn't think I was capable. I'll be honest with you. I hurt like the dickens for three or four days, but it worked! I was much stronger because of having been pushed to my maximum ability.

It is in this same manner that God strengthens us. He knows I can take a lot more than I think I can. Sometimes He allows me to go through pain so that He can build into me that stamina he wants me to have, but which I will not acquire without pain. So in accepting the risk, I must say, "Okay, God, it's in your hands. You know my limits. Keep me from experiencing more than I am able to bear."

Lay Aside Competition. . .

The second step in making friends is to *lay aside competition.* If you seek to be number one, you will be hurt because any time you try and fail, it will hurt. And there will be many times you will not make that top position. If you must be number one, then you're either a winner or a loser, depending upon whether or not you have accomplished your goal. Using that definition, you're probably a loser more often than you're a winner. If you will learn to stop competing—if you will receive and experience that portion of life which is available to you, then you will find yourself enjoying life a lot more. You won't be worried about what Joe over there is doing.

You see, if you're in competition, then everybody else is your enemy and you can't relax for a single moment. Have you ever come home at night and felt totally drained? Perhaps the reason was that you were in competition with everybody else around you. Perhaps you have a habit of speeding, and you arrive at your destination totally exhausted from constantly monitoring your CB and watching out for the black and whites. You *could* take your foot out of the carburetor, you know. You *could* slow down a bit; and although you'll arrive ten or fifteen minutes later, you'll be less tense. The competitive spirit is a real energy drain.

Perhaps you attend a social event, and you're competing to be the best one there—the best looking, the best whatever it may be. The moment you walk in, every person with whom you are competing (generally those of the same gender) is your enemy. You are so busy watching others' reactions that you get uptight, and then you wonder why no one seems to enjoy your company.

Lay aside the competitive spirit. The worst phrase in the English language is "the best." I am so conscious of the harm of that phrase that in describing our church I deliberately avoid the phrase, "the best singles' ministry in the city of Houston," because that would put me in competition with all the other churches. I certainly do not want that.

How do I lay aside competition? I develop brother-sister relationships. These relationships are extremely important. I can have only one wife, but I can have an unlimited number of sisters and brothers.

Foundation of Friendships

The foundation to the establishment of friendships is this: The ultimate love is not romantic love; the ultimate love is the love described in the last chapter as gift love. One does not have to be married to be happy. One must be in meaningful relationships to be happy.

There are several reasons why I use the terms *brother* and *sister* rather than *friend*. For one thing, the word *friend* can be misleading. I have had "friends" who knifed me in the back pretty badly. "Friend" can describe a casual relationship or a very deep relationship. I use the word *brother* and *sister* because it represents a family tie, a relationship of belonging. The Bible is clear in teaching that those who are in God are a family.

Some time ago I heard Jack Taylor of San Antonio say, "You know, I'd like to think there were some Christian appendixes. That is, some fellow believers that I could do without. I could just say, 'Hey friend, drop dead. I'd be a lot better off without you.'".

His remark was tongue-in-cheek, of course. Friends just can't dispose of friends in such a manner. I may have a difficult time liking you, or you may think I'm pretty obnoxious—but if I am your brother, there's a sense of belonging. There is a sense of eternity which gives me the freedom to relate to you in a very meaningful way.

Relating to each other as brothers and sisters alleviates much "uptightness" about male-female relationships. So often people misinterpret the relationship between members of the opposite sex. Married people are afraid to have friendships, or singles are afraid to form relationships with members of the opposite sex, fearing that those friendships will be misunderstood either by the friend or by others. If I have a sister in the flesh, no one would get upset if I wanted to talk to her. I have sisters in the spirit who are as close to me or closer than my natural sisters are. We have a close family relationship. In my counseling ministry I offer brother-sister or brother-brother relationships. By so doing, I am making a commitment of belonging, a commitment of acceptance, a commitment of responsibility. If you need me you can call on me, and I can come to your aid just as I would come to my sister or brother in the flesh.

One man objected to the sister-brother concept because in such a relationship, one couldn't marry his sister. He was hung up on marriage. As I told him, if you form a lot of good brother-sister relationships, and ultimately one of these develops into a romantic relationship, you'll have a good marriage. The tragedy of many marriages is that the individuals did not learn how to be friends first. A romantic relationship built upon a foundation of gift love is stronger than any other kind.

Form Multiple Relationships. . .

So to form friendships, one must accept the risk of vulnerability and lay aside competition. There is another important step. *One must form a multiplicity of relationships.* I worry about singles who immediately zero in on a relationship with just one person as soon as they are divorced. Now, I recognize the validity of a primary relationship. There are many reasons why I can relate to some people better than I can to others. But if someone immediately dives into another relationship before developing friendships, he or she is in trouble. It is especially important that those who are just going through the death of a marriage find several people with whom they can relate.

There are two important reasons for multiplicity of relationships. First, you will be more relaxed in your friendship if you have more than one. If you have only one friend, you're so scared you may lose that person, you'll be uptight in everything you do. Years ago I saw a cartoon depicting two show girls in a dressing room. One said to the other, "I've got to make certain I get my face just like it was last night because he said he liked me just the way I was." That kind of rut, playing the game of pretending to be a certain way all the time, is easy to fall into for people who fear the disapproval of others.

The second reason for multiplicity of relationships is that if something should happen to the primary relationship, I have other friends who can support me. Should I have a need for consolation and my primary relationship is busy, for instance, I can unload some of my burden on another friend, rather than overburden one person. And should that person no longer be a part of my life, I will have others who care and can help ease the pain of a broken relationship.

All people should have friends on those different levels of communication we discussed earlier (i.e., from one to ten). I am very fortunate to have a relationship with my wife which is, if not a ten, at least a 9½. I don't think a person can handle more than one ten. But I am extremely fortunate to have a number of sevens and eights. I have a number of friends whom I can call and say, "Hey, here's where I'm hurting today." I believe that foundation is very important. Certainly I am going to relate primarily to my ten. But there are times when the ten can't handle it for some reason, and I'm glad I have some brothers and sisters with whom I can relate.

People often ask how long it takes to be ready for a romantic relationship after the breakup of a marriage. It takes long enough to establish your foundation. How do you raise the peak of a pyramid? By enlarging its base. The more people you learn to love in a brother-sister relationship, the greater the potential love for the one you love at the top. One must overcome bitterness, develop a healthy self-love, and arrive at a frame of mind where he is open to, but not compelled to, remarry. If one claims he will never remarry, his bitterness level is still so high that he has problems. On the other hand, if one feels he must be married to be happy, he is making the other person responsible for his happiness. When one can say, "I would remarry, but I don't have to remarry," then that person is ready to start finding romantic relationships.

One lady commented that she could see no value in establishing a relationship unless it was with a romantic potential, a potential mate. That lady has been missing out on some beautiful friendships. There can be a one-to-one relationship on a brother-sister level. I have a number of friends of the opposite sex that I could never marry. Their personalities and mine are not complementary, which is the purpose of a marriage relationship. Yet I love to share my feelings and theirs on a deep friendship level. Had I not formed a friendship relationship with these people simply because there was no marriage potential, I would have missed out on some very good friends.

Give Your Friend Freedom. . .

I must be willing to give friends freedom. Yet I may have trouble giving some people freedom because deep down I am fearful they wouldn't really want to come back to me. In my fear of losing them, I will choke them. When I choke them, they panic and retreat from my friendship.

Fear of the loss of a friend can occur in people of the same sex as well as in romantic relationships. Have you ladies ever had a lady friend (or men, a man friend) who, in relating to another person, made you feel insecure because you were afraid the other friendship would become closer than yours? One feels this fear because he or she is putting their security in the other person. But security is not in possessing another. Attempts to possess drive people away. One must learn to trust God to take care of one's needs, and to give one's friends freedom. Even in a romantic relationship—or perhaps I should say especially in a romantic relationship—this freedom is necessary. The couple who does everything together is just as sick as the couple who does nothing together. The do-everything-together couple is paranoid. They possess one another. There must be freedom to do things apart now and then.

Reveal Yourself. . .

To find a friend, one must be a friend. If you wish to learn something about the other person, share with that person something about yourself. Have the courage to share feelings, not simply activities. Rather than simply sharing what happened to you today, tell that person how you felt about what happened to you today.

One word of caution is due about self-revelation. Remember the levels of communication. Do not go more than one level deeper than your friend is ready to go with you. If you have established a new friendship which is, for instance, at a level three—and suddenly you jump to a level seven or eight, not realizing that your partner for one reason or another is not ready for more than a four, then that person will panic and go away. Learn to establish a deep level of communication one step at a time.

Be Sensitive to the Other Person. . .

Establishing depth in communication one step at a time involves being sensitive to the needs of the other individual. Remember that each person is at a given period of growth. There are times when a person is simply not ready for a deep level of communication. Perhaps that person has recently been hurt and needs only a shallow level of communication. If you are insensitive to that person's needs and rush the relationship, that person may retreat in panic. If you can be sensitive and patient and let the person have room to grow, then you may later be able to progress to a deeper friendship.

Convey Warmth. . .

If one is to have ease in making friends, one must learn to convey warmth. Warmth is conveyed both physically and verbally. One can learn to convey warmth. Observe yourself and your reactions. When you are with a group of people, do you linger on the outskirts of the crowd, avoiding eye contact, acting preoccupied or disinterested, perhaps with your arms crossed over your chest or with your hands in your pockets and your head down? People will read your body language, either consciously or subconsciously. And because most everyone has a dislike for rejection, few people will approach those whose body language says they are closed to friendship. On the other hand, if you come into a room of people and look *at,* not through, people, smiling when you catch their eyes, reaching out to shake a hand or embrace a shoulder, you will find people's defenses melting in your warmth. You will find that people will flock to you because you convey an openness to friendship; you make them feel accepted.

The verbal expression of warmth also can be developed. Learn to think more about the feelings of the other person than of your own. Realize that even the most apparently secure person has a need to be appreciated and to be told of another's appreciation. Look for the good in others, and when you see it tell them! By so doing, you'll accomplish two important things: You will make the other person feel great, and begin a friendship with that person. And learn to say "I love you." Those words need not be confined to your ten, nor even to romantic relationships. There are friends whom I love, and if we have established a brother-sister or brother-brother relationship, it can become very natural—and most rewarding—to communicate that love to each other.

Affirm Your Friend. . .

Learn to give your friends affirmation. Accept them where they are. There are days when I get down in the dumps. I'll simply bottom out. At those times I need someone who will be understanding enough to sense that I don't need a sermon. I get those on Sunday. I need someone who will pat me on the back and say, "I believe in you. Go get 'em, Tiger!" Or I may need someone who will just let me sound off. I may know that what I am saying is wrong, stupid and ignorant—and if it is, I don't need someone to tell me. I just need someone who will listen, who will let me get all the garbage out and then say, "I love you, Clyde."

Too often when one expresses negative attitudes, the other will say, "You're not supposed to feel like that. You're not supposed to think that." Well, supposed to or not—I do feel like that, I do think that. Don't condemn me. Understand me. Try to understand where the other person is coming from, and why he is functioning and reacting as he is. Let your friends know that you're still with them, accepting them, loving them, no matter what may be their mood of the moment. Learn to accept and affirm, whether or not you can always agree.

Schedule Time for Dialogue. . .

Friendship is spelled *t-i-m-e*. If you are to establish a friendship, allow time for talking, for sharing of ideas and attitudes. Activities are fine. Movies and tenn· and such can be relaxing, invigorating, enjoyable. But those activities can be done with a stranger. Friendships are built on dialogue. If you are to build a friendship, you must schedule time to talk, to exchange viewpoints, to share feelings. It is in this manner that you truly get to know the other person and can develop from a three or four to a seven or eight, and ultimately find your ten.

Accept Friendship, but Do Not Demand. . .

As you seek friendship, accept it from those who will give it, but do not demand it from those who will not. Some people do not want to relate to you. Sure, it hurts. I'd like to think that everybody would love to relate to Clyde Besson. But some people just don't like me. They don't like my personality, the way I comb my hair, the way I dress or whatever. They just don't like Clyde. I've had to learn to say, "You're missing a blessing, Friend," and keep on trucking. There are people who do want to relate to me. There is no need to spend my time or energy trying to force myself upon someone who doesn't want me.

Along this line, however, I do have a policy in friendship and in love. If I try to establish a relationship with certain people and they don't respond, in love I back away from them. But periodically—say every three months, or every six months—I'll try again. If they still push me away, I accept that they still are not ready for my friendship, and I go on to establish other friendships. Deep down, I would like to have relationships with all people. I believe that's the way each person was created. But while I will not force myself on other people, neither will I shut them out because they shut me out. Two wrongs don't make a right. I will try again at another time to overcome their block to my friendship. Strangely enough, there have been times when a person who repeatedly rejected my friendship ultimately became a treasured friend. I will not automatically shut a door, but neither will I attempt to force one open.

Often I have observed men who have been turned down for a date. Perhaps the lady had other plans, or perhaps she simply did not want to go out with him. There is no need to become obnoxious in an attempt to salvage one's pride. Don't get "bent out of shape" because the lady has other plans or because she would rather go out with someone other than you. Six months from now, knock on the door again. Maybe by that time she will have seen enough growth in you that she will want to go out with you, or perhaps she will have grown to a point that she is ready to accept your friendship. Accept, but do not force, relationships.

Seek to Stop Playing Games. . .

It is very important in developing relationships that a person be real, that one stops playing games.

Admittedly, one cannot be totally real with everybody. Some people will not allow me to be real. An example of this was brought to mind one day by a lady who was a very close friend. She said, "Clyde, I've got a question. When you and I are alone talking, you are very open. In the Sunday school class, you're open, but not quite as open as you are with me. When you're in the pulpit preaching, you are even less open. Why?"

I explained to her that in our friendship we had a mutuality, a depth of sharing. In the class there is a rapport and openness, yet there are some new people who do not know or understand me. I can afford to be open with her because we know and understand each other's shortcomings, and we accept each other's faults. However, if I were as gut level honest in class as I was with my friend, some people wouldn't be able to accept my honesty. It would blow their minds. And when I stand in the pulpit, if I were to be as open in sharing about some areas of single adult problems as I am in class, people who did not understand the plight of the single adult would really come unglued. Some people are not ready to admit there is such a thing as single adult sexuality, for instance, much less accept its being discussed from the pulpit.

In a true friendship you need the kind of openness that allows you to say, "Hey, friend, I want to be courteous, but at the same time I don't want to go around playing games all the time and pretending to be what I am not."

What is a hypocrite? A play actor. The person who has done everything wrong all week, but who comes to church saying, "I acknowledge that I am a sinner, and I am coming to find help," is not a hypocrite. The person who sits in church and is self-righteous, pretending never to make a mistake, is the hypocrite. I can accept a person who admits to all kinds of shortcomings, but who is trying to grow, much more readily than I can accept a person who is self-righteous.

So begin to try to be real. Try to be sincere, honest, open, transparent. That's where true relationships and friendships are made. It is true that not all people will accept me. Just because I am rejected does not mean I am rejectable. Some people will reject me. They will disagree with me to the point that they will not accept my friendship. But in my quest for friends—for brothers and sisters—I develop the relationships that I can, knowing that every time I make a new friend, I become that much richer.

The answer to loneliness is friendship. Now, get busy.

Someone has to take the first step. If everyone waits for the other person to come to them, there will never be new relationships established. Someone has to take that first step and cross into the other's space, saying, "Will you be my friend?" Learning to form friendships is not nearly so expensive as the cost of being lonely.

Chapter Six

Single Adult Sexuality

Without exception, the highest attendance of the seminar "Picking Up the Pieces" will be found the evening I present the unit on single adult sexuality. Also without exception, the lowest attendance will be found when I give the unit on solo parenting. An understanding chuckle always arises from the group when I tell them people seem to be much more interested in how to get children than they are in how to care for them.

As I address this subject, I must recognize the struggle within the reader and within myself as I try to express my viewpoint. Part of my struggle is that I must acknowledge my own sexuality. Often preachers have difficulty with this particular subject, for they seem to pretend that their children were all adopted and that they have never experienced anything of the sexual nature. Often people will say something to the effect that I, being a preacher, cannot possibly comprehend the problem. I have two things to say about that. First, I have three children and none of them are adopted. Second, I have been a single adult and have faced the same pressures and problems faced by any other single person.

At the same time I acknowledge the fact that I come to you from a bias. Let's face it—everything we do comes from some sort of bias, for our actions and beliefs are all based on the foundation upon which they are built. For instance, if I say two plus two equal four, I make that statement from an already accepted bias, using a base-ten numerical system. I acknowledge that I come from a Judeo-Christian background, and that is a bias. Yet I want to attempt to be honest. I want to walk down the middle of the road. I hope to walk not just on the road on this issue, but on a tightrope down the middle of the road. I realize the danger in this position. If one expresses opinions from one ditch, he has all those in that same ditch to agree with him, and he's receiving brickbats only from the other ditch. In attempting to walk that tightrope down the middle, he is open to attack from either side. While walking my tightrope I will be gut-level honest.

Several years ago after attending a state singles' conference, several people complained that they felt the speaker on the topic of sexuality had avoided some questions which had been submitted to him. The man later admitted in my presence that he had done so deliberately because they were too hot for him to handle. That is unfortunate because if a speaker cannot face all aspects of an issue, people have a tendency to doubt the validity of the answers he is willing to give. You may not agree with the answers I give, but I can promise you one thing. I have a desire and will attempt to deal with every legitimate question on the topic of single adult sexuality. My purpose is to enable you as an adult to make an intelligent choice. My purpose is not to condemn you if your actions do not agree with these principles, but rather to share with you truths which you can use to make up your own mind and to choose your own lifestyle.

The Three-Fold Nature of Man

To deal with this subject in its fullness we must realize that man is tricotomous in nature—that is, he is three-part. He has a *body* by which he relates to the external world. You see me and hear me because of my body. I relate to you through my body. Man also has a *soul*—psyche—which is the real person who lives inside that body. The third part is the *spirit,* which is the portion of man through which his soul, or psyche, relates to God. The soul itself may be described as being tricotomous also, for it is comprised of the portion which is the psyche—the intellect and emotions of the person, and the portion which relates through my body to others, and through my spirit to God. You cannot deal with me without dealing with the whole person. Medical science is becoming more and more aware that in the treatment of illness, one's emotions, or psyche, and one's spirit must be treated in addition to one's body. As I deal with the subject of single adult sexuality, I will approach it within the framework of the whole body, soul and spirit—the tricotomous whole person.

With that introduction, let me begin by saying that the biblical concept regarding sex is that it is good. Many people have the attitude that sex is bad. The idea that celibacy is superior is an outlook which says essentially that sex is bad. Some people say that sex is not bad—it is simply neutral. It is neither good nor bad. But the biblical teaching regarding sex is that it is good. When God created human beings male and female (and that is sex) He said, "It is good."

We say that sex is good, because we realize that men and women actually become one flesh due to God's creative action. (Gen. 2:21-24). That is, God is the *source* of our sexuality. He demands its use for the continuation of His creation and the glory of His name. Consequently, our maleness and femaleness reflect the very image of God. (Gen. 1:27). The Bible is very plain that we are cursed if we misuse this sexuality, particularly in the abuse of sex outside of marriage. We are told to control our sexual impulses through self-discipline (1 Cor. 7:9; Titus 2:5-6).

But no one must say that sex, in its proper context, is bad. It is the approach of contemporary culture and of secular humanism to accuse Christianity of being "extremist" regarding sex—meaning that Christians are supposed to be against it. That is not so. We say that sex is good. It was, after all, the consummation of the meaning of sex in marriage which provided Jesus the opportunity to show his glory by his presence at the wedding feast at Cana (Jn. 2:1-11). Sex is good.

Many people disagree with the statement that sex is good. One man actually got up and walked out of a church when I was preaching on sex because he didn't want to hear a discussion of this subject from the pulpit. I must defend my position by saying that the Bible has a lot of things to say about sex. A lot more is said about sex than is said about many other topics which are frequently aired in the pulpit. The Bible says not only that sex is good, but that it is part of God's creation. As such it is to be recognized as something that is valid, good and beautiful.

One thing I believe is important, and that I practice when dealing with young people, is to teach them that sex is not dirty. Some people, having been taught sex is dirty, have a very difficult time adjusting to marriage. They have been taught for eighteen or twenty years that sex is bad, is a no-no; and suddenly they're in a marriage where they must reverse all those years of training. Often the adjustment is very difficult for them. Sex is not evil. It is beautiful and sacred. It is a part of God's creation. It is good.

There is a basic difference between man and animals. Animals are not trichotomous in nature. Sex for animals is purely physical. It involves only their bodies. That is the reason animals seek sex only when there is the possibility for procreation. Human beings, on the other hand, are affected more than just physically by sex. Their sexuality affects the totality of all they are. There must be an emotional involvement. If you doubt that statement, consider the fact that for a male to have a wet dream, he must be dreaming. Even in his sleep he has an emotional as well as a physical involvement. A woman must have an emotional enjoyment in order to have a climax. If she is having sex with someone whom she does not love or enjoy, she will find herself daydreaming of someone else. A valid act of sex also involves the spirit. I personally believe that a valid act of sexual intercourse is and must be as much an act of worship as the singing of a hymn or the saying of a prayer. Unlike animals, which enjoy sex only for the purpose of procreation, humans, because their sexuality involves the totality of the person, are able to have some of their most pleasureable moments when there is no procreation involved.

Four Biblical Concepts for Sex

What is the purpose of sex? I believe that the Bible teaches four basic purposes.

One Flesh.

The first it teaches is the one flesh concept. In intercourse a man and woman establish a new union which breaks down their independence and yet simultaneously enhances their individuality. They become one at the same time they are two. They forever leave a part of themselves with that person. To the degree that they are healthy, they leave more of themselves. To the degree they are unhealthy and cannot fully enjoy it, they leave less. There is no such thing as a casual act.

To understand the principle of one flesh, consider the difference between the bonding processes for wood and for metal. When two pieces of wood are joined, they are held together by glue. If the glue is dissolved or removed, the pieces of wood are completely separated. Two pieces of metal, on the other hand, are joined by the welding process in which the molecules from one piece are actually fused with the molecules from the other. You can saw the pieces apart, but on each a portion of the other will remain. A healthy person leaves a part of himself, forever shared by the other person.

Procreation.

The second purpose for sex is procreation. God provided a beauty and joy which come as two people join together to create a new identity who is a part of both. Each child is a part of both his father and his mother. That new creation brings tremendous joy, but I believe it is secondary. I believe the primary purpose for sex is the one flesh concept and that procreation fits down the line.

110

Pleasure.

The third reason for sex is pleasure. A valid act of sexual intercourse brings pleasure, and the person who does not enjoy a valid act of sex is not fully healthy. The term *valid act* is important here, and I will define it later on. There is tremendous pleasure in sex, but there must be pleasure for the whole person. Sex cannot truly be pleasurable just for the body, it must be pleasurable for the soul and the spirit as well. When there is the total pleasure of all three parts of the whole person, there is not a divorcing of the person, but rather a joining and blending. Excitement and joy result from such a total blending of two people.

Knowledge.

The fourth and final biblical concept for the purpose of sex is knowledge. There are two words used in the Bible which are translated "to know," meaning knowledge. One implies an understanding of concepts or a recognizing of a person's identity; the other, which is the term used regarding sexual intercourse, is the word used describing one's knowledge of God. It implies intimacy. The difference in the levels of knowledge is the focal point. I can say that I know President Reagan. I would recognize him if he came into the room. I know facts about his background, his accomplishments, his policies. That knowledge, however, does not begin to approach the level of knowledge that I mean when I say I know Cathy Besson. I know my wife intimately. It is that level of knowledge to which the Bible refers. In a valid act of sexual intercourse, not only is there pleasure, but there also is a sharing. There is a sharing of who I am and who you are. It is a sharing in which I come to understand more what it means to be male, and the female comes to understand more what it means to be female. You understand the other person more deeply as well. Through the intimacy of sexual intercourse there are a sharing and a knowledge which promote understanding. Whenever one enters into a sexual relationship without consideration of all four purposes—especially the oneness, the pleasure, and the knowledge—the relationship will be defective and there will be consequences.

Valid vs. Defective Sex

In each of the purposes listed, I have used the term *valid act* of sexual intercourse. I have heard three types of sex defined by some speakers: valid, defective and invalid. I prefer to use two: *valid* and *defective*. Some acts of sex are defective to a lesser degree and some to a greater degree; but still to the degree that an act is defective, there are consequences built into it, and one pays the price to a greater or lesser extent. When a sexual act is valid, there is a total pleasure. With that thought in mind, let me attempt to define or describe what I believe the Bible teaches to be valid sexual intercourse.

Several years ago I preached a series of messages on the home. One message was entitled, "The Christian Understanding of Sex." Can you imagine the minister of music trying to choose the hymns for that service? "Why Not Tonight?"—"Almost Persuaded"—"Rescue the Perishing"—"Breathe on Me"—"Revive Us Again"—and "Whosoever Will..." If you are not familiar with the "invitation" in some church services, let me explain. At the end of such services the congregation sings a hymn of invitation which gives a person an opportunity to respond to the sermon and to make a public decision. So what do you choose for the invitational hymn at the end of a sermon on sex? Our minister of music selected a song which I have insisted be used whenever I preach on that topic: "I Surrender All." To me, that which constitutes a valid act is a total surrender of all that one is to the totality of the other, and receiving the same thing in return. Defective sex is anything but that kind of surrender.

I must share an amusing incident which happened after the preaching of the sermon about sex and the singing of the invitational hymn. I called on one of our deacons, a gentleman in his early sixties, to lead the closing prayer. You know how someone will pray, using a well-worn expression without actually thinking about its full meaning. I know he did not realize the impact of his statement when he said, "Lord, help us to go home and put into practice what our preacher has preached about tonight." The church rocked with suppressed giggles. The minister of music had to run outside, and his guffaws could be heard for blocks.

What constitutes a valid act of sexual intercourse? Total surrender. Total commitment of all that one is, surrendering all that one is to the totality of all that the other is.

The Removal of Negatives

In order to achieve a valid act—to surrender all—there must first be the removal of negatives. Two basic negatives which must be removed are guilt and bitterness. When there is a guilt feeling, there cannot be a freedom. When the feeling of guilt is removed, the result is a valid act of sex, which is a part of one's worship of God. When there is unresolved bitterness, particularly if it is toward someone of the opposite sex, the one who is bitter will actually be either using or punishing the other person. This is frequently the case with the man who actually physically abuses a woman in sex because of the bitterness he carries toward some other person—perhaps his mother or a previous mate. Retaining bitterness can be especially damaging to one's ability to have a valid sexual relationship.

Trust must be present in a valid act. Trust is especially important, I believe, to women. Women feel very vulnerable at the point of sexual intercourse; and if there is not a trust level, they become uptight. When a woman is uptight, it is difficult for her to achieve the relaxation necessary for climax. The male must be aware of her need and be certain that he is trustworthy. Trust on both sides promotes an assuming of responsibility for each other—not just physically, but as a total person. The assuming of responsibility must not be just for these thirty minutes or for this night, but rather a commitment to each other which says, "I am willing to assume responsibility for all of you—body, soul and spirit, now and tomorrow.'' It is through the trust and assuming of responsibility for each other that intimacy can develop. I personally believe that one's level of enjoyment is in direct proportion to the diminishing of the negatives and the increasing of the emotional intimacy.

One of the things that disturbs me is that many people in their desire to find intimacy—which we all need—short-change themselves by accepting physical intimacy in lieu of emotional intimacy, which is more difficult to establish. When there is a valid act of sexual intercourse, there is an emotional intimacy evidenced by or demonstrated by the physical transparency or nakedness. Even as there is the physical nakedness, there needs to be the emotional transparency or nakedness. When one establishes a relationship in which there is trust, assuming of responsibility, and openness, there is neither taking nor using; rather there is a giving and receiving. Each person gives to and receives from the other the totality of one's being. Each gives to and receives from the other complete surrender, including the imperfections. Each accepts the other totally.

To the point that there is any deficiency in meeting those prerequisites to a valid act, there is a defective relationship. One thing I have realized through my counseling experience is that many marriage relationships are defective sexually. Frequently my observations get me in hot water. When I preached the sermon about the Christian understanding of sex, I said there were two instances in which marital sex can be defective. One occurs when a man demands his bed right, being concerned not for the other person but for himself. He is not giving love, he is demanding it. The other occurs when a woman uses sex to get what she wants, like a new dress or a vacation. The looks I received from some members of the congregation indicated that some people were very upset with that statement!

We have defined sex which is valid, and have established that it is total surrender. Now let's examine some of the ways in which it can be defective.

When Is Sex Defective?

Sex is defective when I deny my sexuality. Some people have attempted to deny the sexuality of Jesus Christ. Yet the Bible says that Jesus was tempted in every way common to man. If that is true, then he had to have a sex drive. Many people got upset with the song of Mary Magdalene in the rock opera "Jesus Christ, Super Star." But I feel there is a truth in its acknowledgment of the sex drive. Sex is part of God's creation. I will give you ways to deal with it, but denying your sexuality is not one of them. Denying sexuality only serves to suppress it, which pushes you into the opposite ditch.

Secondly, sex is defective when one is not concerned about the total needs of the other person. If a person is concerned simply with the physical need of the other, but is not concerned about the other's emotional and spiritual needs, then he is divorcing the other person in a sense—he is divorcing the totality of the other person and trying to use just one part of that person. Sex is valid to the extent that I am concerned about the total you—all of you. Let me give you another example of what I am talking about. I think it is very defective when a man wants sex with a woman but is not concerned about the totality of all she is, including her children. Her children and their needs are a part of her.

Sex is defective, thirdly, when one is using the other person. One can use another person for physical release. You wake up and you're horny. You're looking for some means of release. You don't want to masturbate, so you just go find someone to have sex with. All you're doing, in essence, is getting someone to masturbate you, using someone for a physical release. You're using, not loving that person—there's no love in it. I'm tempted to say an inflatable doll would suffice as well.

Fourth, sex is likewise defective when it is used as an ego boost. Men who go through a divorce frequently have their egos shattered. They go through a period attempting to prove themselves male. You know, a hundred years ago a man could prove his masculinity by how many notches he had on the six gun he wore at his side. Today, a lot of men try to see how many "chicks" they can make in an effort to prove they are men. In other words, a man becomes a super-stud just to prove he's a man. Some women go through the same thing. A common example is the straitlaced lady whose husband leaves her for a younger woman. She becomes very insecure and goes through a time trying to prove she is still acceptable by seeing how many men she can pick up. Using another person as an ego escape is defective sex.

Using a person to obtain a form of love is a fifth common defective use of sex. The person who is starving to death will eat from the garbage can. It takes a sick person to eat garbage when he's full. It is easy to see how someone who is feeling unloved after the loss of a mate can try to buy love through the use of sex. The act of sex is referred to as "making love." The person feels unloved, and so he or she tries to buy love through the use of sex. The action is easily rationalized. Yes, love can be bought. You can buy it with $50. That's called prostitution. But there are other ways of buying it which are not so blatantly obvious. Men, you can buy it with a $25 meal and a night of dancing. Ladies, you can buy it with a home cooked meal. What I am saying is that whenever one uses another to try to buy a form of love, the sexual relationship is defective. The relationship is defective because that person is trying to find intimacy in a manner which is not complete. Everyone needs intimacy. The primary need, however, is for *emotional intimacy*. Many people attempt to buy with their bodies *physical intimacy* to avoid the pain and hurt that are necessary to know emotional intimacy.

Four Consequences of Defective Sex

What are the consequences of defective sex? We have defined valid sex as a relationship in which each person gives to and receives from the other complete surrender. Defective sex is anything else. Obviously, there will be greater or lesser degrees to which the relationship is defective. To whatever degree the relationship is defective, there are corresponding degrees of consequences. I believe there are four basic consequences: shame or guilt, anxiety, emptiness or longing, and antagonism.

The guilt one feels in a defective relationship is something which many people attempt to deny or ignore, yet it still causes consequences. When I feel guilty, I find myself hiding my real self from you. Let me illustrate. A person may have sex with another, but for some reason he or she has a feeling of guilt which causes a shutting off of the emotional self. The person does not reveal himself emotionally. Many of you know what I'm talking about. You've been in a relationship, you've had sex, and suddenly the relationship stopped growing. There was no deeper development. It seemed that a door closed, and you wondered why you were unable to develop anything else. Because of the feeling of shame and guilt, one shuts up the real self—the emotional self. Real intimacy must be that which includes emotional intimacy.

Why does one experience guilt? I believe guilt is produced because the relationship which was intended to be love—which is giving—is perverted to a relationship which is taking. Let me attempt to phrase this another way because the concept is very important. Love is giving to another. If I am using you and taking from you something which you are not giving to me—not *receiving* love, but *taking* whatever form of love I can get—then I am in effect robbing you. I am not experiencing love; I am robbing. It is in this area, where I am taking that which is not freely given, that the guilt is produced. Perverting that which is a vehicle of expressing love will create guilt.

Anxiety, the second consequence of defective sex, is evidenced in several areas of our lives. The first area where one experiences anxiety is in a feeling of lack of security. There is such an emphasis on sexual performance is our society today that men feel compelled to be super-studs, and women feel they must be promiscuous in bed. If the sexual relationship is present without the emotional commitment, and that is the foundation for the relationship, then a person may feel insecure. He may wonder what would happen if something happened to the ability to perform. A woman may experience this type of anxiety after a mastectomy or a hysterectomy when she fears she is no longer fully female. A man may fear he will suffer injury or illness which will render him unable to have sex. When a man or woman has a defective sexual relationship in which he or she is not loved for the total person, there is an anxiety which can impair sexual performance and that, in turn, may result in divorce or desertion. In a defective relationship, neither party experiences the security of being loved as a whole person.

Another anxiety factor is competition. If a person is loved simply because the physical relationship is good, then he has a fear that someone better may come along and may replace him or her. A woman sees another woman who has a better figure, and she becomes anxious that her partner will prefer the other woman. A man sees super-stud come to town, and he becomes anxious that his partner will be attracted to him. Anxiety promotes rigidity. Rigidity, in turn, diminishes the capacity for sexual enjoyment. Diminished capacity creates more anxiety about the relationship. A chain reaction can begin which creates a deep anxiety and seriously affects the person's capacity for sexual enjoyment.

Fear of failure is the third form of anxiety. If there is not that commitment to the total person, then sexual performance can be blown out of proportion. One gets uptight, fearing he or she may fail to perform. Again, the result is a vicious circle —the more uptight, the more likely to fail. Frequently people with whom I am counseling share that because they had a poor sexual relationship in a former marriage, they want to be certain the physical relationship is good in the new relationship they are forming. There are problems in this area for both the male and the female.

Men frequently have problems with premature ejaculation. I have read that there are two basic causes for this. One is unresolved bitterness toward a previous mate and/or a mother. In this case, a man is simply using the woman. The other cause is a fear of failure to be a super-stud. This creates an anxiety which makes delay impossible. The answer to his problem is to relax; but the more he feels he must produce, the more uptight he becomes, and the more severe the problem. Conversely, the more he learns he is loved for himself as a total person, the less anxiety he will feel, and the more effectively he will be able to perform sexually.

Women often have a problem with frigidity. The causes are the same as those for premature ejaculation. If the woman has unresolved bitterness toward some man in her past—either father or mate—she will be uptight and rigid. She may not even want sex. In either case, frigidity results. Often a woman's bitterness is a carry-over from her upbringing. If a woman has been taught sex is dirty, then her subconscious tells her she is not supposed to enjoy sex, and she will have a problem achieving a climax. This kind of problem can usually be traced to a mother who was bitter and conveyed that bitterness to her daughter. It must be dissolved if the daughter is to have a maximum enjoyment of sex. The fear of failure to perform is also a cause of frigidity. If the woman does not have a valid relationship—one in which she feels the security of total commitment—she may be so uptight over fear of failure she will be unable to reach a climax. It is especially important for a woman to feel the security of commitment in a relationship because insecurity produces anxiety which diminishes enjoyment.

Sex is something beautiful when two people are so committed and interwoven that they are not worried about what they must do or how they must produce. They are sharing their inner being. The have no fear of having to prove thenselves. Let me tell you something—you don't prove love. Love is demonstrated, but it not proved.

The third consequence of defective sex is a longing or emptiness. Do you remember the diet concoctions Metrecal and Sego? They had all the vitamins and minerals and calories you needed for a meal. You ate the wafer or drank the liquid. Physically you were supposed to have all you needed, but there was something within you saying, "I haven't been fed yet!" There was something missing. You were still hungry. Something just did not taste right. It didn't feel right. In a defective relationship, you don't "feel right." You're left with an emptiness.

Do you remember the commercial, "Are you smoking more and enjoying it less?" Well there are a lot of people who are engaging in sex more and enjoying it less. One reason we are seeing the heavy emphasis on increased sexual promiscuity—even to the point of the bizarre—is that people cannot find satisfaction in defective relationships. Feeling unsatisfied, they try far-fetched things to find something which will make them happy and fulfilled; yet they wake up just as empty as when they went to bed. Deep down, everyone wants that sense of contentment.

Several years ago an excellent description of that feeling of emptiness appeared in a column called "Frankly Female," a regular feature of the *Phoenix Gazette*. Marcy Brockman, the writer of the column, had interviewed a man who gave his prototypes of the people who frequent singles' bars. There's the "gate guard" who stands by the door to be the first to survey all the new young chicks that come in; there's "Willie off the shrimp boat" who is waiting to be attacked by a woman; and there's the regular straight guy who is there because he is lonely. All three have one thing in common: They go out, they spend the night with a woman, but something is still missing. In response to her query of just what they were seeking, the man replied, "It's the 'Saturday morning feeling.' It's that special feeling of waking up on Saturday morning next to somebody and not wanting to get up, knowing that you don't have to get up, knowing that you are next to someone who loves you."

There is an important, driving need to love and to be loved. Without fulfilling that need, it doesn't matter how many climaxes a person has, or how many times one has sex, there's still something mising. There's an emptiness.

The final and ultimate result of defective sex is antagonism. The ultimate illustration of antagonism is prostitution. Psychological studies have shown that most prostitutes are women who had poor father images and have tremendous bitterness toward men. They start out trying to buy male approval with their bodies. Then they become resentful and bitter because they realize they are not being loved, but simply being used. By the time a woman becomes a full card-carrying prostitute, she hates men. She is inwardly laughing, saying, "You've got to pay for it. You can't get anybody to love you, can you?" She is mocking men because she feels so much antagonism.

What are some of the ways the world offers to deal with one's sexuality? The first is, "Take a cold shower." That's all wet. All it does is get you wet. It doesn't do one bit of good for your sex drive. It has never cooled off a person, and I mention it here only tongue-in-cheek. The second solution is masturbation. It can meet the physical need, but not the emotional need. There is still something missing—a feeling of warmth. You find yourself dreaming, trying to fulfill that emotional need. There is using a prostitute. All that really amounts to is having another person masturbate you. It leaves the same emptiness. There is a relationship with a casual acquaintance. Maybe one is just physically horny, and the other is just trying to buy love. They go to a bar on Saturday night, meet each other, and spend the night together. They may wake up physically satisfied the next morning, but deep down they will still be looking for something more.

Then there is that relationship between two people who have a deep relationship going. Being honest, this is, at least, much less defective than the others; but it still has consequences in feelings of anxiety, emptiness or of being used.

Having examined the world's options, I found myself wondering what I could say to people—what I could propose as an alternate. Each of the world's solutions has its degree of defectiveness. Mine is not a fool-proof solution, but one day I think the Lord gave me an interesting alternative. I'll share it with you. It's called my "red beans and rice" approach.

Red Beans and Rice

I wake up and I'm hungry. When I'm hungry, some days I'd love to have a good rib eye steak or some crawfish *etouffe*. I can't always have what I want, however, because I can't always drive over to a nice restaurant for some good *etouffe;* and with the price of beef I cannot often afford the price of rib eye. I have learned that my hunger drive can be met and satisfied with a good plate of red beans and rice.

My sex drive is a valid drive. Just because I'm single does not mean that it does not exist. Just because it's there, though, doesn't mean that I must have sexual intercourse to fulfill it. It may be that I can take a bowl of red beans and rice. So I got to thinking, if that's true, how can this need be met in my life? What can I do to provide a physical "red beans and rice" answer to the sex drive?

I realized that the first thing I must do in dealing with my sex drive is to acknowledge it. I must be able to admit it to God. I travel at times in my ministry. Let's say I wake up one morning in New York City, and my wife is at home in Houston, and I'm horny. I'm not going to pretend I'm not, I'm not going to deny it, I'm just plain old horny—that's the only way I know to describe it. "Now, Lord, because you've said in all things to give thanks, I'm going to praise your name. I'm going to give you thanks. Lord, I'm going to praise you, not necessarily because I'm horny, but because I'm going to trust this sex drive to you to allow you to meet it in a viable and valid way." Once I've acknowledged it, praised God, thanked Him in advance, and given it to Him, I've said, "Now, Lord, it's yours. You meet it."

An amusing sidelight at this point occurred when I was doing a singles conference in Rockport, Texas. On Friday after the sessions, a lady took me aside and confided she was having a real problem with her sexuality. I explained to her that we would be doing the unit on sexuality the following day, but that I would share some concepts briefly. When I shared that we first must acknowledge and praise the Lord for our sexuality, she said with a loud voice and a laugh, "Hallelujah! Praise the Lord!" The others in the room had not heard our conversation but did hear her exclamation, and they looked at her as if she were crazy. When I gave the seminar the next day, the group immediately understood, and the whole bunch broke up in laughter!

As I further explored the problem in my mind, I realized the sex drive is composed of three primary needs: There's the need for affirmation of maleness/femaleness. There's the need for affection. And there's the need for intimacy. Okay. So I wake up in New York and I'm horny. I acknowledge my feeling and put the drive in the Lord's hands, expecting Him to meet that drive in a positive way. I go downstairs for breakfast at the cafe, and some lady gives me a look which says, "Boy, you are one sexy-looking dude!" I have put the drive in the Lord's hands, and He knows what my problem is. God looked and said, "Okay, today Clyde is doubting his maleness for some reason." So He sends this woman by who gives me that look that says "I've got it all together."

I can have one of several reactions at this point. Do you remember the ditches? The handling of our drives can fall into either of the two ditches. If I deny my sexuality and pretend she didn't look at me that way, or if I feel guilty about my sexuality and wish she had not looked at me that way, that's one ditch. By doing either of those denial reactions, I have devalued the very thing that God has given me to meet my need. On the other hand, I can fall into the other ditch and say, "Hey Honey, when do you get off work?" But if I have actually put the situation in God's hands and that person gives me that look, I'll admit it's not crawfish *etouffe;* but it does satisfy the need which I had at that moment to know that I am an "okay" male. Every man or woman has a need at times for an affirmation of his or her attractiveness. If anyone says he does not like for someone occasionally to give him a look which says, "Hey, Babe, you're one hunk of a woman," or "Hey, Man, you've got it all together," that person is lying either to me or to himself. We all have that need. Pardon me if I'm being gut level honest with you. When God knows you are feeling insecure, He can send someone to give you that look, and you can think, "Thanks, I needed that!" and go on.

Maybe God knows that my need is not for affirmation, but rather for affection. We never outgrow our need for affection. Studies have shown that the reason breast feeding a baby is better than bottle feeding is not the formula. It is the fact that to breastfeed a baby the mother must hold and cuddle it in her arms. She can't just pop him in the crib and prop up his bottle.

Touch is very important. That's the reason both Peter and Paul said to greet the brethren with a "holy kiss." I can't tell you how that can translate as "shake hands." I think there's much more to that statement than shaking hands. There's at least a "holy hug" in it. There may be some unholy kisses, but I believe there needs to be a lot more holy hugging. I think one reason why some singles find themselves jumping into bed is that they need physical touch—they need a hug, and they're getting nothing.

I'll never forget speaking once at a state singles conference at First Baptist Church of Houston. I was sitting in the foyer of this building—a gigantic lobby. A woman came in whom I had known for some twelve years. She was involved in a singles organization when I first became involved in singles work. We hadn't seen each other in about a year. When she saw me, she ran across the lobby and threw one big hug on me. Do you know what? I liked it! One morning I wake up and God says, "Clyde's problem today is that he just needs a holy hug." So I walk down to a meeting, and there is a woman who is a holy hugger. She has a real talent for giving a holy hug. She walks up and gives me that hug, and I say, "Thank you, Lord, I needed that!"

Perhaps God looks down and sees that our need is intimacy. I'm alone and have no one to share with. Perhaps I meet a stranger, and all of a sudden we develop an emotional closeness. Or perhaps someone whom I have known for a long time but have not seen recently drops by for lunch, and we begin to talk and to share where we are in our lives. Our need for intimacy is being met.

Sure, I still look for that rib eye steak, but a hunger drive is not driving me up the wall. When I put my sex drive in God's hands and thank Him for red beans and rice, I feel a peace and a satisfaction. I do not have that feeling of emptiness or longing which I experience as the consequence of a defective relationship.

Now I've shared with you some truths—an ideal. If I were to decide to violate all of these truths, it would not nullify what I have said. It would only acknowledge my own humanity. Sometimes preachers have a tendency to forget that they are human. I was once tempted to write a seminary professor who wrote an article stating that a minister who had been divorced could not preach on the sacredness of marriage. I wanted to point out to him that all preachers are sinners, each with his own area of weakness. If his statement were true, then no preacher could preach on the areas of his particular deficiency. If he has the sin of impatience or of being judgmental, for example, he could not preach on those subjects. But that simply is not true. Even though a preacher is imperfect, he can recognize and communicate God's truths and ideals, for they always remain the same.

I want to share one last thought with you. God loves us in spite of our sin or imperfections. If we make a mistake or violate God's ideal, we ask His forgiveness and go on. God accepts us where we are. One day a lady told me, "Clyde, you know, I get horny some Saturday night, and I go out to a dance, and I spend the night with some guy. I know I need to be in church the next day, but I feel too guilt-ridden. I just tune in a religious program on T.V."

My reply to her was along these lines: If you've blown it on Saturday night, you just climb on out of bed and come on down to Sunday school. You see, you and I come together, both of us struggling to be more of what we were intended to be. I have my areas of imperfection; you have yours. If I will accept you where you are, and you accept me where I am, we can both grow together. I accept you. God accepts you. It's your choice how you will deal with your sexuality. You'll make the choice; but I hope that no matter what choice you make, you know that I accept you as my equal and that I'm your fellow struggler working through life. You'll be faced with choices. Sometimes you'll make one which will not be defective and will carry no consequences; other times you'll make a defective choice and there will be consequences. Either way, remember that God loves you, and I love you, no matter what decision you make.

Chapter Seven

The Battle Between the Sexes

God made male and female to complement one another. The word *complementation* or *complement* comes from the word meaning "to make complete or make whole." The idea is that one is to be strong where the other is weak, in order that the whole—the relationship—may be full and that each may bring the other to fulfillment.

When I look at something and see white, I know that all light is being reflected. If I see black, I know that all light is being absorbed and nothing is being reflected. I know that there are complementary colors, like blue and orange. When I see blue, I know that certain rays are being reflected and others are being absorbed; I know that orange is the relfection or absorption of the opposite. To make a perfect gray, one combines the basic color, mixes it with its complement, and adds a little white. That is how God made male and female—not to be in competition, but to be complementary.

The failure to understand the principle of equal but different can create a tremendous amount of competition. Competition creates conflict, which can ultimately destroy a relationship. The "battle between the sexes" is simply a failure to recognize and understand the basic difference between males and females, and to utilize those differences to form a stronger relationship, rather than allowing the differences to destroy the relationship.

One evening when I gave the verbal delivery of this chapter, a lady in the audience became highly irritated. She interrupted me to state very emphatically that all differences are sociological. She hassled me the whole time I was speaking. Though I would not have embarrassed her publicly, I was tempted to simply say, "Ma'am, if you don't believe there are differences between males and females, I suggest that you strip." For if there are the obvious physical differences, there are the just as obvious emotional differences. Neither is superior or inferior to the other. Superiority or inferiority is not the issue; the issue is that the differences were created so that through a relationship with the other, each may be made complete.

A football team is a good illustration of the principle of different but equal. A team can have a lot of problems if it has too many running backs and not enough blockers. A good team must have a good running back and a good blocking back. That blocking back is just as important as the running back. He may not get all the glory, but without him, nothing is accomplished. As with the male and female, the best team has the best complementation.

Intellect vs. Emotion

To understand the basic battle between the sexes, one must understand some basic concepts. Man (the species) is tricotomous in nature—that is, he is body, soul and spirit. The *body* is the means by which the *soul*—the real me—relates to the external world. I cannot relate to you without my body. Even when I send non-verbal communications, they are communicated by my body. The soul—the psyche, again, is the real me. The *spirit* is the means by which the soul—me—relates to God. Body, soul and spirit.

Now, the soul—the psyche—is also tricotomous: intellect, emotion and volition. The *intellect* and the *emotions* assimilate the facts and give their input to the *volition,* which makes a decision. Another word for *volition* is the *will.* Every decision made or willful act committed is based on a combination of information which has been furnished by the person's intellect and emotions.

God intended ultimately that we be perfectly balanced between intellect and emotion. I believe that the only person who was perfectly balanced between intellect and emotion was Jesus Christ. As a person grows in his or her spiritual maturity, the balance becomes more complete. In the creation God made men to lead with their intellect and, to a greater or lesser degree, verify it with the emotion. Women, on the other hand, were created to lead with their emotions and, to a greater of lesser degree, verify with their intellect. God then created a relationship between a man and a woman, a relationship in which the insights of one were to bring balance to and be balanced by the insights of the other. Thus, as each cooperated with the other, a perfect union would evolve—the kind in which each individual would grow in the likeness of Christ.

It is through a misunderstanding of this created difference that the battle begins. For instance, there are some men who are prone to think that intellectual reasoning is the ideal or the better way. That's a lot of tommyrot. There is reasoning that is emotional as well as reasoning that is intellectual. Men, have you ever known a woman to make the right decision by intuition, even though she may be completely unaware of the facts? That is called emotional reasoning. It is just as valid as intellect and facts.

The balance between intellect and emotion varies with each person. Some men are very strongly intellectual and have very little emotion. These men often work in the realm of such jobs as engineering or accounting. There are other men who are intellectual, yet have a depth of emotion. Many of these men often hold jobs in a sales related field.

Again, there is a balance of good and bad in these characteristics which make them different but equal. Frequently women will wish their mates would be more emotional. The emotional man can have more warmth about him, but he is less likely to be faithful. The engineer-type, on the other hand, may not know emotion, but he's as faithful as a clock.

There are some women who are almost all emotions and very little intellect, while there are others who originate with their emotion but are also very intellectual. Before I get myself in trouble here, let me quickly define that *the intellect of which I speak has nothing to do with intelligence.* I am talking about intellectual reasoning vs. emotional reasoning—the predominance of which forms the basis for one's decisions.

As you recognize this truth, you will begin to observe it at work in relationships. Those who are in the middle of the emotion-intellect range normally gravitate to one another. They find a complementation there. And those who are on the extreme ends gravitate to each other as well. Invariably you'll find that very emotional woman who is married to that coldly intellectual male. The goal should be that through time each will balance or moderate the other. Unfortunately, however, we frequently fail to understand the different-but-equal basis; and the very differences which were created to be made complementary wind up creating competition instead, and that destroys the relationship.

It is vital that we understand and accept the created difference that men lead from the intellect and verify to a greater or lesser extent with the emotions, while women lead from the emotions and verify to a greater or lesser extent with the intellect.

There are a couple of illustrations of this principle at work. One is that women are more prone to admit illness and consult a doctor than men are. In their "I can do anything" stubbornness, men will often refuse to see a doctor unless the illness appears terminal. You'll see women who go to the doctor every time they get a sniffle, and men who won't go until they're about to die of a heart attack.

Another illustration is in the realm of sports. This principle can be observed at any little league event in the country. Little Johnny has a sprained ankle which has mostly healed. Mom and Dad are sitting in the stands watching the game. If he's typical of many fathers I know, Dad has the attitude, "C'mon! Get tough! You can make it!" Mom, on the other hand, is fighting to control a panic that Little Johnny will hurt himself again. The man is leading from his intellect, with the attitude of conquering the problem; the woman is more gentle and tender, leading form her emotions.

Differences in Basic Concepts

There are four areas of basic attitudes or concepts in which men and women differ. Again, each individual will vary to the extent which he or she falls into the extreme of the female or male tendency; but the tendencies are prevalent just the same.

Abstract vs. Concrete

The first difference in attitude is that the male mind is more theoretical and abstract, whereas the female mind is more practical and concrete. A man will dream great dreams; the woman wants concrete examples. A man will say, "Honey, one of these days we're going to have a big house up on the hill with a swimming pool, and a beautiful back yard with a palm tree. . ." The wife will reply, "Can I just have a potted geranium in the meantime?"

Often a man will express a concept or idea. I have done this in the counseling field. I'll be thinking simply of a concept but a woman will want to know who it is I'm talking about. She can relate much easier to a specific person that she can to an abstract concept.

Speech Habits

Speech is another area in which there is a basic difference between men and women. Men speak to reveal facts. Women speak to reveal emotion. If you don't believe it, think about telephone habits. There are very few men who will pick up the phone and call a friend to talk for an hour, unless it's a female friend. Seldom do you hear a man call his friend and ask, "How are you doing? How do you feel?" He'll call up a buddy and ask him to go play golf, or he may relive every stroke of a golf match——but their conversation will be a discussion of an event. Women, on the other hand, talk to reveal emotion.

A typical example of this speech difference occurs at the end of a day. A man comes home and is greeted by his wife, asking what he did today. His reply is something like, "I worked."

"What did you do?"

"Oh, nothing really important." Then he may tell her briefly that he worked on such-and-such project most of the day. He has reported an event.

The woman will then talk for thirty minutes about the fight between their son and the boy next door that lasted a total of thirty seconds. In the process, she will describe the other mother's coming outside, what she was wearing, what she said, and what she thought. The woman is revealing all her inner feelings about the whole event. She is talking to reveal the emotions she felt about the encounter.

Success vs. Security

A man's primary drive is for success—for the accomplishment of a job. A woman, on the other hand, finds her basic fulfillment in security. A man wants to be loved for what he does. To him it is important to receive approval and recognition for what he accomplishes. A woman is more concerned about approval for who she is, rather than for what she has done. A man likes to be complimented for the job he's done; a woman likes to be complimented for who she is. It is far more important to tell a woman she's a beautiful person or she looks nice, than it is to tell her she cooked a good meal.

One of the problems in today's society is that so many men don't know how to give approval to their wives. Many women are entering the working world to get the satisfaction and approval they fail to receive at home. The tragedy in this situation is that frequently these women begin receiving approval at work, and they are tempted to move into a romance situation with that person who shows them the approval for which they long. They are hungry for someone to notice them.

Love: Physical vs. Emotional

The fourth area of basic attitude differences between male and female is in their concepts of the meaning of love. To a male, love is primarily physical; to a woman it is primarily emotional. In one of his books, Charlie Shedd states that in a good relationship, a man can teach a woman how to love with her body, and a woman can teach a man how to love with his soul.

You see, to a man, love is primarily physical, therefore primarily sexual. To a woman, however, love is primarily emotional, and it is the things done before and after the actual act of intercourse that are far more important. It's the little "sussies" (a southern term meaning *warm compliments)* that mean so much. It's things like offering to do the dishes or helping her with some task without putting the make on her. These things mean a lot because they deal with her emotional need.

Basic Areas of Male-Female Frustration

Understanding the basic differences in volition and attitudes between men and women, I want to share with you some of the ways in which males and females frustrate each other when they do not recognize and utilize these basic differences. Rather than make a list for men first and then women, or vice versa, I will alternate between the two, so that neither sex will feel that I'm picking on them.

Male Difficulties with Communication

First of all, men frustrate women by their refusal or inability to communicate. I want to examine both sides of the issue. Women want to know what men are feeling. But there are three reasons I believe that men often have trouble communicating.

Admitting Weakness

The first reason is that men often have that mistaken idea that they must be perfect in order to be loved. We have difficulty admitting weakness. Sometimes a man is scared stiff—but rather than communicate this, because he would be construed as less than a man, he chooses to keep it all within. If he has a problem of any kind, he is afraid to share it with his woman because he thinks he's supposed to be perfect.

Male Ego

A second reason for hesitancy in communication is the male ego. Ladies, the most vulnerable part of a man is his ego. If you ever want to really wipe a man out, all you have to do is to hit him in his ego.

Here is a typical example. A man comes home from work, and he's got a problem. He hasn't been able to solve it all day. He's been working on it for a week. This problem has got him whipped, so where is his ego? About half an inch high. So he comes home from work and begins to share his problem with his wife. With her emotional reasoning, the answer is obvious to her. "Oh, that's silly. The answer is. . . ." What does this do to his ego? Bam! Knocked him dead!

It's fine to take a cancer out of a patient who has cancer. But if you kill him in the process, what good is it? A man's ego is very vulnerable. Ladies, your understanding of this truth is very important. I don't believe in playing games, yet I think love necessitates meeting needs. If I recognize that a person has a need to have his ego boosted and supported and strengthened, then in love I'm going to do something which will support that person, not defeat or destroy him. Let's reexamine the options in the above situation.

Here comes the male, dragging in from work because nothing has gone right. He looks like a little whipped puppy dog with its tail between its legs. You have two choices. You can do as everybody else has done to him all day and jump down this throat or put him down or make fun of him. If that is your choice, your chances of his staying married to you for the rest of his life are slim to none. He may be sick, but he's not stupid. The other choice is that you can serve as a complementation to him. You can let him know you believe in him, that you're confident in him, and thus build him up again so that the next day he can go out and lick a tiger. He can take the world on again for you.

Now, after you have boosted his ego by saying that you believe in him, and that you can understand how he could have been defeated by wrestling with such a difficult problem all week, but that you know he will find the answer—then, if you have some insight into the problem, you can "accidentally on purpose" slip it to him so that he thinks it's his idea. By so doing, you preserve his ego and his masculinity. There is nothing as good in love as a man's making a woman feel she is all woman—and a woman's making a man feel he is all man.

Female Moralizing

Another reason why men have difficulty in communicating is that women by nature are more moralistic than men. You find more women in church on Sundays than men. Men have a tendency to compromise more and let things ride. Women are more prone to stand for the facts.

134

So here is this man who has been at work all day with his young secretary who has worn a micro-mini skirt and a see-through blouse. She has been "flaunting it" all day, and he has had one heck of a battle. He walks in that evening and says, "Honey, I'll be honest with you. Today I've had a real battle. This secretary has just really been throwing it at me all day, and I'm all in a tizzy."

What will be the reaction of the average woman? "Honey, I understand. I can feel for you today. Can I help in any way?" Hardly. She will be more likely to suggest dismissal of the secretary and disappointment with him for even looking at another woman.

An amusing thing along this line happened to a preacher I know. In preaching a sermon on the Ten Commandments, he, of course, got to the subject of adultery. Knowing there were some people who considered divorce to be the unpardonable sin, the preacher attempted to jog their thinking by turning to the passage which says that if a man lusts in his heart, he has committed adultery already. To drive the point home, he then suggested there was not a married man in the congregation who had not, at one time or another following a spat with his wife, entertained the thought of what it might have been like had he married that old sweetheart, or someone from work or from the church. Remember the illustration about the man thinking in abstract ideas and the woman thinking in concrete applications? The first thing this minister's wife wanted to know when they were alone was which woman he'd thought about. Needless to say, the preacher didn't feel the freedom of honest communication.

Male "Tuning Out" Female

Part of the communication problem is that men seemingly refuse to listen. Any full-fledged male has long since learned to say "uh-huh" and "uh-uh" at the right moment and never hear a word that is spoken. And any female has learned to take advantage of that by trying to trick her man into an "uh-huh" response over a new dress or something of the sort, without his realizing what he agreed to.

Let's face it, men—we have a problem. In a Catholic telespot commercial that appeared on television several years ago, a woman was talking to a man when suddenly the sound went off. Just about the time I reached to adjust my set, a narrator came on and said, "Has this ever happened to you?" Men seemingly are not concerned about the emotional input and sharing that a woman is giving.

On the other hand, ladies, it would be a lot easier if you would use the principle of the *Reader's Digest Condensed Book*. If you'd reduce that thirty-minute tirade to a fifteen-minute discourse, you would have your man's attention. Also, let him have his cup of coffee when he gets home before you start in on it.

Men, I agree with the ladies. We need to be listening. We fail to listen because we're not caring enough to understand what the other person is saying, what she is feeling. Feelings are real, and not having them considered or listened to is a frustration. In counseling, I spend a lot of my time just listening to women unload because their husbands will not listen. They pour out their feelings, go home, and are happy for a couple of weeks. Then they are back, pouring it out again. Hey, men! I need some help! If you'll learn to listen, you'll find your woman a lot more warm, a lot more receptive to your love and concern.

Female Domination

On the other hand, women frustrate men by their attempts to dominate, or by appearing to do so. Domination does not mean that you crack a bull whip. Domination is an attempt to control. In defense of the woman, let me say that this problem is a natural result of the mothering instinct. Part of that instinct is to help a child to grow up. In so doing, the mother guides and controls the child, putting boundaries out so that the child can become full grown without facing unnecessary disasters. Sometimes it is difficult to change gears.

Picture a young married couple. The woman is a teacher in second grade; the man is doing graduate work. He comes home from having spent eight or ten hours discussing intellectual subjects in the learned halls, and his wife talks to him as if he were a second grader. She hasn't changed gears. Or the woman has been at home talking to this two-year-old all day. When you walk in, don't be surprised if she talks to you as if you were a two-year-old.

But there is often another reason for appearing to dominate. Many women tend to view men as diamonds in the rough, and themselves as gem cutters and polishers. A woman will think that if she can have just six months or a year with that glob of coal, she'll have him polished into the most sparkling diamond imaginable. Then she can boast, "Look at my husband!" The problem here is that the moment she gets into the cutter-polisher role, she has moved from the wife role to the mother role. I observe this situation frequently in my counseling. More and more men are getting tired of being polished and are walking away. The women come in for counseling, wanting to understand why—just as everything seemed to be going so well. . . just as he had begun to behave in the manner for which he had been trained—he just walked out. Frequently I discover that the woman has been playing the part of the mother—the gem-cutter—and the man has felt stifled. When he's finally had enough, he walks out.

Male Interests Outside the Home

Men frustrate women by their preoccupation with interests outside the home. Or stated differently, men frustrate women by their disinterest with things regarding the home. The woman asks, "What furniture should we get for the living room?" Male response: "I don't care." "What color drapes should we get?" "I don't care." "Do you prefer print sheets, colored, white, or what?" "I don't care." But he'll sit and talk all night about the job or that stupid golf game or that fish that got away. The woman is hurt because she feels that his interests are always out somewhere else, never at home with her.

Men, all people, male and female, have some creative drive. Women often find their creative drive being expressed in cooking or decorating. If we are not showing any interest in what they are doing, we are thwarting that creative drive, and they become very frustrated. They are interested in receiving our input because they want to please us in what they are doing, even though it is an expression of their creative drive. They are frustrated by our inability or refusal to talk about things at home.

Female Emotionalism

Women frustrate men by their tendency to become emotional in an argument. Perhaps a man is arguing with his wife. He starts sounding off with all his facts, and the next thing he knows, she's crying. He's totally frustrated. Men have been taught how to argue with words, how to argue with fists—but we've never been taught how to argue with tears. We don't know what to do. The male doesn't know whether to say, "I'm sorry, Honey," and give in and feel manipulated, or to say, " Well, if you're going to cry, I'll give you something to cry about," and whop her alongside the head! Either way, he's frustrated. He wants to say, "If you'll argue fair, then I've got a chance. But you are using a weapon I don't have. That's not right."

But men, remember this: Women by nature are more emotional. Those of you who are cold, intellectual engineer-types are most likely to be married to that lady who is just the opposite. She is going to resort to tears a lot more than even the average woman, and you're just going to have to learn to deal with it.

"Little Things Mean a Lot"

On the other hand, men frustrate women by their failure to understand that little things mean a lot. Men, the unpardonable sin is to forget an anniversary, a birthday or some such date. It is

not the price of the gift—it's the thought. But even more important than anniversaries and birthdays are those little unexpected
"sussies"—that little card you drop in the mail, that bouquet of
cut flowers that cost you $2. So many times the man thinks it's
got to be something big. He doesn't have $50 to spend on a bottle
of fancy perfume or a new dress, so he does nothing. The woman
is concerned about that little thought—just a card or a flower,
something small.

Men, I'm going to tell you one other thing. If your lady ever
tells you she doesn't want anything, don't believe her. She may
be trying to warn you that even though she doesn't feel she can do
very much for you, she does want that thought.

Another thing which is very important to a woman is a little
call once in awhile. Just say, "Hey, I'm just thinking about you.
Bye." No big conversation, just an "I'm thinking about you"
thought.

"Dreams of the Everyday Housewife"

Another way in which women frustrate men is by their
refusal to abandon girlhood dreams. Every young girl dreams of
being swept off her feet by a knight on a white charger, only to
wake up and find she was knocked off her pins by a kicker in a
pick-up truck. The problem is that she continues to hold forth
this dream of Robert Redford or Burt Reynolds, or whoever it
might be, with all his perfections. The man wants to say, "Hey, I
can't live up to that. I'm not Burt Reynolds." The man is
frustrated because he feels totally inadequate, unable to measure
up to her standard. He wants to fight back and say, "Why don't
you love me? Don't try to make me into this person—into this
dream. Just let me be me—the kicker. Let me put on my boots
and go out and kick for awhile, but love me for what I am!"
When she refuses to do so, it becomes a frustration. Many a man
finally gives up and says, "The hell with it!"

There is a real problem from the woman's standpoint in this
attitude. She has dreamed her dream and has elevated her man to

a lofty perch so often that when she finally admits or realizes he is not Robert Redford or Burt Reynolds—that he has his "warts"—she doesn't let him stop in the middle of the road. She carries him all the way into the other ditch and has no respect for him at all. She loses respect for him, not because of who he is, but rather because he did not become what she had dreamed of making him.

Female Mood Fluctuations

Men frustrate women by their inability to understand the somewhat more volatile mood swings of a woman. Someone has said that the body chemistry of a male changes four times a month, but for the female it changes seventeen times a month. The woman will be in one mood, her husband will recognize it; and before he can change his mood to meet hers, she's changed again. He has difficulty understanding that for no apparent reason, she can go up or down. She can't explain it—he can't understand it. He wants to say, "Hey, wait up! Level out once in awhile and let me see where you are. I get tired of this kissing-on-the-go type thing."

The woman is frustrated because she is not having these mood changes deliberately. She can't explain it, but a while ago she was happy, and now she is sad. She needs her man to give her some time, to have him understand her changes of mood, to have him realize she'll be happy again after awhile.

Inconsequential Issues

Another situation in which women frustrate men is the woman's tendency to attack on issues that seem to the man to be inconsequential. For instance, some women get really upset about socks in the middle of the floor. Men can't understand it. Why?

Men, a woman's home is her domain. When you come in and toss your socks in the middle of the floor, you're telling her,

"I don't care about things which are important to you." You are also telling her that all she is is your slave. Go pick up your socks.

When the woman complains about seemingly inconsequential things, frequently what she means is that you really don't seem to care about her and her place and her needs. But she can't come right out and say that you don't love her. What she does is pick some little issue and complain about it. The man becomes frustrated because, again, he wants to deal with facts, not emotions. He would rather have a woman say what's *really* bugging her so he can deal with it. When she chooses an emotional issue which is beside the question, he doesn't know what's going on. When he finally does figure out what the problem really is—*if* he does—he's frustrated that she didn't deal with the issue head on.

So we have seen the many areas in which the natural tendencies of the male and female can lead to frustration. Hopefully I've generated some chuckles now and then, as you have recognized yourself or your mate in a situation.

Again, the issue is this: Complementation or competition—which is it? A man and woman can compete with each other—each contending their method of dealing with life is the better—or they can recognize that the natural differences between male and female viewpoints can enable them to work as a team, each complementing, each counterbalancing the other person. In love they can each contribute to the other's growth as a person, acknowledging their different but equal creation, allowing those very differences to bring each person to a more balanced, more Christlike personality. I believe it is through the understanding of each other's natures that we can learn to relax and help each other grow.

Chapter Eight

Solo Parenting

Some people tend to think that a child is permanently crippled by being reared in a solo parent environment. That assumption is not the truth. As a matter of fact, it is better for a child to be reared by one healthy parent than by two parents in an unhealthy situation. Just because a child is in a solo parent home does not mean that the child cannot grow up to be well adjusted.

As we examine the role of the single parent, I want to share with you some basic ideas on meeting the needs of the child, and then we shall examine the role of a step-parent. Many solo parents will find themselves in the role of a step-parent in the future, and it will be important to have some guidance in dealing with that situation.

Understanding the Child's Feelings

If you are to be a good parent and meet the needs of your child, you must begin by getting in touch with the feelings the child is experiencing. The more experience I have in dealing with the children of solo parents, the more I am convinced that the children feel the same emotions that are experienced and felt by their parents.

Feelings of Confusion

One of the most evident feelings of solo-parent children is that of confusion. The child is feeling all the array of emotions which are also felt by the parents; and when their youth and inexperience are added to those conflicting emotions, a great deal of confusion is created. A young child will be confused because he doesn't understand why Daddy or Mother is not coming home. In a divorce situation, the child experiences confusion due to his own emotional state. At times he actually wants Mother and Daddy to divorce, and at other times he does not want them to divorce at all. The confusion of conflicting emotions is very frustrating to children.

Feelings of Anger

In the midst of their confusion, children feel angry. In the case of the death of a parent, the child will find himself experiencing a sense of anger, feeling that he has been cheated, that he has been deprived of the support and love of that parent. In the case of a divorce, the child will experience anger toward both parents. There is an anger in the midst of the arguments between his parents; or if there are no visible arguments, there is an anger about the coldness and lack of affection which is evident. The child will feel that the parent's energy is being wasted, and that no loving warmth is being given to the child.

The child will feel an anger toward the parent who left. Frequently, however, the child in a divorce situation will not express his anger toward the missing parent, but rather toward the parent who has custody. Even in a case where the father or mother walks out and never comes back, the anger will be expressed to the parent who remains. If the child sees the absent parent only once every six months or once a year, he will not risk venting his anger toward that parent. He will, instead, vent his anger upon the parent who has custody, the parent with whom his is living, because there is that fear his anger might cause the absent parent never to return. He will vent his anger on the parent with whom he feels more security. His anger must be released, must be expressed.

Feelings of Rejection

One of the deepest feelings a child experiences in a solo-parent situation is rejection. Whether the parent has left by death or by divorce, the child still experiences a sense of rejection.

At first glance it may be difficult to understand how a child feels rejection in the death of a parent, but that feeling is very real. The premature death of a parent can be a very real form of rejection to a child. Charles Sullivan of Denver, Colorado, says that the worst possible form of rejection which can be experienced is that felt by a child in the suicide of a parent. Death by natural causes or by accident cannot be prevented; but a child feels that suicide could have been prevented. He feels that the parent just gave up on him, that the parent didn't care enough to stay and fight for and with the child.

A child feels rejection if a parent simply walks away. At one time it was always the father who deserted his family; but any more, the woman frequently is the one who walks away. Even if the parent does not totally desert the child, there is still a feeling that the parent is not there all the time, and that his or her absence means that the parent does not care about the child. The feeling of rejection is very real.

Feelings of Bitterness

Feelings of anger and rejection produce bitterness. In the death of a parent, the child will experience bitterness toward the missing parent. There is another bitterness in the death of a parent that a child feels, but is often denied the privilege of expressing, and that is a bitterness toward God. Some well-meaning friend will say, "Honey, God needed another angel in heaven, so he took your father to be one of his precious angels."

The child's feeling, though he may not express it, will be "Big deal. Why didn't God take Joe's father? I needed my father!"

Because the child is not given the freedom to express an anger or bitterness toward God, he will internalize that anger or bitterness. When bitterness is internalized, it will be expressed toward friends and family. There may be a hostility that seems just to boil within the child.

The bitterness felt by a child of divorced parents is very real. I personally am becoming more and more convinced that, even as it is impossible for an adult to go through a divorce without bitterness, so it is impossible for a child of five years of age or older to experience the divorce of his parents without bitterness. Your child feels the same bitterness you felt in the divorce. He feels a bitterness toward the missing parent, toward God, and toward you. The child is bitter because he feels you could have worked things out. Frequently the bitterness will be expressed toward the mother because the child feels she ran his daddy away. The child will not understand all the intricate argument reasons or all the problems; he simply knows that one parent is missing, and he is resentful of it.

Feelings of Guilt

What does bitterness produce? Guilt. The child will feel guilty about his bitterness or anger toward his parents. But the child will also feel guilt from other sources.

In the death of a parent, the child may believe himself to be responsible for the death, and such a responsibility will create guilt. The child may have heard Mother and Daddy arguing or talking about Daddy's working so hard to provide for the children. The child wants something, and is told by the parent that there's just not enough money. So Daddy gets a second job and dies of a heart attack. What does the child feel? "I caused Daddy's death. If I had not been so demanding, if I could have been happy with less money, then Daddy would still be here." He feels guilty.

In the case of a divorce, the children never are the cause. The children may be a surface issue, but they are never the problem. But in most divorces, one of the points of disagreement is in the management of the children. The children hear these arguments. You don't argue in front of your children? Listen, children are not dummies. You and your mate suddenly have the sparkle in your eyes—not of love, but of anger—and you walk into another room and lock the door. When you come out, one of you is teary-eyed. The children know you have been arguing, and they feel you were arguing about them. They feel they are the cause. Or they may overhear you say that if you didn't have the children, the two of you might better be able to work out your problems. The child then experiences a guilt, believing himself to be the cause of his parent's separation.

The child's feeling of guilt may be fostered unintentionally by the custodial parent. Perhaps in a fit of frustration the custodial parent makes a statement like this: "That sorry Daddy (or Mother) of yours. He's out running around and chasing every skirt in town, having a good time, while I have to stay home and prepare meals and wash clothes and carry his responsibility." Every single parent feels such a frustration at times. The child will feel very guilty because he thinks he is choking the parent with whom he is staying. Guilt is a very real emotion which is experienced by the child.

Expressions of Feelings

When a child is experiencing all these emotions, his behavior will be affected in one or more of several ways. Frequently the child's interest in his school work will decline. I wish I could go to every school teacher, especially of the elementary grades, and tell them that when a child's grades begin to drop, rather than jump on that child, find out what is going on at home. Pick up the phone, call the parent, explain that the child seems to be having problems and ask, for the child's sake, whether or not the parents are having personal problems. The parent may say it is none of the teacher's business; but if that is their response, it is probable that there are some problems in the child's home. Rather than reprimanding the child for his declining grades, the teacher really needs to give that child an extra helping of understanding and support.

Some children may become the most vicious child on the playground, taking out their anger on other children around them. Other children may completely withdraw, going into their bedrooms and simply staying there, playing games. The child may be playing a game of wishful thinking that the parent is coming home.

No matter how bad the situation may be, the child will wish most of the time that his parents get back together. The child is a composite of both parents. He will feel that if they cannot get along with each other, and as he is a composite of both, then neither parent will be able to get along with him. He will feel torn apart because if his mom and dad cannot be one, how can he be at peace with himself?

Emotional confusion is felt by the child whose parent has abused him. The child will feel a tremendous anger toward that parent, at times wishing the parent would drop dead, but at the same time, wishing the parent could change and that his parents could get along with each other. There is a tremendous amount of confusion felt by the child, and it may be expressed in most any change of behavior.

Creating a Healthy Parent

When you begin to understand what emotions your child is experiencing, then you can be concerned with how you can meet his needs. You may ask, "So my children have problems. What can I do?"

What is the most important thing you can give your child? Love? Affection? No. While those are important, the most important thing you can give your child is a healthy parent. Just giving yourself is not enough. Until you have a healthy self, it is difficult to give yourself. Let me repeat: *The most important thing you can do for your child or children is to give them a healthy parent.*

Becoming a healthy parent involves two very important things: first, resolving any and all bitterness, and second, developing a healthy self-love.

Resolving Bitterness

Bitterness can be very damaging to your effectiveness as a parent. A first-hand example of the destruction of such bitterness is the young man whose case I discussed earlier. He preferred staying in the detention home to going back to his mother.

The Juvenile Officer and I talked him into going home, and we tried to work with the mother. I wish I could say there was a good, happy ending to the situation. But Mother has never worked through all of her bitterness. The boy was in Houston International Hospital for awhile, and the last report I had of him, he was on drugs and apparently was pushing drugs to support his habit.

Mothers, it is very important that you heed what I am saying at this point. You child is a part of his father as well as a part of you. *Any* bitterness that you maintain toward your former mate will automatically be transferred to your children.

Another incident which happened a number of years ago illustrates this principle. A girl of fourteen attempted suicide. As I counseled with the girl, the story quickly came out. Her dad, from all sources I could find, was one hell-raiser. The mother frequently made certain the daughter knew what a rotten person her father was. The girl attempted suicide to force her mother to let the girl live with her father.

I cannot stress this point too much. Any unresolved bitterness that you have in any area will be transferred to the ones you love, and especially to your children. The number one thing you must do as a parent is to make certain you have dealt with all your bitterness toward your former mate and/or your parents.

A Healthy Self-Love

The second thing you must do to give your children a healthy parent is to develop a healthy self-love. You must have a healthy love for yourself because until you are truly able to love yourself, you will be upset with your children as they attempt to find out who they are. You will be threatened. Your authority will be threatened. You will find yourself relating to those children in a way which is negative rather than approving.

If you are going to genuinely compliment, or build up, other people—especially your children—you must have a healthy self-love. If you do not, you will push your children to excel so that you can ride their coattails and say, "That's my child. That's my son; that's my daughter." I previously mentioned that I worked in little league baseball as a manager. If I could have gotten rid of the parents, I could have had fun and could have taught the boys a lot of baseball. But the game was spoiled by the parents who were pushing their kids, and the dads who never quite made it were the worst.

Yes, you must give to your child a healthy parent. To do so, you must get rid of your bitterness and develop a healthy self-love. Please, for the sake of your children, if you are having difficulty in either of these areas, turn back to Chapters Two and Three and reread them until you learn to put their principles into practice.

Meeting the Child's Needs

Once you have given your child a healthy parent, or at least have started working toward that end, then you are ready to give him love to meet his needs. Love is meeting needs. That's the best definition I know. What are the needs I should fulfill in my child?

A Sense of Acceptance

The first need you must meet in your children is to give them a sense of acceptance. Remember, love equals acceptance; like equals approval.

When I give my child acceptance, the first thing I give to that child is a sense of belonging. The child has experienced a form of rejection whether it has been intentional or unintentional. The child needs security. He needs to know that no matter what, you will never disown him. I think every child needs to know that he or she can never do anything that would cause his parent to disown him.

Personally, I have always tried to say to my children, "I love you. I may not always agree with what you do, but I want you to know that you are important to me." I think one reason preacher's kids often go sour is that preachers are more concerned about their own reputations than they are about the needs of their children.

A pastor friend of mine once gave me his insight in this area. His son was on drugs, and my friend was very uptight about it. He said he kept trying to impress upon his son that the young man could get a record which would jeopardize his getting jobs and so forth. Then one day it dawned om him that the real issue was not what would happen to the son, but rather what people would think if they knew the pastor of the First Baptist Church had a son who was busted for drugs. He realized that his first concern was not for his son, but rather for his own name. Children pick up on that attitude very quickly.

It is very important to let your children know that there is nothing they can ever do which will cause you to stop loving them. You may not always approve, but you must always love them. You must make certain your children know beyond a shadow of a doubt that you'll always love them, and that they always will have a place in your life.

In conveying your acceptance, you must be aware of the messages you may unintentionally convey. Sometimes in your frustration and anger, you verbally and non-verbally tell your child that you're tired of housework, tired of cooking—that you wish you could just be free like people who have no children. Or the child misbehaves. He threatens to go live with Daddy. If your response is, "If Daddy treats you so much better that I do, then go live with him!", your child experiences rejection. He feels uncertain. Will she send me away? Does she really mean it? He's scared. He may find himself being just a little mean sometimes, just to find out if you meant it. You must care enough to stick by that child, even through the problems he can give you.

When you accept your child, accept him as the unique person he is. I have six children—one of each kind. That sounds a little weird, I know. I have two daughters and a son, and a step-daughter and two stepsons. I have tried to let each one of my children be himself or herself, not necessarily to make them what I wanted them to be.

A number of years ago my younger daughter had a real identity crisis. Her older sister had finished high school in only three years. In her junior-senior year combined, she was co-captain of the girl's swim team. (She had placed in the regionals during her sophomore year but was unable to compete during her senior year because of a torn cartilage.) Not only that, but she was awarded an endowed academic scholarship because she had a 4.2 average. Further she was voted most beautiful. My younger daughter was upset because she felt she could not live up to the image of her sister. I told her, "You don't have to live up to your sister. You're not a jock. You never swam that much, so don't try. Just be the best *you* are capable of being. You don't have to live up to your sister." The younger daughter was in the fifth grade at the time and she had the lead in both school plays that year. Acting was her forte.

My older daughter was a motivated self-starter. She had to be at school every morning at six-thirty to swim competitively, and she got herself up and ready. She was the type who would lay out the clothes she planned to wear the next day so that she could get dressed, wake her brother, and get off to school. My son, on the other hand, was just the opposite. Frequently he would awaken me in the morning by stumblimg into my room to get forgotten lunch money. Or he would have to wash clothes at the last minute and get them out of the dryer because he had kept them hidden where they couldn't be found on wash days. It would have been so easy to say, "Why can't you be like your sister?" But I could not do that to my son. I accepted him for what he was, for his strengths. Our children each have unique personalities. Some are extroverts, other introverts; some are organized, others disorganized. We must learn to accept our children for the uniqueness of what they are.

One thing parents find difficult is to accept the children *with* their warts. Sometimes their warts have warts on the warts. Thank you, Lord, for the warts. Learn to accept your children just for what they are, as they are. Do not try to remold them into something else. As I said, the word *education* comes from the Latin word *dus,* which means to lead forth. Education is not pouring facts into a child and shaping a child. Education is equipping the child or enabling the child to become what God created him or her to be. My job as a parent is not to mold my children into the image I have for them, but rather to equip them to become what God intended them to be. In order to accomplish that goal, I must learn, first of all, to accept them as they are.

A Sense of Approval

A second, and very crucial, need which children have is for approval. It troubles me that most parents spend four times as much time, effort and verbiage criticizing their children as they spend complimenting them. Stop to think about it. If your child does something good, you simply say, "Honey, that's good." If he does something bad, that's bad, that's ugly, that's bad. We go over and over and over again how bad it is. We may ignore that child when he is good, but let him do something bad, and we certainly pay attention!

When I was in seminary, one of the graduate assistants was busy working on his dissertation. His wife was working to put him through school. When he was not in class, he would go home and type. They had a five-year-old and a two-year-old. He noticed that whenever he was home, the five-year-old was always bad, especially to the two-year-old. One day the five-year-old took a broomstick and whopped the living daylights out of the two-year-old. Naturally, Daddy immediately grabbed his five-year-old, and as he proceeded to lay one on the child's rear end, he asked, "Why did you do that?"

The child's reply was, "So you'd pay me some attention."

It dawned on the father that because the two-year-old was not yet potty trained, Daddy was always paying attention to him. "Do you need to go to the bathroom? Do you need a glass of water?" But the five-year-old was "old enough to take care of himself," so Daddy ignored him. The child soon learned that he could get attention by being bad.

A person must have strokes, even if they are negative strokes. Your child needs approval. Approval is the taproot of the soul. Without it, the soul withers and dies. I am a firm believer in positive reinforcement. There are times when children misbehave because they've learned that misbehavior is the way to get attention. You know the old principle: The squeaking wheel gets the grease. I recommend that parents ignore such children when they are bad, especially if they are throwing a temper tantrum. But when the children do something right, just praise and love and praise them again. When a child throws a temper tantrum, many times the most effective remedy is to put the child in a room and let him throw his fit. Lock the door and let the child scream and yell until he makes himself sick. He'll learn that he doesn't get attention that way. On the other hand, when he does something good, praise him profusely. The child will realize that the best way to get attention is by being good. It is very important that you give your children approval.

Give Them Understanding

It is important that we give our children understanding. One important part of understanding is *time.* You must spend some time with your children. Singles, let me say something to you. Do you remember the highway and the ditches on either side? If you spend all your time with your children, that's one ditch. If you spend all your time on yourself, that's the other ditch. You must have time with them and time for yourself.

When you are with your children, it is necessary to learn a very sensible principle. It is not the amount of time you spend which is most important; it is the quality of time. Time is a relative thing. Do you realize that to a four-year-old, a year is one-fourth of a lifetime? Five minutes of good quality time can sometimes be the most beautiful thing in the world.

A pastor who worked in the Haight-Ashbury district once decided that Friday nights would be Daddy-Stay-at-Home night. He had observed the hippies and recognized their children needed time with their fathers. After a while he noticed the children's attitude was, "Oh, no. Not another Daddy-Stay-at-Home night. I wish Daddy would go somewhere else so I could have some fun." He realized he had defeated the purpose of this night at home, for the fathers weren't giving those children quality time.

One evening as this pastor was talking with one of the church ladies who didn't know how to get off the phone, a car horn blared in the driveway and two deacons shouted, "Come on, preacher—we've got a committee meeting!" Further, the man's five-year-old son was pulling at his tie, saying, "Daddy, Daddy, Daddy!"

It dawned on him that his child needed his time, right then. He asked his wife to tell the men he'd join them at the church in a few minutes. He told the lady he had an emergency and had to get off the phone. He pulled loose his tie and said, "Okay, Son, what do you want?" It took the boy less than five minutes to tell him something which had happened during that day. He was one happy little boy, for he had a king for a daddy. He knew his daddy loved him. The father went on to his meeting five minutes late, but his son was left feeling he had spent an eternity with his dad. The father had fulfilled that boy's need for quality time.

There is also a need for private time with the child. Every parent should spend some time alone with each child periodically. When your children are together, they are competing with each other to see who will get the most of your time. But alone, when there is no competition, you have an opportunity really to get to know each child. Schedule the time. Do something the child wants to do. You'll both get to know each other better.

Freedom of Expression

Another part to understanding a child is to give that child the freedom to express what he is feeling. Some of his feelings may not be "right," but if they are what he is feeling at the time, they are valid.

There are two areas where I believe it is important to allow a child to express his feelings. One is the freedom to express his feelings about the missing parent. Ladies, when your child comes home from visiting your former spouse, and he talks about the new house Daddy just got, or Daddy's new travel trailer, or about Daddy's new wife, and all those feelings are boiling up in you, you know what it is, don't you? It's unresolved bitterness. Don't tell your child you don't want him to talk about the other parent. The child needs to have that freedom. That is a part of him, a part of his life. Give your child the freedom to talk about the other parent. For children to grow up healthy, they must have a healthy love for their missing parent. Even when they are able to acknowledge the fact that the man or woman is not all he or she should be, children need the freedom to talk about and love that parent. If you have trouble listening, you need to get to work on your bitterness.

There is another area where freedom of expression is important, and that is the freedom to express negative feelings without condemnation. Some time ago while I was doing a seminar at First Baptist Church of Houston, a lady in the group shared an experience with us. Her son began to toss around a few four-letter words, especially of the sexual type. She asked him to sit down and talk with her. She explained to him she would prefer that he not use those words and began to tell him why. After they had visited for a few minutes, the boy began almost to cry with joy. He said, "Mom, I'm glad you're my mom. I'm sure glad I don't have Billy's mom." When the mother asked why, he said, "Well, Billy used those words and his mom washed his mouth out with soap. But you explained why I shouldn't use them. You let me talk. You understand. You didn't put me down."

Give your children understanding. Give them the freedom to talk and to share their feelings. If the language comes out descriptive, let them know your feelings about their language, yes—but be careful not to condemn the person who used the language.

The Need for Discipline

Disciplining their children is one area where single parents tend to get in one of two ditches. One ditch is in spoiling the children, and it usually comes from a sense of guilt in the parent or of pity for the child. In an attempt to make up for the loss of one parent, the other parent will go overboard in giving the child anything he or she wants.

The other ditch is in overdisciplining, and this is a really sticky area. The custodial parent may feel as if he or she was a failure as a mate, and as a result may become overly concerned about being a failure as a parent. This parent will overreact to everything the child does and overdiscipline the child until either the child's spirit is broken or the child rebels, depending upon the nature of the child.

Grandparents often are a real problem in the proper discipline of the single-parent child. They seem especially prone to spoil the children if it was their son or daughter who was primarily to blame in the breakup of the marriage. They will spoil the child in an attempt to make up for the actions of the missing parent.

One day as I sat in the waiting room at Women's Hospital, I overheard a lady talking about how she had never been able to afford to do a lot for her children. But now they were grown; and since she had plenty of money, she was really spoiling her grandchildren. She would give them anything they wanted. I turned to the lady and said, "Ma'am, excuse me for interrupting, but I am a counselor, and I'm going to ask you to please reconsider." The lady said, "No, that's a grandparent's prerogative."

From the row in front of us, a lady turned around with tears in her eyes. She said, "Ma'am, please listen to him. I was married to a young man whose grandparents had spoiled him. It spoiled our marriage. Please listen to him."

Do not attempt to make up for the loss of a parent. You can't. Instead, learn to be fair in your discipline. Children need discipline. They need to know their bounds, their limits.

When you discipline your children, make certain there is a clarity of understanding. As children grow older, there needs to be a setting down of rules. It is helpful to write out those rules and to post them in a place where they can be seen. If you write down the rule, the child cannot misunderstand or pretend to misunderstand the rule. It is there in black and white.

There is a principle one needs to recognize when setting forth rules for one's children. A young twig can easily be bent and shaped, but when that twig becomes older, that same pressure would break it. I think parents often reverse the proper stringency of discipline. Have you ever noticed how a parent will laugh at a young child's mistakes, and yet when the child becomes a teen, laughing matters suddenly become matters for discipline? That attitude is just the reverse of what it should be. One should be tighter and more restrictive with a young child and more freeing with the older child. Your goal is to help your children grow to the place where you can set them free.

Applying that principle is especially difficult if you have teenagers right now and you were too loose when they were younger. Suddenly you find you have a problem on your hands. Your tendency may be to crack down all of a sudden. Let me warn you: Don't try to work too fast. If you have been loose in the discipline of your child when he or she was young, and suddenly you try to put that teenager into a pattern of discipline, that child will rebel. You'll have an even more serious problem. Proceed with caution and tighten your discipline gradually. Ask God for wisdom *and* help.

Another important principle about discipline is to enforce, rather than threaten. Do not threaten your children. How often have you heard a frustrated parent whose child misbehaves, saying, "Don't do that! If you do that, I'll do so-and-so." Recognizing that the threatened punishment is so severe the parent really won't carry it through, the child will do the same thing again, if for no other reason than to show the parent up. So the parent threatens again. The child misbehaves again. Finally the parent becomes so angry s/he carries out the threatened punishment. The child has learned that the only way to get the parent's full attention is to push that parent to the point of anger.

A good rule of thumb is never to tell a child to do or not to do something more than twice. The first repetition may be necessary to make certain the child has understood the request. If the child does not comply with the next request, then reasonable punishment should be enforced. It is important to set a reasonable discipline or punishment so that it may be enforced consistently. Every time you postpone the discipline beyond the second request, you are creating a monster. Save yourself a lot of anger and wasted energy by setting forth principles, establishing reasonable discipline procedures for the failure to adhere to those principles, and consistently carrying forth that punishment by enforcing, rather than threatening.

When I was about twenty years old, I had the privilege of being a counselor in a teenage camp in the state of Washington. The dormitory was a long building, with a dining hall and assembly room on the first story and a dorm upstairs. Separating the boys from the girls was literally a knotty pine wall. I was downstairs in a staff meeting one evening when I noticed that the girls' side of the dorm upstairs was noisy, but the boys were totally quiet. I thought surely there must be some devilment going on for the boys to be so quiet, so I calmly slipped up the stairs. All the boys were sound asleep.

Earlier, of course, I had made the rule and set the punishment for breaking it. I guess I just didn't believe the boys had taken me seriously. But they had learned the principle: Do; don't threaten.

Discovering Your Child's Identity

Helping your children to discover their own identities is a very important part of parenting. It is important to recognize that children are a composite of both parents. Each child is a unique person. It is not the parent's job to force a child into a mold, but to assist that child in finding out who God created them to be.

One part of helping a child to discover identity is in the area of understanding male/femaleness. There is, admittedly, a great deal of artificial role discrimination; yet there are also some basic differences between males and females. Those differences are more than just physical. As a child grows, he needs to encounter and experience the differences in roles and attitudes. This is one area which is especially difficult for the solo parent. There is a great deal being said about the fear of homosexuality in children of solo parents. I believe homosexuality to be the result of a poor parent image. That image can come from a boy's being reared by an overly-cruel father or an overly-dominant mother, or vice-versa with girls. I believe that children reared by healthy, loving parents and given opportunities to have the influence of healthy identity figures of both sexes, can adjust properly to their male/female roles.

There is one problem area with a child's identity which deserves special mention. The custodial parent's oldest child of the opposite sex often has a tendency to take the role of the missing parent. In other words, you ladies who have sons may find the oldest will try to become the man of the house. If he is man of the house, he is man of the bedroom. Let me explain. Have you ever heard a six or seven-year-old boy ask his mother, "What's that bill for?" or "Who's that letter from?" That's the question his daddy used to ask, right? And the young man heard someone say that since Daddy has gone, he has to be the man of the house. Since Daddy is not here, the boy will have a tendency to move into the bedroom emotionally. It may be with the statement, "I'm scared, Mommy," and the child will slip into the bedroom. Listen, ladies—that boy may be validly afraid and may come in to your room one night; but it is best if you don't let him stay the whole night. I don't care how afraid he is, you'll do him a greater injustice. Comfort him, calm his fears, but then let him know that he is to return to his room, that his place is not in yours. I believe it is best even for a baby to be reared in a separate room. Mother can sleep much better when she doesn't hear every little turn of that child, and the child will not develop a dependency by sleeping in the room with Mama. If you have a teenage boy who has become man of the house, or if you have a seven-year-old who has become man of the house, I advise you to have a mother-to-son talk with him and inform him that he's son, and you're mother. If you don't, you are crippling him; and when he gets to the age where he normally would make a transition to other women, he will find that transition difficult. He will feel that his first obligation is to his mother, and emotionally he will be married to her. He will have difficulty relating because he will feel that he is being unfaithful.

The same principle applies to fathers and their daughters. Don't let that daughter take the role of woman of the house. That is not her place. You are father; she is daughter.

Parents, take careful heed of this principle. If you fail to do so, you are not only crippling your children's capacity to form healthy relationships, but you are creating a possessiveness which will make it difficult, if not impossible, for those children to relate to a stepparent if you should remarry.

A second important principle in helping your child discover his identity is to provide good male/female images, especially when there is a missing father or missing mother. Then it is absolutely essential that you provide a healthy image of the missing parent role. I get annoyed with singles' organizations which ought to be self-help, but frequently become hustle organizations. Because of the hustle, the children are the ones who suffer. Both the men and the women are so busy hustling each other, they fail to form valid friendships which can provide a stable role model for their children.

A dear friend of mine agreed to serve as a deacon in a church with the understanding that he would be assigned only to solo parent families. He gets involved with the boys and girls. He takes the boys to their athletic events. He and his wife bring the children into their home to let them observe a man and woman working together. Another example of this type of role model occurred when a man in the singles' Bible study class took his daughter and the boys and girls of three ladies in the class to see the Blue Angels. The children had an opportunity to see a man and to go and do something with a man.

Several years ago a young man in my congregation came up to me and said, "Clyde, will you come and see me play baseball tomorrow night? It's my last game." I happened to know that his father had not seen him play a single game. Even one Saturday, when the young man had a rain-out game scheduled, the father refused to go, saying the young man could call and let him know how it went. Although I had a meeting scheduled, I never told the boy. I had the privilege of seeing that boy play. He was voted to the All Star team, and I watched him play in that game as well. One of my fondest memories is that a couple of weeks later, on Father's day, that young man and his brother brought a potted plant to my office on Sunday morning. I will always treasure that memory.

In every singles' group there is a potential to meet the needs of your children. Some time ago our church had a singles' roller skating party in the gym. Out there skating were kids who I don't believe had ever been on skates. I hadn't been on skates for years. We skated for a couple of hours, and then someone had the bright idea of playing hockey. Imagine adults, both male and female, and kids playing hockey on roller skates—no broken bones, but a lot of falls, holy hugs and hellacious crashes. At one time there were five people—a combination of children and adults—all tangled up in the netting, skates going every imaginable direction. Everybody who wasn't brave enough or crazy enough to be participating was rocking with laughter. The kids as well as the adults were having a ball.

There is a tremendous need for solo parent children to interact with adults in this manner. Let's turn to the organizations where you have group activities and try to meet that need. It is important to meet those needs elsewhere in the church also. In every classroom where there are solo parent children, for example, teachers should have a special awareness of the needs of these children and be sensitive to meeting those needs.

Dating Relationships and Your Children

Frequently the question of parental behavior in dating situations arises. The matter of showing affection is a special area of concern. Let me give you a couple of observations in this area.

First of all, when you begin to date, your children most likely will attempt to interfere. Children have an innate desire that Mom and Dad get back together. When you begin to date, your children will take every opportunity to place themselves physically between you and your date. You might as well expect it. There are times when it is okay to let that child sit between you, for it is important that he feel secure in his place of importance. But there are times you must insist that the child sit on the other side of you, that the child share you.

Regarding a show of affection, let me say that while a parent should not "make out" in front of the child, I do believe the child needs to see healthy affection. When you have established an ongoing relationship, it is healthy for the child to see the holding of hands, an arm around the shoulder, a hug or a kiss. A child who does not see affection in the home will have difficulty in learning how to be affectionate in marriage.

What About Visitation?

To those of you who have visitation rights, not custody, let me make a couple of observations. First, don't spoil. Love your children, but do not try to buy their love. Do not create for them an artificial world. Don't be the kind of dad who gets the children once every two weeks and tries to spoil them by buying them things and lavishing time. Involve your children in a normal environment; give them a realistic idea of life rather than overindulge them.

Secondly, do not pry. Ladies, it is none of your business who that "ex" is dating. If you were still married to him, it would be your concern; but you are not, and it's none of your cotton-pickin' business—so don't ask the children. If the children come home and talk about it, be understanding and let them talk. But don't you dare make one prying comment. Men, when you pick up those children on Friday, don't you start asking questions like, "What's Mommy been doing? Where is she spending her money?" It is none of your business. That's putting it bluntly, I know—but you get the point.

What about dating of the visiting parent who sees the children only every other week? The same thing applies to you about visitation which applies to the parent who has custody all week long. Spending all your time with the children or no time with the children can be equally unhealthy. If you are constantly involved in dating, that is unhealthy because you are not spending any time with your child. On the other hand, if you never date when the children are there, the children will not get a realistic idea of life. I believe there needs to be some dating. It is very good to take the children along. By taking the children, they get an opportunity to share with a new person, and it can be fun for all of you. Sometimes you may have to leave them to go out on a date. It is important that your children know that you love them, but that they do not control your every move.

Stepparenting

The key to successful stepparenting is one word: *adoption.* I am not talking about legal adoption. I am talking about emotional adoption. Never marry until you are able to release your children to the new mate as if they were his or her own (or in other words, until you have that kind of trust in that person), or until you are able to emotionally adopt that person's children.

This may sound like a simplistic statement, but I do not believe that children are ever the cause of the break-up of a marriage. The problem lies in the parents and their distrust of each other; that's what causes them to fight over the children.

For instance, I have seen knock-down drag-out battles about child support. The new wife will complain that her husband is paying out all this child support, but her former husband is not paying any; consequently, the two of them are supporting two sets of children. That argument would never occur if she had come to the place where she had adopted his children. If you have adopted your mate's children, ladies, you'll want those children to have the best. You'll make certain the child support is one of the first things that is paid. If it is not paid, it's *your* children who are suffering because you have adopted them.

Not only is the adoption important in the area of finances, but also in the area of discipline. You might as well recognize that in the area of discipline, you and your mate will disagree in some areas, no matter who you are. Children pick up on the differences, and they'll play one parent against the other. If it's "your children" and "my children," they are more able to divide you. When it's "our children," it is much easier to work through any difficulties. Together you must work out the basic rules of discipline. One comment in this regard: Don't disagree in front of the children. When you disagree on an issue of discipline, wait until you are alone, talk it through, and come to a compromise if necessary. But whatever you do, support each other.

Another important thing to remember in a stepparenting situation is not to force yourself on the children. Simply commit yourself to love them as if they were your own children, and in time they will accept you.

I must share an amusing personal anecdote here. As I have mentioned, I have three stepchildren. Cathy's youngest child, Chris, had a lot of difficulty accepting me when we first started dating. Someone told him, "Chris, if your mother marries a preacher, he'll make you memorize the Bible for fifteen minutes every day." Not only that, but at one time she had dated a cowboy—a bullrider, and Chris liked the bullrider type better. It was really difficult for him to learn to accept this preacher named Clyde. On one occasion, Chris had overspent his allowance, and he came whispering to his mother that he needed more money. He seemed afraid to approach me with the problem. Cathy laughed and said aloud, "Oh, that's what you need." She let me know about the situation, and I said, "Hey, Chris, if you need some money, talk to me, too." Cathy and I were working together. But I cannot force my way into Chris' affections. I must earn his love and respect. If I have the attitude that these are my children, then that affection will develop and mature quite naturally.

Again, let me stress the word: *adoption*. Whenever someone adopts a child, that parent doesn't mind doing whatever is necessary to earn the right to be called whatever he or she may be called. Chris still hasn't decided what to call me. One time he'll call me Daddy, the next time he'll call me Clyde, and then he'll call me "Cajun Cook"—just whatever comes to mind at the time. We all laugh about it. But again, the key is the commitment for adoption.

There was no question in my mind when I married the second time, that those children were just like my own. I have hopes that if the children want to go to college, their father will see to it that the money is there. But I have told Cathy and the children, if he doesn't, it doesn't matter; for as long as I have a penny, they and my children have equal rights to the money allocated for college educations. As far as I am concerned, Cathy's children are just as much mine as they are hers. Because I have accepted her children, they are not a burden. Being their parent is simply a part of the marriage. It is a part of my love for my wife that I am willing to accept that responsibility.

Chapter Nine

Preparations For Remarriage

One does not have to be headed for marriage in order to have a need for this chapter. No matter where one happens to be in a relationship, there are steps which are helpful in directing the growth process. Together we will examine the theology of remarriage, how to prepare oneself for remarriage, how to find the person who is exactly right, and what to expect when that person is found and the marriage vows are exchanged.

Theology of Remarriage

I have found through many years of dealing with previously married singles that the question most frequently asked is, "What does the Bible say?" Even for those who are not actively involved in their churches or who have pushed God as far away as possible, there is this concern which is a result of their religious backgrounds.

Single by Death of Mate

First let me address the issue of the theology of remarriage to those who have lost a mate by death. The Bible is quite clear in teaching that marriage is for this life only. When one's mate dies, one is free to remarry.

You may recall the occasion when Jesus was questioned about a Jewish custom. The custom was that if a man died and his wife was left without a child, she remarried very quickly the next of kin, normally her husband's brother. The question was posed, what if the woman were to experience the death not only of her husband, but, in succession of each of his seven brothers? Then whose wife would she be in heaven? Jesus' answer was clear: There is no giving or receiving of marriage in heaven. In heaven, we will all be brothers and sisters. When one who loses a mate by death comes to grips with that fact, then he or she realizes that at that moment of death, one is free to move forward.

Single by Divorce

The theology on remarriage after divorce is much more complicated than the theology on remarriage after death. There have been many disagreements in churches of all denominations about this topic. What I am going to share with you is the belief to which I have grown, starting from a base of a seminary which was more or less blocked to remarriage of divorced people, and building on that theology from my personal study of God's word and of individuals and society over a period of more than fifteen years.

The more I have studied the Bible, the more I have become convinced that God gives no reason for divorce. Divorce takes place because of the hardness of the heart. It is the ultimate failure of people to work together or to make it, whatever the reasons. God's ideal is that there be no divorce.

When looking at modern life realistically, however, one must recognize that divorce is a reality. One writer on this subject points out that divorce is the better part of valor when the relationship makes one bitter rather than better. A marriage is not two people coexisting. Genesis 2:18 says that marriage is for the purpose of a man and woman coming together as helpmates, or complements. Another way to say it is that marriage is two people joined together in order to enhance and enrich each other. When one or both parties no longer enhance, but rather destroy the other person, then divorce becomes a reality. Although they may stay together under one roof, they are spiritually divorced because one's destruction of the other prevents their fulfilling the purpose of marriage. There are many people who live under the same roof, but who are spiritually divorced because they are not building up, enhancing, enriching each other, fulfilling the purpose for marriage.

Most divorces actually take place anywhere from one to fifteen years before they go to court. All the judge does is give legal recognition to something which has already transpired. When a doctor signs a death certificate, he doesn't kill the person—he simply declares that person legally dead. In the same manner, a divorce judge simply declares a marriage legally dead. The divorce transpired long before the signing of the paper; it took place when two people stopped working together to enhance and build up each other.

One of the most frequent symptoms of spiritual divorce is the "put-down." One or both parties to the marriage will take every opportunity to belittle the other, to destroy the other's feeling of self-esteem. A continual, habitual attitude of put-downs indicates that there is a divorce, a destructiveness.

I do not like divorce. I am certain that divorce is not in keeping with God's ideals. Yet sometimes divorce is the lesser of two evils. When the relationship becomes destructive rather than beneficial or enhancing, then divorce may become a necessity.

There are times when divorce may be a matter of self-defense. Earlier I mentioned an illustration of this point—the woman whose husband was putting arsenic in her food every day, slowly building up the dose to be enough to kill her. Few people would advise that woman to stay in that marriage. There is an emotional or psychological destruction that can be just as devastating as a fatal dose of arsenic. When one begins to receive that kind of emotional trauma, one's only hope for self-preservation may be divorce.

I believe that divorce is sin. Divorce is contrary to God's ideal, and anything contrary to God's ideal is sin. Yet the Bible says, "Where sin did abound, grace did much more abound." God's grace gives one the opportunity of forgiveness—not because one deserves it, but because it is God's nature to provide for man. Therefore, when one comes to a place where one bows before God, acknowledging those mistakes and shortcomings which contributed to the death of the marriage—at that point, God will forgive that person. Now, you will recall, when God forgives, He marks the slate clean, "paid in full." When He washes us clean, He justifies us, and we are just as if we'd never sinned.

It is vital that you understand the full implication here. If you tell a lie and confess it to God, God forgives you. He accepts you and treats you just as if you never told that lie. When one murders, and later comes to God and confesses that murder, God forgives that person. That person is then just as if he'd never committed murder. Now, one who has committed murder does not have to resurrect the dead person to be forgiven, right? That may sound stupid to you, but bear with me—I want to show you something. When one has committed murder and confesses it to God, God forgives even though that person does not resurrect the dead. Are you getting the picture? A divorce is the death of a marriage. Both parties have contributed to the death of a marriage. When a person bows before God and says, "God, here is what I did that contributed," at that point God forgives and justifies. He does not justify only if we are able to resurrect the dead marriage. He justifies period. He cleanses. At that point one becomes as a spotless virgin.

When Cathy and I married, I stood before the people and shared with them remarks which I am in the process of incorporating into wedding ceremonies for divorced people. As I said in our cermony, "We come at a time of a new beginning. We know that we both contributed to the deaths of our marriages. But because of God's love and God's grace, as we have bowed before Him in honest confession, He has forgiven us and justified us. Because of His grace and mercy, we now stand before him clean, given a new opportunity—a time of new beginning. And so we commit ourselves to this new relationship, ever giving thanks unto God for the opportunity that He gave us to start over." God's grace is the secret. When God forgives, He washes one clean. At that point one becomes a virgin.

As I have said, what I have shared is what God has led me to believe over a period of fifteen years. When I was a young pastor, having come from a background more or less forbidding conducting weddings for divorced people, a man came to me and asked if I would be willing to conduct the wedding for him and his fiancée. Both were divorced, and the man's former wife was remarried and was a member of my church. Faced with a new situation, I asked the man to wait a week for my decision, to give me time to pray about it. I prayed, and I consulted with the former pastor of the church, who was an area missionary. I sought his prayers and guidance. After a week of prayer, studying scriptures, and coming to an understanding of forgiveness, I agreed to conduct the wedding. Shortly events occurred which validated the fact that the marriage was a good marriage. It seemed to me that God was saying, "Clyde, I approve."

Since that time I have thought, studied and prayed a great deal over the question of remarriage of divorced people. I am convinced that God does not approve of divorce, but he still accepts the divorce. I am also convinced that when the divorced person has found forgiveness, he or she is clean, and God will approve a new relationship. I believe that God can look down upon that new marriage and say, "Yes, I disapproved of the divorce; but of this marriage, I approve." I am sharing with you what I have studied, researched and experienced. You may not agree with me; but I believe this is the word the Lord has brought to me, and it has given me real peace.

Preparing Oneself for Remarriage

Having acknowledged, then, the right to remarry, one must make some self-preparation. There are attitudes and relationships which must be reformed before one is ready for a new relationship.

Dealing with the Former Mate

If one is to remarry, what is to be his attitude toward his former mate? It is very simple. Put that former mate in the heavenly relationship. The Bible teaches us that we are all going to be brothers and sisters in heaven. If you can put your former spouse in the heavenly relationship of brother and sister, then you are in a healthy situation. You can share with that person, be happy for and communicate with that person. If the two of you have children, communication will be necessary for a lifetime; for even after your children are adults, there will still be occasions when you must be involved with your former mate. If you can consider him or her to be your brother or sister, you can have a healthy relationship.

On a personal note, some time ago Cathy and I needed some financial advice about real estate. Cathy's former husband is a finanical wizard, able to make money when nobody else can. So we called on Jim for advice. We had the freedom to do this, you see, because Cathy and he are brother and sister, and he and I are brothers. He and his new wife can discuss their relationship with us, and Cathy can honestly help her to work through a problem or to understand Jim better. When one can arrive at that relationship, there is a freedom. I don't need to feel threatened by Jim.

An amusing thing happened when Cathy and I first started dating. One Sunday I made a big pot of gumbo at Cathy's. On Tuesday night I came over to visit, and that same night Jim had come by to visit the boys. When I walked in the door, there sat Jim at the dinner table, eating some of the leftover gumbo! He even complimented the chef. We were both comfortable. We can relate because Cathy and Jim have come to consider each other as brother and sister. We did not feel any competition. You know, if you have a healthy marriage, you do not feel competition with your brothers-in-law and sisters-in law. They are a part of the family, and you accept them as such.

Thus if you are again single, whether it is by death or by divorce, you must put your former mate in the heavenly relationship—that is, accept that person as a bother or a sister. Until you have established that heavenly relationship, you will not be free to move on; for as long as you are thinking "married to" that person, you will remain emotionally married even though you may become physically married to someone else. Put that former mate in the heavenly relationship.

Getting Your Act Together

In addition to reforming your attitudes toward your former mate, you also must get your own act together. Many people fail to realize that the most important part of the marriage is a happy "me." Unless I am happy, I cannot have a healthy marriage. As a marriage counselor, I treat individuals rather than the marriage. Many counselors treat the marriage; I treat individuals because until you have healthy individuals, you cannot have a healthy marriage. What are the ingredients to happiness?

Your Attitude Toward Marriage

First of all, do you have a healthy attitude toward marriage? A healthy attitude says, "I am open to, but not compelled to remarry." If one is not open to marriage, that person is acknowledging a lot of unresolved bitterness. If you are saying, "I'll never marry again," you'd better check your bitterness level. On the other hand, if you are saying, "I must marry again," you are making someone else responsible for your happiness. You are healthy only when you are able to be open, but not compelled to remarry.

View Past Mistakes Honestly

The second step toward happiness is to be able to be honest about what went wrong with the first marriage. If you do not acknowledge your mistakes of the past, you will most certainly repeat them in the future. The reason twice as many seond marriages as first end in divorce is that most people do not deal with what went wrong. They run from it.

Someone may say, "Well, Clyde, I honestly don't know what went wrong with my first marriage." You don't? I'll give you a hint as to how you can find out. Ask your former mate. She or he will tell you if you will listen. If you are honestly wanting to know, and your former mate does not think you are being blase, he or she will be glad to tell you what went wrong and what you did to contribute to the death of that marriage. You may hear more than you want to hear. But get honest with the Lord and find our what went wrong in that first marriage.

Deal with Resentments

Third, deal with all your resentments. Any unresolved resentments you may have toward your former mate are going to be transferred to the next one. Rid yourself of all resentment toward that former mate so that you can have an honest brotherly love for that person.

You can know your resentment is gone when you can honestly be happy for your former mate when good things happen to him or her. When you get to that place, you are in good shape.

I promise you—any unresolved resentment you have toward that former mate is going to be transferred to the new mate. For the first six months of your new marriage, you'll be on a honeymoon and you won't say much. But after that, every time he or she does anything that reminds you of the faults of that first or former mate, you will get very edgy. And you won't stand for the treatment you put up with the first time; you'll tell your new mate about it in a hurry.

A Healthy Self-Love

You must make certain your self-love is at least on a level seven or above on a scale from one to ten. This is a very important point. It's not easy to measure—but if you don't have at least a 6½ (that rounds off to seven, right?), you will be in trouble. What you will do is draw more out of the relationship than you put in. You will be depending on the other person for your happiness. You will depend on that person to reassure you to such an extent that it will have a seriously detrimental effect upon the marriage.

Stand Alone

To make certain your self-esteem has risen to a good level, you must be able to stand alone. The problem with many first marriages is that many women simply go from daddy to daddy. The young girl goes from a total dependence upon her father, directly into a marriage where she is totally dependent upon her husband. She has never really stood alone. I have a little eccentricity when I perform a formal wedding in that I insist that the father who escorts the bride leave her at the second pew, letting her take the last few steps by herself as a symbol of the fact that she can stand alone.

When my older daughter was married, someone asked me who was going to walk her down the aisle since I was performing the service. We had already talked about it. She understood her daddy. My daughter walked all the way by herself. She said, "Daddy, my husband is walking out there by himself. No one is holding his hand. I can do the same thing."

Are you able to stand alone?

As we have seen in another chapter, there is a ditch on each side of every road. Sometimes after one has gone through a divorce and has been forced to stand alone, he or she will find being alone to be most enjoyable. That person will assert his or her independence and, once single five or more years, will have difficulty letting go of that independence. If you are such a person, you will have a little more difficulty when you marry. Letting go of your independence may be difficult for you.

An amusing anecdote comes to mind regarding this point. One day I met a couple for whom I had conducted the wedding some time before. Both were in their sixties and both had been single for a long time prior to their marriage. They confided that their biggest arguments had been over how to stack the silverware in the drawer and whose towels to use. They had been independent so long they had established their own patters, and they were having to compromise and work together. It was creating a problem.

One observation, however. Even though being overly independent may create a tension, it is much better to have a mate who can stand on his or her own two feet, than to have one you must drag all the time.

Develop Friendships

Development of a good circle of friends is essential. No one should get involved in a primary romantic relationship until one has a basic group of friends—at least four or five, including at least two of the opposite sex. And you will need to maintain those friendships. Some couples isolate themselves when they marry, and then they wonder why they freeze to death. When they have no influx, no warmth flowing back in, problems can multiply.

The old marriage vow said, "leaving all others to cleave to you only." I have changed that vow in the ceremonies I perform, using instead "to give myself without reserve to you." God never intended for us to leave all other friendships. He intended us to be involved in relationships. I need my friends, and Cathy needs her friends. You will need yours. Develop them before you begin

to form your primary relationship. That foundation of friendships will be a support factor in your life.

Get To Know Yourself

You must understand yourself before you are ready for a
marriage relationship. A marriage is a complementary relationship. It is true that personality-wise—not-character-
wise—opposites attract. The reason for that is that I need the opposite kind of person to balance me. An introvert will almost invariably marry an extrovert. And the more introverted he or she
may be, the more of an extrovert he or she will marry. An
organized person will marry a spontaneous person. A "hyper"
person will invariably marry a "laid-back" person.

In most areas of life, people are trained to know what they
are doing before they actually must perform. Yet in the second
most important decision we make in our lives—the selection of
the person with whom we are to spend our lives—we have little or
no training on the basis for making that selection. We never train
people to understand themselves and to understand the complementary nature of marriage so that they will look for someone
who will complement or balance them. You must share some
qualities, yes. But if I am way out on an extreme in an area, I need
someone who can balance me. In order to know what qualities
will balance me, I must get to know myself. It's time to start finding out who you are so you'll know how to go about looking.

What To Seek in a Mate

Now that you are beginning to find out who you are, it's
time to determine what you're looking for. Do you remember the
description of the psyche—the intellect and emotions? In order
to have a healthy relationship, I have to tie together my intellect
and my emotions. I think the tragedy is that some poeple go
"dear hunting" with their emotions, and others go "dear hunting" with their intellects. I think you should do this type of hunt-

ing with a two-barrel shotgun.

You know, if I were going to buy a car, and I was going to be emotional and intellectual about it, one of the things I would do first is determine what kind of car I wanted. I'd do some preplanning so that I would be less likely to find myself two days after purchase saying, "Why did I let that salesman talk me into buying that car?" I would buy and get what I was really looking for.

In making my choice of a car, one of the first questions I would answer is, "For what purpose do I want the car?" If I want prestige, I'll select a Mark VI or a Cadillac. If I want economy, I'll select a compact. I'd decide first what I wanted, what I needed.

After I made that basic determination, then I would decide what options I wanted on the car. In selection of options, I must establish some priorities because I know that the likelihood of my finding a car exactly like I want is very slim. So I must decide which options I could do without and which are necessities. You know, some things are negotiable, some are not. For instance, I had heat exhaustion a number of years ago. An air conditioner in a car is not a negotiable item with me; it is a necessity. Now, Cathy is so cold-blooded that an air conditioner would be something she could do without. So, you see, my priorities may differ from yours because our needs may be different.

You are ready to go "dear hunting." What are you looking for? I can't tell you exactly what you should look for, but I will share with you some thoughts I jotted down when I was looking. Perhaps these will help you to work out your own "dear hunting" list.

Resolution of Bitterness

One of my most important priorities was to find one who had resolved her bitterness toward her former mate. I knew if she had not, she would transfer it to me.

One point of advice I will give to you. As you start dating, *listen*. If that person is constantly critical of his or her former mate and reflects bitterness toward that former mate—run, don't walk, to the nearest exit. Don't think that you are going in to save them. Suggest they read "How to Trust After Being Burned" or get some counseling. Let them get well, and then date them again.

A Healthy Self-Love

Another of my priorities was that she have a healthy self-love. How can you tell? Again, listen. If that person always talks about his faults, and never his good qualitites—or if he always talks about his good qualities and never acknowledges his faults—his self-love is usually somewhat deficient. If that person can talk equally freely about good qualities and deficiencies, then that person probably has a healthy self-love. You don't have to ask a lot of questions. Just listen when they talk. One dates for three purposes: to have fun, to discover what qualities turn us on and turn us off, and to find that person who had the most number of turn-ons and the fewest number of turn-offs.

Optimism

Another important item on my list was a person who was optimistic. I am certain that optimism is high on my list due to the nature of my work. When I hear people share their problems with me, I must come home to someone who has an optimistic outlook. But there is another important reason. I don't think a Christian has room to be pessimistic. We have the most beautiful news in the world. I've turned over to the end of the Book, and I know how the story ends; I'm not worried. I don't care what happens today or tomorrow; I know that ultimately God is going to win. Why should I get uptight about it all day long? I want someone who has a positive, optimistic attitude toward life because if she's negative, she's going to bring me down. Have you ever been around someone who was so down-in-the-mouth or depressed that you felt as if you were in a whirling hurricane when you were around them? I think life is meant to be fun, and I personally don't want to be around someone who enjoys gloom.

Acceptance

I need someone who can be accepting of me. I am not perfect. I know it. Some of my faults I know; others I do not. I want someone who can lovingly help me grow—who, most of all, can accept me and not try to change everything about me. In other words, I am not looking for a diamond cutter. I have one of those already; his name is Jesus Christ. You've possibly heard John Anderson's song "A Diamond Someday," which says, "I'm an old chunk of coal, but someday I'm going to be a diamond." God is my diamond cutter. I will let him do the cutting. I don't want my mate to be my diamond cutter. I need her to be loving, supporting and accepting of me.

Emotional Intimacy

It is important to me to have someone who is willing to be emotionally intimate—who will share with me what she is feeling and thinking. She can share with me when she is happy, or when she is sad or angry. I want her to tell me what is going on, rather than my having to pry out communication. I want a person who day by day, week by week, can show more and more of herself to me—who can be a real person. She must use the freedom to be open and honest and intimate.

Sense of Humor

Another important quality to me is a sense of humor. In a book entitled *The Humor of Christ,* Elton Trueblood points out that Jesus is a master at the pun-type jokes. For instance, I like to tell Cajun stories. I may not be the best joke-teller in the world, but I love to tell jokes. I tell jokes in my sermons. I may break out into a Cajun dialect to tell a story. To me, humor is a part of life.

180

The person who shares my life must have a sense of humor; it makes life much more fun.

Physically Attractive

I want a mate who is attractive. There is a difference between "beautiful" and "attractive." Attractive means that one makes the most of what one has. I cannot determine whether I will be six-foot-six or five-six, or whether I will be narrow or big-framed. I can't determine whether I will have classic lines that make one beautiful or handsome. But I'll tell you what I can do. I can make the most of what I have. I can make the most of my appearance by keeping my body in the best shape possible. I can make the most of myself by being sure that I look neat. If my mate were sloppily groomed, I would feel she did not care enough about herself or about me. One doesn't have to spend a lot of money; one simply has to take a little time. This is an area where I have a very strong feeling. I realize that some people cannot help their appearance because they have medical problems. I feel that only under that circumstance can unattractiveness be acceptable. I have often observed that when people are single, they get themselves into the best shape. When they get married, within six months to a year many of the guys have a pot belly. To me, that pot belly says that men don't care about themselves and the people they love.

Pardon me if I am direct and to the point—but I want a lady that I am proud of. I believe ladies feel the same way. It gives me a great deal of satisfaction to walk into a place and know that others find my wife attractive. I really get an ego boost from this, and I am really glad to be with her. Perhaps this is important to me because I am involved where people are, and I think it is a priority. I am sharing with you my list; you can make your own.

Share a Dream

I want someone who has a dream. I have a dream. Now, my

dream and the dream of my wife do not have to be the same, but they must be dreams we can mutually share. My dream is that *Picking Up the Pieces* will one day be shared with people throughout the world, and that I will have the privilege of traveling to share these truths with people around the nation. Cathy's ulitmate dream is for a log house on five acres of land with two horses. I love it. I can share that dream, and she shares mine. If you don't have a dream, you are drifting. I want to be going somewhere in my marriage.

A Total Person

It is important to me that my wife be a total person. There are several things which comprise what I consider to be a total person.

Prior to one of my seminars, a lady I knew said, "Clyde, where are the men? All I see here are a bunch of panty-waists." Now, I think she was overstating, because I was there, and I don't consider myself a panty-waist. But I understood what she meant. She went on to say, "Clyde, I come to a meeting like this, or to church, and I find a lot of guys who are gentle and kind, but they are not tough or macho. I can go into a bar, and I'll find guys who have lots of macho, but no tenderness or kindness. Where is the person who is both? I come from a ranch out in West Texas," she continued, "and I see cowboys who are really attractive, but there is no Christianity in them. I see these guys in church, and they are Christians, but I don't see any cowboy qualities in them."

She got me to thinking in terms of the Christian Cowboy, or the qualities that make up a super-sexy Christian male or a super-sexy Christian female. There is that total person who is both—who is comfortable and at home in both dimensions. There is that type of person who is heavenly bound and heavenly minded, but who also knows that he or she lives here on earth and can walk here on the face of it without being upset. That person has several qualities. He or she can dress up and go to an opera, for instance, and feel comfortable. It may not be their favorite place, but they are comfortable in a tux or a long dress. But that same person can also put on a pair of jeans and boots and walk through the barnyard and occasionally step in it without getting paranoid.

Another way of saying it is that the total man is one who has those Christian qualities of gentleness, kindness, sensitivity and understanding, but also has those qualities of the cowboy who is tough and independent—who can act alone, who is ready to stand up and fight when necessary. He has a gentleness and also a toughness about him.

That total woman is one who feels comfortable in silk and satin, who had the qualities of gentleness, softness and sweetness, but who also is able to understand the earthy things of life, things like finances, and reality of life, and sex. Are you getting the picture? The total person is that person who has the better qualities of both worlds.

I have very strong feelings about Jesus Christ. One of the things that always bothered me was that all the painting and pictures I saw of Jesus as I was growing up were almost—pardon the term—effeminate. They showed no toughness. In my study I have hanging a newer painting of Jesus. It depicts him as a rugged man—a man's man. I believe that Jesus was a man's man. But he also had the quality of tenderness so that both men and women were drawn to him. That is the total person I am talking about. And one of my priorities was to find a total person.

Approval

A very important characteristic to me is approval. I need a person who is warm and approving, who can make me feel that there is no better place to go than to where that person is. When I come in after a bad day, and I am drained, I need a person like my wife who can sense my state of mind and make me feel as if I'm king of the world. Warm, supportive and understanding, approving.

Complementary Personalities

I mentioned earlier that in getting ready for remarriage, I needed to get to know myself. Because I need someone who complements me, I first must find out who I am, and then, I must seek that person who balances me in all the areas where I need balancing.

You see, I looked at myself, and knew first that I am an extrovert, that I needed an introvert to balance me. I have a very dear friend, and she and I talked several times when I was single. We are very close friends, but we would have killed each other in a marriage because we would have been competing for center stage. She is an extrovert, too. I need someone who can balance me at that point.

Also, I know that I am not organized, so I need someone who is. And I'm a very "hyper" person—I get going and have a hard time slowing down—so I need someone who is kind of "laid-back." When I once shared that combination of needs, someone said, "Clyde, what you need is an organized ding-a-ling." When I shared that thought in Cathy's presence, she smiled and said, "Clyde, ain't that what you got?"

So, what I am saying is that you need to find that person who complements and balances you. Recognize that some people whom you love dearly you could not successfully be married to. It has nothing to do with love, nothing to do with respect — it has to do with complementation.

Kick a Few Tires

Now that you have your list made, go out and do some car shopping. One friend who heard me make that comparison said, "Yes, Clyde, you have to go out and kick a few tires."

As I told him, what you will do is go out and kick a few tires. Then you'll slam a few doors and then you will drive a few models. But there is one thing I want you to give yourself permission to do. When you get out on the street and drive a block or two, and you realize this is not exactly what you thought it was, don't be ashamed to take it back to the showroom, give back the key, and go drive another model. Who knows, after you have driven two or three, you might come back to the first one. But don't feel as if you have to buy the first one you get the keys to. It's better to move into a relationship and then back out a bit—it's better to break up beforehand—than to go through another divorce. So don't be ashamed of doing a little car shopping or car driving.

I don't mean to be flippant by this illustration. I've simply found that often if I get people thinking along hopefully humorous lines, they will catch the truths and apply them. As singles, you kick tires every day. It's okay. The process of car shopping is dating. Date a few people. Drive a few cars—kick the tires, slam the doors, try the air conditioning. Then find the one that has the best combination of things you want to buy. As I said, there are negotiable and non-negotiable items. If I wanted a Sunbird, preferably blue, with an air conditioner and am-fm stereo radio, I would set out with that list in mind. Suppose I found a blue one that had an air conditioner but no am-fm stereo. On the other hand, I found another that wasn't blue—it was turquoise—but it had an air conditioner and an am-fm stereo. Hmmm. I'd have to decide which one I wanted. Well, knowing me, color is not as important as the radio and air conditioning. I would choose the turquoise rather than the blue one. Now, to some people, blue is more important. You must establish your own negotiable and non-negotiable items, but find the one that best suits your needs.

Another important point to remember, though, is to choose according to what you have to offer. You know, I might like to go down and buy a Mercedes; but I'm sorry, I don't have the money. It is just as important that a person recognize his or her limitations, and not frustrate himself or herself by struggling to obtain that which for them is unobtainable. On the other hand, it is just as important for a race car not to be forced to drive in city traffic, but instead to seek a companion who can lap the Indy 500.

What To Do When You've Found "Mr. Right"

So you've gotten to know yourself, you've found that right person—now what? I want to share with you a few practical things you need to consider as you move toward a marriage relationship.

Role Expectation

First of all, you need to talk openly and honestly about role expectation. Each one of us goes into a marriage with a set of ideas as to what we expect from ourselves and what we expect from our mate. These expectations are determined by our past—our childhood and our previous marriage. These are often subconscious expectations, but they are based on what we have seen from life. Thus we expect them.

This is one area which is often not recognized as a ground of conflict. But suppose, for sake of illustration, that a man from the Czech community of Schulenberg were to marry a lady from over in East Texas. The Czech family is patriarchial; Daddy rules the roost. The East Texas family is matriarchial; Daddy is the figure-head, Mother rules the roost. Now, you let those two get married without discussing expectations, and what is going to happen? The East Texas woman and the Schulenberg man are both expecting to be leaders, and you can't have two people leading the same band. They are going to have trouble.

Regarding this point, the most vivid illustration I have ever seen involved my former neighbor. His daughter had come home after a year of marriage and had said, "Dad, I'm going to get a divorce. My husband doesn't love me." My neighbor began to inquire as to why she felt her husband did not love her. No, he did not beat her; no, he did not run around; no, he didn't say he didn't love her. Finally, she said, "Well, Daddy, he doesn't come home from work and cook the meals and wash the dishes and wash and iron the clothes."

My neighbor had been left with the responsibility of rearing that young girl and her brother by himself, because his wife left them when the girl was quite young. Since she had grown up seeing Daddy do all these things, she just assumed her husband should do them, too. The young man's mother had done all these things. Fortunately, the girl's father was able to recognize the problem and explain it to her. She and her husband were then able to work out their relationship.

The way to deal with role expectations is this: Don't discuss it first. When you realize you are getting serious, each of you sit down and write out what you expect your role to be and what you expect your mate's role to be. After you have made your list, number them as to priorities. Then swap lists. You may find that one has listed things that the other has not listed; or you may find that on one list a given priority is #1, while on the other list it is #8. After you have seen each other's lists, then talk about it and work out a compromise. You can work from that compromise—but always keep the originals because you will have a tendency to revert to the original on occasions. If you are aware of the differences in expectations, then you can understand what's going on.

By the way, I think couples should do this about every two or three years because priorities change as you change. You are changing every day of your life.

Children

Children are the second area where you need mutual understanding and planning. As I explained in the chapter on solo parenting, the secret in stepparenting is emotional adoption. If you have children, do not marry until you are willing to yield the children to the new mate as if they were his or her own. On the flip side on the coin, do not marry until you can accept the other person's children—whether or not you'll have custody—as if they were your own. The reason is clear and very important. If you can accept and emotionally adopt each other's children, then discipline will not be a problem. Yes, you will have the same problems any parent has with discipline. You will have some basic disagreements. But because it's not "your children" and "my children," but "our children," the burdens will be shared rather than multiplied. There will be no feeling of needing to protect one's children from the treatment of the other. There will be no problem about child support. Just as your children are yours when they're away at college, they are yours when they are living with their other parent; the child support is a means of caring for them.

You also need to sit down together and work out a basic set of rules for the children. Here, too, you will have a different set of expectations, based primarily on your upbringing and previous relationships. One may come in with the military spit and polish. The other will feel that children are to be cared for, that they should be allowed to have freedom just to drift along. You must work out a compromise which is mutually acceptable. You need to talk about your areas of agreement and disagreement and work them out.

Finances

Finances are an area about which I have some strong convictions. Many people may disagree, and that is fine. Everyone is entitled to his or her opinion. But I have drawn these conclusions through counseling and observation of hundreds of marriages over a period of many years, and I believe them to be correct.

The secret of a successful marriage is love and trust. To the degree that I do not have trust in you, the marriage is restricted.

I think we all agree that basically, for the children's sake, anything brought into the marriage is protected in a sense. But if I am not willing to say that anything I have is to be used with and for my mate, then I should never marry. A lot of lawyers may differ with me, and I know why: They are lawyers and I am a counselor. They are thinking about protection of material possessions; I am talking about what is necessary for a good marriage. Let me tell you something I have observed. If you go to a lawyer and draw up a pre-nuptial agreement, a pre-marriage agreement about finances, I'll give you odds that you will have to use it. Please understand what I'm saying. If you go to the trouble of consulting a lawyer to draw up arrangements about finances, your odds are 99 to 1 that the marriage will end in divorce.

Let's face it—a divorce financially devastates both parties. Occasionally one may come out a little better than the other, but normally both are devastated. If you are seeking someone or some way after a divorce to put you back immediately into the same financial status you had, forget it. When you have gone through a divorce and you remarry, you must recognize that the two of you are going to have to work together to rebuild. It will take time. Probably both will come into the marriage with debts. One may come in with many assets, while the other has very few assets. Finances will become a problem if you do not have a basic understanding and love for one another, and a basic trust. To me, "his and her" bank accounts are just like "his and her" beds. If you are going to have separate beds, why marry? (The question applies to those who do not for various reasons *need* separate beds.) If you are going to have separate bank accounts, the same question can be asked.

Changing names and bank accounts is a lot of trouble. Some ladies prefer not to change their names. A change of name has different implications to different people. To me, the change of name or the consolidation of accounts and all the time-consuming details that are involved with such matters, represent a desire to be identified with the person to whom I am married. I want to be a part of that person.

By way of personal illustration, when Cathy and I married, she had more assets than I had. Yet she couldn't wait to get to the bank to open a joint account. She wanted to say, "It's ours. We are together."

Now, beyond the feeling of sharing, you need simply to talk

and be open about finances. Some ladies have confided to me that they really don't know what the person is doing financially, and they fear that the man is pulling the wool over their eyes. I want to tell you ladies something. I had no qualms about talking finances to Cathy before we were married—even to the point of showing her what I owed and what income I was making. I know women who have been married to men for years and do not know what income their husbands are making—or vice versa.

It is important to a successful marriage that each person be honest. If you have honestly communicated your finances, then you have nothing to hide, nothing to worry about. If there are problems, then you can talk through the problems and agree on a course of action to solve those problems. Trust and communication are the keys.

Areas of Adjustment

There is one other thing I will tell you. Be ready for the little adjustments after you get married. Normally, one person has been single longer than the other. The one who has been single longer will have a more difficult time with the adjustment. You see, two people are different, and you must learn to get along with these little things. Some differences are very small, yet they can be very important.

One example of difference is in people's waking up patterns. Some people wake up as soon as the alarm goes off, get out of bed, grab a cup of coffee and get on the move. For others, waking up is a long, slow process. Cathy is one of those people who likes for her clock radio to go off thirty minutes before she has to get up. I am one who's wide awake when the radio goes off. I had to learn how to snooze!

On the other hand, when some people get up in the morning, they like the house to be quiet. So here is a guy who likes quiet in the mornings, and he's married to a gal who prefers her radio blaring above the noise of her hair dryer. These are little things, but you must be ready to communicate your preferences and to negotiate a mutually aceptable compromise. I could go on about dozens of little things. One likes a lot of salt; one does not like much salt. One likes it hot; the other likes it cold.

Just a note here, mentioning hot and cold. If you are cold-blooded, and your spouse is not, please understand that those of us who are hot-blooded burn up at your comfortable temperatures, and there is a limit, you know, to how much we can take off! It is much easier for you to add clothes than it is for your mate to subtract them.

Are you getting the picture? There are many little things on which you will need to compromise. In these little things, you may not be as honest before marriage as you should be. You simply may not be aware of the problem. I'll give you a hint: Before you marry, it is very advisable to do a work project with that intended mate. Do something like paint a room in the house or work in the yard together. In such a project you will find a lot of adjustments you can make before you are in the marriage and have to make them.

As you can see, preparing for remarriage is much more complicated than simply finding someone willing to say, "I do." It involves the complete process of letting go of the old relationship, giving oneself permission to seek a new relationship, getting to know oneself and learning what qualities in that other person are complementary and vital to your happiness. Once it appears you have found that person, you will need a great deal of understanding and communication to work through areas of potential problems. But I can tell you something from my years of experience in advising others, as well as from my own personal experience: If you will take the time to follow each of the steps described in this chapter, your chances of finding your "ten" will be greatly enhanced, and chances of experiencing the devastation of another divorce will be kept to a minimum. Use both your intellect and your emotion to verify the information you are receiving about that other person. Take the time to listen and prepare *before* the marriage takes place. Believe me, it is worth the delay to wait for that complementary relationship and the joy it will bring.

Chapter Ten

I'm Not Perfect,
But I'm Improving

Perfection is a state toward which we are continually growing, but which we shall never achieve. Many singles become discouraged because they have so many areas of imperfection in their lives. However, as long as we are growing and improving, we are successful. Success is the progressive realization of one's goals.

In this chapter we will take a look at some keys to success in managing finances, overcoming depression and dealing with stress. All these things are very important to singles. Each could be an entire chapter in itself; but for our purposes here, they will will be condensed and combined into one.

In all these areas, it is important to remember that we are successful if we are improving—if we are moving in the direction of coping more successfully with these areas of our lives than we were last month, or last year.

Keys to Financial Freedom

One area of great difficulty for at least ninety percent of the singles I have known is in the area of finances. The economy creates financial burdens even for families with two incomes, and it seems that the single person or single parent families frequently have even greater difficulties in this area than does society as a whole.

One cause for the financial stress is often the expenditures which couples make in the latter portion of their marriages, trying to buy their way to happiness. Often I have seen couples who, in trying to solve problems in the marriage, buy a new home, thinking that a better place to live will help matters. They spend six months to a year in that home, then they split because, of course, the home does not solve their problem. They then find themselves having to maintain two separate residences on the same income they had before. And financially they're backed up against a wall.

Another cause for financial stress can be the unwise spending of insurance monies following the death of a mate. Sometimes a widow, for example, is shocked to learn how fast one can go through a sizeable settlement. In the loneliness and insecurity, she is tempted to purchase things to replace the mate, and that which seems to be a limitless supply is thus dissipated in a few short years. Such a person needs to think twice before making major purchases and to adhere to the financial principles discussed in this section of the chapter.

I want to share with you first some philosophical concepts regarding financial freedom. Those concepts are not going to be concretely applicable, yet they will help one form an attitude or foundation upon which practical applications may be built. Then I will share several practical steps to financial freedom.

My wife, Cathy, was single when she first heard *Picking Up the Pieces* in its seminar form. Since she was unable to attend the last unit, she asked me to give her the essential ideas. That was in November, and she began to put the principles to work. The following summer, she bought a home. Now, the purchase of a home by a single lady is sometimes difficult, though not all that unusual—until you take into account that when Cathy began to apply the principles in November, she had outstanding debts from her divorce which were considerable. I won't go into the details of how God worked out her finances, but I really believe He did. Less than a year later, she was able to buy her home. I believe the principles work.

Key #1: Recognize that God possesses all the wealth of the world.

Key #2: Recognize that all of God's wealth legally belongs to us as His children. He promises to supply all our *needs* abundantly.

Key #3: The source of your income is God—not the company for whom you work. The company is just the pay agent. If you become frustrated with your company, remember that when you meet all of God's principles, He will bless you more than you think. The company is not the provider; God is the provider.

Key #4: As good stewards, in evidence of our faith in and our commitment to God, we should never purchase anything we are not willing to give away. The reason for this is quite simple. If I ever purchase anything I am not willing to give away, that item becomes my god. Since we are to worship only the one true God, we must not "cling" to material possessions.

Key #5: The way to appropriate God's resources is to give. Luke 6:38 states that Jesus says, "Give, and it shall be given unto you." In like measure as you give, so shall you also receive. If you have ever wondered why you have not received much, perhaps it is because you have been giving with a quarter of a teaspoon. Learn to throw in a tablespoonful or cupful. The Bible states simply, as you give, so shall you also receive.

Because the secret to receiving is giving, one should actually seek ways to give. But there is a danger here. There is a difference between swapping and giving. In swapping, you have a pay-off; you are expecting approval or recognition from the person to whom you give. In giving, one gives purely for the joy that giving brings. Try giving an anonymous gift to someone who has a need. If someone needs money, send a cashier's check. There is a joy in knowing you have met the needs of another without seeking reward or recognition for yourself.

Key #6: Give not according to your apparent wealth, but rather according to God's real wealth. So often we give out of what we think we have rather than from what God can provide for us to give.

A number of years ago I was counseling with a young man who had been part of a satanic cult. He had made a change in his life and was trying to put it all together. One problem he was facing, however, was that while he was in the cult, he had written some hot checks. Payments were due on the checks; and he knew that if he did not make those payments, the next knock on his door could be the police. Convinced that he was sincere in his efforts to straighten out his life, I prayed, "Lord, what can I do to help him?"

At that moment I remembered a wedding I was to perform the next Friday evening, and was impressed that the Lord was saying, "Clyde, why don't you give him what you receive from the wedding?"

You know, sometimes I really question the Lord when I receive impressions such as these. I do not charge for weddings. Whatever I receive is strictly a gift. Normally a preacher gets a gift of $15 to $25. I said, "Now, Lord, you know that amount will not even begin to scratch the surface; but if that's what you want, I'll do it."

The wedding was a small and informal one at the church. It was a brief ceremony, and thirty minutes later I was on my way with a check in my pocket. When I reached my car, I thought, "Well, let's see what God has given to my young man." I opened the envelope and there was a check for $100! I had planned a sum of $15 or $25, but God gave four or five times as much. When we give, we should do so with an attitude not of our own resources, but rather of what God in His resources may provide.

Key #7: Be willing to be used as the instrument for meeting someone's needs. Too often people pray for God to meet someone's needs, but they are unwilling to initiate the action.

Key #8: Save money only as directed by God, and then only

if you would be willing to give everything away if God so directed.

Key #9: Give cheerfully. Perhaps that is the hardest item on the list. The Bible says in 2 Corinthians 9:7, "God loves a cheerful giver." The word which is translated as *cheerful* actually means more like *hilarious*. God loves a hilarious giver. Have you ever attended a worship service in which the happiest portion of the service was offering time? I wonder what would happen if everyone gave cheerfully, not grudgingly—if the attitude was not, "Here comes the plate again, and I have to give something to God," but rather, "Here, God—thank you because you have blessed me. Everything I have is from your resources." Thank God for your resources, and give to Him and to everyone else, not grudgingly or from a sense of duty, but cheerfully, happily, hilariously.

The aforementioned principles have been philosophical. The following are practical suggestions.

Key #10: To keep yourself financially free, never borrow money to purchase depreciating items. There are several biblical concepts which relate to this key. Romans 13 states that one should owe no man but to love him. As the book of Proverbs points out, the borrower is a slave to the lender (Prov. 22:7). When I borrow money from another person, or from an institution, I become that person or that institution's slave. Owing money puts a pressure on you. So many people borrow money on depreciating items, and then when the paycheck comes in, they are already in a bind because it has already been spent. There won't be money to meet current expenses or emergencies because all those bills have to be paid. That's no way to live.

When you obligate yourself to make payments on depreciating items, you are presuming on the future. The Bible teaches in James 4:13-17 that one does not know what he will do tomorrow. One should not make an obligation which presumes on the future.

Key #11: Give God a chance to provide for you before you buy an item. In Philippians 4:19, the Bible says, "My God shall supply all your needs according to his riches and glory in Christ Jesus.'' God may want an opportunity to give to you, to express His love and concern for you. He may provide as an answer to prayer; or He may provide something much better than you would buy. Ephesians 3:20 states that God ''is able to do exceedingly abundantly above all that we ask or think.'' More often than not, if we are willing to wait for Him to provide, we will receive more than we could have provided for ourselves.

I admit that I am impatient. Often, however, the Lord has illustrated to me the principle of waiting on Him. I have often bought something for myself, only to have a friend or relative say, "Clyde, I'm sorry you bought that because I was going to buy one next week and give it to you." Once I needed a tape recorder. I found one on sale so I put it in lay-away. A short time later, my wife gave me the same tape recorder for my birthday. Then I had one more than I needed. So you see, the principles I am sharing are those which I have learned, often through my own weaknesses, and which I have found are really true. Give God a chance to give to you.

Key #12: Get out of debt. If you are ever going to live financially free, you must begin to get out of debt. You must start that effort. How do you do it?

First, list all your expenditures, and then number them in priority order.

Second, discontinue all expenditures that are not necessary. If you are to get out of debt, you must tighten the belt. If you are overweight, how do you lose? You push away from the table and cut back on your intake. To trim an overage in debts, you must learn to discontinue all that is not necessary. Consider selling depreciating items on which you have no debt. Eliminate credit cards except those used to keep records, and pay those upon receipt of your bill. The current rate of interest in Texas on charge cards is 18%; yet we fuss about a 14% rate on home mortgages. We are paying through the nose on interest charges.

Third, begin buying on a cash basis. So often singles get on a big kick thinking they're going to get themselves out of debt. The income tax refund check comes in and they pay off all their bills, setting nothing extra aside. One day they decide they deserve a given item so they go out and charge it. Before they realize what has happened, they have two or three cards up to the $500 or $800 limit, then they don't know how they're going to make ends meet because of their monthly payments.

If you are one of the many who have fallen into this rut, the only way you will get out of debt is to pay all your monthly installments. Then next month, rather than charging an amount equal to your previous payment, either don't buy the item or pay cash. The only way you will reduce that credit card balance is to pay on it every month and then pay cash for what you buy. You may need to consider additional work until you get your debts paid off. One caution here, however: Don't get an extra job and spend more because you have a second income. Consider additional work to pay off the debt, the priority being to get out of debt.

Key #13: To learn how to manage your money, do a study of your spending habits. I discovered one day that I was nickel-ing and dime-ing myself to death. No big items — but no money. I noticed that I would pick up a little blouse here, a shirt there, a meal or something else — and my money was all gone. Do a study of your spending habits. For a month, keep track of everything you spend. Not only will it prove interesting, it will also help you learn to manage your money.

Key #14: Learn to spend wisely. Make a distinction between *needs* and *wants*. You know, sometimes my "want" gets out of whack. What I think I *need* is actually just what I *want*. It is important to be able to make that distinction.

Another part of learning to spend wisely is to learn how to shop. Just because something is a bargain doesn't mean it is necessarily good. If you want to learn to shop, my wife could give you a few insights. She can get more out of $10 than anyone I have ever seen. Some of her most elegant clothes are things she has purchased for under $10 at a fire sale outlet. She will go to a fire sale weekly, and for several weeks she won't find a thing.

Then she will find a $180 dress for $8. She knows how to select quality in clothes.

Ladies, I recommend this kind of shopping. You don't have to tell anybody where you got your dress.

Another place to shop is a resale shop. One lady I know shopped in an exclusive area of Houston and bought a mink coat at a tremendous bargain through a resale shop.

Another idea is to wait for regular sales. Every company has sales on its merchandise from time to time. One suit on which I receive more compliments than any other suit I own was bought a week after Easter for one-third off. I had seen it earlier but decided to wait. Learn to wait for sales.

In learning to spend money wisely, beware of vanity buying. People often pay twice to three times normal prices simply to have the prestigious name brands. The clothes don't fit a bit better, but everybody thinks, "They're 'with it'." If you have that kind of money, fine. But if you are complaining about not having enough money to make ends meet, and you are buying all the prestigious lines, then you need to learn to shop for something other than your vanity.

Take advantage of seasonal buying. When a season ends, you can catch some really good deals. For items like summer shoes, for example, wait until summer is nearly over. While you may not get exactly the shoe you want, you can save a lot of money. The same thing applies to clothing. Items like lawnmowers may be purchased at a bargain during pre-season sales; but if you can wait to buy at the end of the season, when the stores don't want to carry over their money in merchandise until the next year, you can save even more.

All these suggestions are to illustrate one point: If you can learn to spend wisely, you can get four times the mileage out of a dollar.

Building, then, on biblical philosophical concepts in the use of finances, and the blessings available to those who apply God's principles in this matter, one may then take those practical steps toward financial freedom. What a pleasant state that is! Try it. It works!

Preparing a Budget

I believe it is important that every single person prepare a budget to determine how his or her money is to be spent. In so doing, one must determine needs and priorities.

My first suggestion is that you make allowances for some recreation money in that budget. Don't start paying off your bills so fast that you don't save some money for fun. Don't try to pay your bills faster than needed. I know one couple who almost ruined their relationship by doing just that. The couple had just married. The woman was debt-free conscious, and her husband had accumulated a lot of bills. She prepared a budget by which, using both their incomes, they could be free of debt in six months. But she failed to allow money for an occasional movie or a night of dining out. About the fourth month, they were really at each other's throats. It would have been far better had they planned an eight-month payout with a bit of fun included, instead of that six-month payout with no fun whatsoever.

One item which often puts singles into debt is the car. If you are having a problem getting out of debt, you might consider trading that big sporty Trans-Am for a less conspicuous '78 or '79 Toyota. If you need a Trans-Am, a 280-Z, or a Corvette to impress people with your importance, your self-esteem is very low. You are treating the symptom rather than the problem. I don't mean to be critical of those who own the more expensive, sporty cars; I went through that stage. I had my Firebird. But you know, the '77 Capri I'm driving now runs just fine, and I have no monthly payments.

Dealing with Depression

The second most common problem for singles is depression. Frequently singles become morbid in their thinking and attitudes. The problem is almost universal. Let us examine the causes for depression and then find some ways to cope with it.

What causes depression? There are several factors. I believe some depression is to be expected by one whose marriage has ended in death or divorce. There is a grief reaction involved with such a trauma, and a part of a natural grief reaction is a period of depression. It is when the depression continues beyond the natural period of grief that it becomes a problem.

A second cause of depression is being physically tired. Many singles I know are physically tired all the time. In a few pages you will find an exercise to help you eliminate a tremendous amount of stress and thus offset that tiredness.

Self-pity is a third cause of depression. I like to call it "pity-pot." What happens when one uses the "pity-pot"? One develops a bad case of negative thinking. Zig Ziglar calls depression "stinkin' thinkin'." If you have stinking thinking, or self-pity, you are allowing yourself to live with negative ideas.

Someone else has said that depression is inwardly-directed anger. It occurs when one is angry at others whom he cannot tell, and so he directs it at himself. Following that line of thinking, I began to wonder what causes anger. I believe the primary cause of inwardly-directed anger is a feeling of being trapped. Perhaps you feel trapped in a situation you don't feel you caused, one which you don't like, and you see no hope for ever getting out of it. You may direct that anger toward God. You may feel like saying, "God, I didn't ask to be single; I didn't want this divorce. But here I am, and either I have to remain single or go back out there in that meat market and try to get a date. I detest it." So you retain a vicious anger toward God and toward the person who left you to fend for yourself. You literally feel you have no hope, no way to go, no one to tell off. So you become depressed and remain so.

How can you reverse the cycle and overcome depression?

Find Positive Friends

The first action I would share is that you must find some positive people to be around. I believe I'd have climbed the walls had I been subjected to six months or a year of some of the singles' groups I've seen. In these groups there are basically two types of people: the kind so busy having "fun" they don't stop and work through their problems, and the kind always complaining about how bad life is. In all honesty, I don't want to be around negative people when I am depressed. They only compound the problem. I want to find some people whose attitude says, "The rest of my life is before me, and I'm going to learn to make it good!"

Dream a Dream

The second thing I would recommend is this: Have the courage to dream a dream. Begin to look forward. Believe that because God promises He will work good in everything, the best years of your life are before you. Remember, a person is old when he has more to look back on than he has to look forward to; he's old when he can no longer dream dreams. I have difficulty relating to elderly people who want to do nothing but talk about the good old days. When you stop to think about it, the good old days weren't perfect. There was no air conditioning, travel was by horse and buggy, there were mosquitoes and no window screens. In other words, rather than look back to yesterday, I believe you've got to look forward to tomorrow. Start trying to dream some dreams.

How do you learn again to dream dreams? Take the basic hope that God will keep his promise to work in everything for your ultimate good. Consciously make a decision to believe that promise, to trust God and to say to him, "God, I am excited about what will happen tomorrow." When you become excited about the future, you will find your depression leaving in a hurry.

You know, you can *choose* your mental attitudes. How do you look at the day? Do you wake up and think, "Ugh! I have to go to work and face that bunch of brass, face the boss, answer that telephone!" Do you work on thinking positive or thinking negative?

You wake up and it's raining. What do you think? Once during an especially dry year I fertilized my yard one day, and two or three days later there was a good all-day rain. I was delighted that my grass was getting badly needed moisture, not to mention all the other plants in the area needing water. Yet I heard people complaining all day long because it was raining. You see, we can choose whether to look at the bad side, or whether to look at the positive and get excited about what is going to happen afterwards.

If you realize you are depressed because you are on the pity-pot, look up and say, "God, you promised something good through all these problems. I am going to look for the good. I am going to start to claim the good." When you are able to do that, you will replace negative thinking with positive thinking. When you start thinking positively, you will find you will be drawn to positive people. By associating with them you will have a positive support group, and that support can turn pessimism into optimism. Only positive people can dream dreams.

Set a Goal

One of the best definitions of success I have heard is "being and doing all that you were intended to be and to do."

That takes establishing goals. A problem I find with many singles is that their primary goal prior to the death of the marriage was that relationship itself; and when that no longer exists, they do not form new goals. Many women, for example, have no goals other than to be good wives and mothers. Those goals are certainly worthwhile; but when they have been shattered, and there are no others, life has little meaning.

Of each person I counsel I will often ask this question: "Just what kind of person do you want to be?"

The answer often goes something like this: "For the last twenty years, I was the person I thought my mate wanted me to be. I never gave myself permission to be the person I was intended to be. Now that my mate is gone, I don't really know *what* I am going to do."

I have been seasick only once. I was on a ship in San Jacinto Bay on a very calm day when we ran out of gas. We were not rolling—just gently rocking, going nowhere. Now, I have been on a cruise and had no problem at all. But that gentle rocking, going nowhere, caused me to make my contribution to the Bay. Many people are emotionally seasick because all they're doing is drifting. Another word is *existing,* not living. One of the most important things some people need to do is to begin asking themselves, "What are my goals? What do I want to accomplish? What do I want to be? What do I want to do?" The day you have nothing to strive for, you die.

What kind of goal should you set, and how should you go about it? For years I had difficulty with goal programs which were created by success motivation, because all those goals were goals of acquiring. I simply was not comfortable with that approach.

In one of his books, Jess Laird said that he, too, had fallen into the acquiring rat-race. He wanted to be successful, and success to him was making $75,000 a year. He decided the best way to accomplish that goal was to become an advertising executive. He went to school and prepared for his career. He started working toward the realization of his "acquiring" goal. Three heart attacks later, he began to ask himself what life was all about.

There is a tragedy involved with goals of acquiring. If what I am *doing* is not in keeping with my *being,* I am discontent. I am so discontent, I think if I could just acquire more possessions I'd be happy. So I work harder at the job I don't like. I acquire more things—I am still discontent. *Being* must come first. The first goal one should set is what kind of person he wants to be. Out of one's *being* will flow one's *doing*—that which is in harmony with one's being.

There is nothing wrong with acquiring, but it must be the result of being and doing, not the primary goal. The only people who make money are those who work in a mint. The rest of us have money given to us as a reward for a product or service we provide. If first I am being, and then I am doing, then I will receive the reward. I can then decide how I will utilize that reward—what I'll acquire with it. Happiness comes from setting goals of being, doing and acquiring—in that order.

In setting goals for being, consider the whole self—body, soul and spirit. I challenge you to define the goals for each and to write them down. About the body, for example, what are your plans weight-wise? Nutrition-wise? What do you need to do to increase energy, firm the muscles? What about the appearance? One of my goals is to maintain a certain weight limit. Whenever I go above it, I put myself on a diet.

The soul is personality. What kind of personality do you want to have? What kind of character do you want to have? I challenge you to think about your definition and put it down on paper. You can have a goal which is concrete. Work toward the realization of that goal.

Finally, the spirit is the part of you which relates to God. Set a goal for development in your spiritual life. What type of relationship do you want to have with God? Establish that goal and spend time with Him to work toward its realization.

Coping with Stress

A common problem in today's society is stress. Many people do not understand stress and do not know how to cope with it.

First of all, if we are to deal with stress, we must remove unrealistic expectations. Too many of us seem to demand perfection from ourselves. When life does not go as we had planned, we find ourselves feeling rejected or feeling failure. The Bible clearly teaches that none of us will be perfect on this earth. If you have a problem with perfectionism, consider this statement. Better yet, commit it to memory and quote it when the occasion calls for it: "Only God is perfect. Since I am human, *I give myself permission to make mistakes.* When I do, I will claim God's forgiveness, and I will forgive myself and go forward just as if the mistake was never made."

You know, I deal with human lives every day. The misunderstanding of one word can cause me to misunderstand an individual. I *must* give myself permission to make mistakes. When I do, and I am aware of it, I simply say to that person, "Hey, I misunderstood. I'm sorry." I could go around browbeating myself. I choose to give myself permission to be human.

Secondly, I give myself permission to play. Most American adults do not give themselves permission to play. Many adults know how to play only in rebellion. You see what appears to be play, but it is actually rebellion. You can tell it's rebellion when they feel they must justify their play for reasons of business or health, or when they must get slightly inebriated. Often I do not take as much play time as I want to take, but I do give myself permission to play. Play is okay. I act crazy sometimes, tell crazy or corny jokes. I don't have to justify playing tennis because it is good for me. To deal with stress, I must give myself permission to play.

A place to escape from the cares of the world to be recharged is a tremendous advantage in coping with stress. I would love to go to Colorado about every other week and get back in the mountains, leaving all the pressures and problems of the world behind. Some folks have the means to provide such an escape; they are fortunate. But what if I have neither the time nor the resources to go to Colorado every other week? How can I escape? I have learned a secret about relaxing. If my mind takes me away, it can be almost as good as the real thing, and I don't have to pack a suitcase or stand in a ticket line.

Relaxation Technique

Let me take you with me on such a trip. You just sit back, relax, and leave the driving to me. As soon as you have completed reading this chapter, close your eyes and try as completely as possible to do what I suggest.

Picture yourself in a field of wildflowers. There are beautiful, full bluebonnets. Picture the field full of purple, mauve and white flowers in full bloom, with a brush of brilliant orange peeping through now and then. The blue of the sky is very clear and there are a few white, puffy clouds. The temperature is about 72 degrees and the sun is bright and warm, but not hot. You are dressed in casual jeans.

As you picture the field of bluebonnets, and you see the gentle rolling of green hills in the distance, visualize your best friend coming toward you. Perhaps you can picture Jesus coming to you. He is not dressed in a white robe, but in a pair of blue jeans—comfortable, somewhat faded jeans. As he walks up, picture him just reaching out and giving you a good hug of greeting.

You begin to walk together, and after a short distance you sit down. With the cushion of bluebonnets beneath you, you feel as if you are almost sitting on air. In the next few moments, picture yourself sharing with your best friend the problems that you face—your fears, your concerns. Picture Jesus listening intently, then reaching out and taking each burden as you tell it to him. Imagine that you have placed those concerns in his hands, knowing that he is going to take care of them. You now feel as if a weight has been lifted from your shoulders. As you are lying there in the bluebonnets, you feel a lightness—as if you're suspended in air—as if you are beginning to float.

As you share with Jesus, you will note how very interested he is in you. You will feel his love. I want you then to picture Jesus getting up, reaching down for your hand, helping you up, and again walking with you through the bluebonnets. The two of you are lighthearted now. As you walk together, listen to him as he simply tells you how much he loves you, and what a beautiful person you are. Feel the warmth of the sun as it heals every ache and pain, and the gentle blowing of the breeze through your hair. Feel the tension leave you.

Suddenly you begin to skip as a child would skip in joyful play. Picture a stream in front of you. You and Jesus run up beside the stream, and Jesus, with a little mischief in his eyes, splashes water on you. You laugh and splash back at him. Gently he trips you, and you fall into the water. You reach out and grab him and he, too, falls in. Both of you are soaked to the skin. You laugh together. Together you leave the stream and run playfully through the bluebonnets, having a joyous time of laughter. You are laughing as you have never laughed before—laughing from pure fun.

You're out of breath. You slow to a walk. You approach a small bush, and Jesus points to a butterfly which has just emerged from its cocoon. Look at the butterfly and its beautiful colors, stretching its wings to dry in the sun.

Jesus says, "That's you. You are just emerging from your cocoon. Remember how that butterfly was first a caterpillar, and how for a time it was seemingly trapped in its cocoon? During its entrapment, a great change was taking place—a metamorphosis. The same thing has happened to you. You are emerging now into the most beautiful time in your life."

Picture the butterfly, its wings now dried and full, flying gently from the bush, delicately floating on air, the sun catching the beauty of its colors as it experiences for the first time the fullness of being a butterfly. Picture yourself as if you were flying with the butterfly, moving your arms in graceful motions which carry you gently upward. You fly for a few moments, then you return. Jesus says, "You see, you are a promise. Your future is before you."

With that warm feeling flowing through you—with that outlook of a beautiful tomorrow—picture you and Jesus walking to the back of the field of bluebonnets and coming to a lake. Jesus looks at you with love in his eyes, and then he smiles. He says, "You know, sometimes you worry about who is going to take care of you. I'll do that."

Jesus takes a fishing pole and catches some trout, cleans them there in the lake. He builds a fire, places the fish in a pan and begins to fry them. The aroma of the fresh fish cooking there by the lake is carried along by the gentle breeze. It reaches your *nostrils. It smells good. Suddenly you realize how hungry you are. Picture yourself eating until you are filled. As you eat, Jesus says to you, "I'll meet your every need."*

The sun is beginning to set. You look out over the hills, and before you is the most beautiful sunset you have every seen, with its oranges, mauves, blues and greens. "Those are the colors of promise," Jesus tells you. "The promise of tomorrow. A beautiful day—a new day. See your potential, your possibilities."

Now, as the coolness of evening descends, Jesus builds the fire higher and says, "Take a nap. Sleep, that you might be rested for tomorrow—for your new challenge."

Picture yourself contentedly drifting off to sleep. After you have slept for a while, picture Jesus coming to you, gently awakening you. "This is your day. Go. Meet it. Meet your challenge. Join me again this afternoon, and we will relive your day. It is yours. Claim it."

If you will allow yourself five quiet minutes per day for a trip to your favorite escape with your best friend, Jesus, you will find your stresses melting away. Tell him you are not perfect but you know that you are improving; and with His help, your burdens do not seem nearly so heavy. Ask Him to help you pick up the pieces of your life so that you may begin anew—each day—refreshed, restored. Whole. Please close the book and try it, right now.

Clyde C. Besson is an ordained minister and a graduate of Louisiana College and New Orleans Baptist Theological Seminary. He has served as a pastor for nineteen years and is the founder/director of *Christian Growth Ministries,* a marriage and family counseling ministry with special emphasis directed toward the formerly married.

Interested parties may arrange for a "Picking Up the Pieces" seminar in their locale by contacting author Besson at

CHRISTIAN GROWTH MINISTRIES
P.O. Box 7823
The Woodlands, Texas 77387
(713) 367-9881

Seminars are held on a Friday evening and all day Saturday, with an optional Saturday evening banquet. Subjects presented parallel those covered in this book.

MAIGRET
ET LE VOLEUR
PARESSEUX

OUVRAGES DE GEORGES SIMENON

AUX PRESSES DE LA CITÉ

COLLECTION MAIGRET

ROMANS

MÉMOIRES

GEORGES SIMENON

MAIGRET ET LE VOLEUR PARESSEUX

PRESSES DE LA CITÉ

OUVRAGES DE GEORGES SIMENON

AUX PRESSES DE LA CITÉ (suite)

« TRIO »

★

PRESSES POCKET

★

A LA N.R.F.

ÉDITION COLLECTIVE SOUS COUVERTURE VERTE

SÉRIE POURPRE

CHAPITRE

1

Il y eut un vacarme pas loin de sa tête et Maigret se mit à remuer, maussade, comme effrayé, un de ses bras battant l'air en dehors des draps. Il avait conscience d'être dans son lit, conscience aussi de la présence de sa femme qui, mieux éveillée que lui, attendait dans l'obscurité sans rien oser dire.

Sur quoi il se trompait — pendant quelques secondes tout au moins — c'était sur la nature de ce bruit insistant, agressif, impérieux. Et c'était toujours en hiver, par temps très froid, qu'il se trompait de la sorte.

Il lui semblait que c'était le réveille-matin qui sonnait, alors que depuis son mariage, il n'y en avait plus sur sa table de nuit. Cela remontait à plus loin encore que l'adolescence : à son enfance, quand il était enfant de chœur et servait la messe de six heures.

Pourtant, il avait servi la même messe au printemps, en été, en automne. Pourquoi le souvenir qui lui en restait et qui lui revenait automatiquement était-il un souvenir d'obscurité, de gel, de doigts engourdis, de chaussures qui, sur le chemin, faisaient craquer une pellicule de glace?

Il renversait son verre, comme cela lui arrivait souvent, et Mme Maigret allumait la lampe de chevet au moment où sa main atteignait le téléphone.

— Maigret... Oui...

Il était quatre heures dix et le silence, dehors, était le silence particulier aux plus froides nuits d'hiver.

— Ici Fumel, monsieur le commissaire...

— Comment?

Il entendait mal. On aurait dit que son correspondant parlait à travers un mouchoir.

— Fumel, du XVIᵉ...

L'homme étouffait sa voix comme s'il craignait d'être entendu par quelqu'un se trouvant dans une pièce voisine. Devant l'absence de réaction du commissaire, il ajoutait :

— Aristide...

Aristide Fumel, bon! Maigret était éveillé, à présent, et se demandait pourquoi diable l'inspecteur Fumel, du XVIᵉ arrondissement, l'éveillait à quatre heures du matin.

Et pourquoi, en outre, sa voix sonnait-elle mystérieuse, comme furtive?

— Je ne sais pas si je fais bien de vous
téléphoner... J'ai tout de suite averti mon
chef direct, le commissaire de police... Il m'a
dit d'appeler le Parquet et j'ai eu le substitut
de garde au bout du fil...

Mme Maigret qui, pourtant, n'entendait que
les répliques de son mari, se levait déjà, cherchait ses pantoufles du bout du pied, s'enve-
loppait de sa robe de chambre ouatinée et se
dirigeait vers la cuisine où on entendait le
sifflement du gaz, puis l'eau qui coulait dans
la bouilloire.

— On ne sait plus trop ce que l'on doit faire,
vous comprenez ? Le substitut m'a ordonné de
retourner sur les lieux et de l'attendre. Ce
n'est pas moi qui ai découvert le corps, mais
deux agents cyclistes...

— Où?

— Comment?

— Je demande, où?

— Au bois de Boulogne... Route des Poteaux... Vous connaissez ?... Elle donne dans
l'avenue Fortunée, pas loin de la porte Dauphine... Il s'agit d'un homme d'un certain âge...
Mon âge à peu près... Pour autant que j'aie
pu en juger, il n'a rien dans les poches, aucun papier... Bien entendu, je n'ai pas bougé
le corps... Je ne sais pas pourquoi, il me semble
qu'il y a quelque chose de bizarre et j'ai préféré vous téléphoner... Il vaudrait mieux que
les gens du Parquet ne le sachent pas...

— Je te remercie, Fumel...

— Je retourne là-bas tout de suite, des fois qu'ils arriveraient plus vite que d'habitude...

— Où es-tu?

— Au poste de la Faisanderie... Vous comptez venir?

Maigret hésita, toujours enfoui dans la chaleur du lit.

— Oui.

— Qu'est-ce que vous direz?

— Je ne sais pas encore. Je trouverai.

Il était humilié, presque furieux, mais ce n'était pas la première fois depuis six mois. Le brave Fumel n'y était pour rien. Mme Maigret, dans l'encadrement de la porte, lui recommandait :

— Habille-toi chaudement. Il gèle dur.

En écartant le rideau, il découvrit des fleurs de givre sur les vitres. Les becs de gaz avaient une luminosité spéciale qu'on ne leur voit que par les grands froids et il n'y avait pas une âme boulevard Richard-Lenoir, pas un bruit, une seule fenêtre éclairée, en face, sans doute dans une chambre de malade.

Maintenant, on les obligeait à tricher! On, c'était le Parquet, les gens du ministère de l'Intérieur, tous ces nouveaux législateurs enfin, sortis des grandes écoles, qui s'étaient mis en tête d'organiser le monde selon leurs petites idées.

La police, à leurs yeux, constituait un

rouage inférieur, un peu honteux, de la Justice avec une majuscule. Il fallait s'en méfier, la tenir à l'œil, ne lui laisser qu'un rôle subalterne.

Fumel appartenait encore à la vieille époque, comme Janvier, comme Lucas, comme une vingtaine environ des collaborateurs de Maigret, mais les autres s'accommodaient des nouvelles méthodes et des nouveaux règlements, ne pensant qu'à préparer des examens afin de monter plus vite en grade.

Pauvre Fumel qui, lui, n'avait jamais pu monter en grade parce qu'il était incapable d'apprendre l'orthographe et de rédiger un rapport !

Le procureur, ou un de ses substituts, tenait à être le premier averti, le premier sur place, en compagnie d'un juge d'instruction mal éveillé, et ces messieurs donnaient leur avis comme s'ils avaient passé leur vie à découvrir des cadavres et connaissaient mieux que quiconque les criminels.

Quant à la police... On la chargeait de commissions rogatoires...

— Vous ferez telle et telle chose... Vous appréhenderez telle personne et vous me l'amènerez dans mon cabinet...

— Surtout, ne lui posez pas de questions ! Il faut que cela se passe dans les règles...

Il y en avait tant, de règles, le Journal officiel publiait de si nombreux textes parfois contradictoires qu'ils ne s'y retrouvaient pas eux-mêmes, vivaient dans la terreur d'être pris en faute et de donner prise aux protestations des avocats.

Il s'habillait, grognon. Pourquoi, les nuits d'hiver, quand on le réveillait ainsi, le café avait-il un goût particulier? L'odeur de l'appartement était différente aussi, lui rappelait la maison de ses parents quand il se levait à cinq heures et demie du matin.

— Tu appelles le bureau pour qu'on t'envoie une voiture?

Non! S'il arrivait là-bas avec une auto du quai, il risquait qu'on lui réclame des comptes.

— Téléphone à la station de taxis...

On ne lui rembourserait pas la course, à moins que, si meurtre il y avait, il ne découvre l'assassin dans un délai très bref. On ne remboursait plus les taxis qu'en cas de succès. Encore fallait-il prouver qu'on n'aurait pas pu se rendre autrement sur les lieux.

Sa femme lui tendait une grosse écharpe de laine.

— Tu as tes gants?

Il fouillait les poches de son pardessus.

— Tu ne veux pas manger un morceau?

Il n'avait pas faim. Il semblait bouder et pourtant, au fond, c'étaient des moments qu'il aimait bien, peut-être ceux qu'il regretterait le plus une fois à la retraite.

Il descendait l'escalier, trouvait un taxi à la porte, avec de la vapeur blanche qui sortait du pot d'échappement.

— Au bois de Boulogne... Vous connaissez la route des Poteaux?

— Ce serait malheureux que je ne la connaisse pas, après trente-cinq ans de métier...

C'est ainsi, en somme, que les anciens se consolaient de leur vieillissement.

Les banquettes étaient glacées. On ne rencontra que quelques voitures, des autobus vides qui se dirigeaient vers leur tête de ligne. Les premiers bars n'étaient pas encore éclairés. Aux Champs-Elysées, des femmes de ménage nettoyaient les bureaux.

— Encore une fille qui s'est fait descendre?

— Je ne sais pas... Je ne crois pas...

— Je me disais bien qu'elle n'aurait pas trouvé beaucoup de clients au Bois par un temps pareil.

Sa pipe aussi avait un autre goût. Il enfonçait les mains dans les poches, calculait qu'il y avait au moins trois mois qu'il n'avait rencontré Fumel et qu'il connaissait celui-ci depuis... à peu près depuis sa propre entrée dans la police, à l'époque où il travaillait dans un commissariat de quartier.

Fumel était déjà laid et, déjà, on le plaignait tout en se moquant de lui, d'abord parce que ses parents avaient eu l'idée de l'appeler Aristide, ensuite parce que, malgré son physique, il avait perpétuellement des drames de cœur.

Il s'était marié et sa femme, après un an,

était partie sans laisser d'adresse. Il avait remué ciel et terre pour la retrouver. Pendant
des années, son signalement avait été dans la
poche de tous les policiers et de tous les gendarmes de France et Fumel se précipitait à
la morgue chaque fois qu'on repêchait dans la
Seine un cadavre de sexe féminin.

C'était passé à l'état de légende.

— On ne m'ôtera pas de la tête qu'il lui est
arrivé malheur et que c'est à moi qu'on en
voulait...

Un de ses yeux était fixe, plus clair que
l'autre, presque transparent, ce qui rendait
son regard gênant.

— Je l'aimerai toute ma vie... Et je sais
qu'un jour je la retrouverai...

Avait-il encore le même espoir, à cinquante
et un ans? Cela ne l'empêchait pas, périodiquement, de tomber amoureux et le sort continuait à s'acharner sur lui, car chacune de ses
aventures entraînait des complications invrai-
semblables et finissait mal.

On l'avait même, avec toutes les apparences
de la raison, accusé de proxénétisme, à cause
d'une garce qui se moquait de lui, et il avait
évité de justesse d'être rayé des cadres de la
police.

Comment s'y prenait-il, si naïf et si mala-
droit en ce qui le concernait, pour être cependant un des meilleurs inspecteurs de Paris?

Le taxi franchissait la porte Dauphine, tournait à droite dans le Bois et on apercevait

déjà la lueur d'une lampe de poche. Un peu
plus tard, on voyait des ombres, au bord d'une
allée.

Maigret descendait de voiture, payait la
course. Une silhouette s'approchait.

— Vous arrivez avant eux... soupirait Fumel en tapant des pieds sur le sol gelé pour se
réchauffer.

Deux vélos étaient appuyés à un arbre. Les
agents en pèlerine battaient la semelle, eux
aussi, cependant qu'un petit monsieur à chapeau gris perle regardait l'heure à sa montre
avec impatience.

— Le docteur Boisrond, de l'état civil...
Maigret serrait la main distraitement, se dirigeait vers une forme sombre, au pied d'un
arbre. Fumel braquait la lumière de sa lampe
de poche.

— Je crois, monsieur le commissaire, expli-
quait-il, que vous allez comprendre ce que je
veux dire... Pour moi, il y a quelque chose qui
cloche...

— Qui l'a découvert?

— Ces deux agents cyclistes, en faisant leur
ronde...

— A quelle heure?

— Trois heures douze... Ils ont d'abord cru
que c'était un sac jeté au bord du chemin...

Par terre, en effet, dans les herbes durcies
par le gel, l'homme n'était qu'un tas informe.
Il n'était pas étendu de tout son long, mais
ramassé sur lui-même, presque roulé en

boule, et seule une main sortait de la masse,
encore crispée, comme si elle avait tenté de
saisir quelque chose.

— De quoi est-il mort? demanda Maigret
au médecin.

— Je n'ai guère osé y toucher avant l'arrivée du Parquet mais, autant que j'en puisse
juger, il a eu le crâne fracturé par un ou plusieurs coups portés avec un objet très lourd...

— Le crâne? insistait le commissaire.

Car, à la lueur de la lampe de poche, il
ne voyait en guise de visage que des chairs
tuméfiées et sanguinolentes.

— Je ne peux rien affirmer avant l'autopsie, mais je jurerais que ces coups-là ont
été donnés après, quand l'homme était mort,
tout au moins mourant...

Et Fumel, regardant Maigret dans la demi-
obscurité :

— Vous voyez ce que je veux dire, patron?

Les vêtements étaient de bonne qualité, sans
luxe, des vêtements comme en portent par
exemple des fonctionnaires ou des retraités.

— Tu dis qu'il n'y a rien dans les poches?

— J'ai tâté prudemment et n'ai senti aucun objet... Maintenant, regardez autour...

Fumel éclairait le sol autour de la tête et
on ne voyait aucune tache de sang.

— Ce n'est pas ici qu'il a été frappé. Le
docteur est d'accord, car étant donné ses
blessures, il a dû saigner abondamment. On
l'a donc apporté dans le Bois, sans doute en

voiture. On dirait même, à la façon dont il est recroquevillé sur lui-même, qu'il a été poussé de l'auto sans que ceux qui le transportaient se donnent la peine d'en descendre.

Le bois de Boulogne était silencieux, figé comme un décor de théâtre, avec, de loin en loin, ses lampadaires qui dessinaient un cercle régulier de lumière blanche.

— Attention... Je crois que les voici...

Une auto arrivait de la porte Dauphine, une longue voiture noire qui cherchait son chemin et Fumel agita sa lampe électrique, se précipita vers la portière.

Maigret, fumant sa pipe à petites bouffées, se tenait à l'écart.

— C'est ici, monsieur le substitut... Le commissaire de police, qui a dû se rendre à l'hôpital Cochin pour un constat, sera ici dans quelques minutes...

Maigret avait reconnu le magistrat, un grand maigre, d'une trentaine d'années, très élégant, qui s'appelait Kernavel. Il reconnaissait le juge d'instruction aussi, avec qui il avait rarement eu l'occasion de travailler et qui était en quelque sorte à cheval entre les nouveaux et les anciens : un certain Cajou, brun de poil, d'une quarantaine d'années. Quant au greffier, il se tenait aussi loin que possible du cadavre, comme s'il craignait que le spectacle le fasse vomir.

— Qui... commença le substitut.

Il regardait la silhouette de Maigret et fronçait les sourcils.

— Pardon. Je ne vous avais pas vu tout de suite. Comment se fait-il que vous soyez ici?

Maigret se contenta d'un geste vague, d'une phrase plus vague encore :

— Un hasard...

Et Kernavel, mécontent, affectait désormais de ne s'adresser qu'à Fumel.

— De quoi s'agit-il au juste?

— Deux agents cyclistes, en effectuant leur ronde, ont aperçu le corps, il y a un peu plus d'une heure. J'ai alerté le commissaire de police, mais il devait d'abord passer, comme je vous l'ai dit, à l'hôpital Cochin pour un constat urgent et il m'a chargé de prévenir le Parquet. Tout de suite après, j'ai appelé le docteur Boisrond...

Le substitut cherchait le médecin autour de lui.

— Qu'est-ce que vous avez découvert, docteur?

— Fracture du crâne, probablement fractures multiples...

— Un accident? Vous ne croyez pas qu'il a été heurté par une voiture?

— Il a été frappé plusieurs fois, sur la tête d'abord, au visage ensuite, avec un instrument contondant.

— Vous êtes certain, donc, qu'il s'agit d'un meurtre?

Maigret aurait pu se taire, laisser faire, laisser dire. Il ne s'en avança pas moins d'un pas.

— On gagnerait peut-être du temps en prévenant les spécialistes de l'Identité Judiciaire?

C'est à Fumel, toujours, que le substitut donna ses instructions.

— Envoyez un des agents téléphoner...

Il était blême de froid. Tout le monde avait froid, autour du corps immobile.

— Un rôdeur?

— Il n'est pas habillé comme un rôdeur et, par le temps qu'il fait, il n'y en a guère dans le Bois.

— Dévalisé?

— Pour autant que je sache, il n'y a rien dans ses poches.

— Un homme qui rentrait chez lui et qui a été attaqué?

— On ne voit pas de sang par terre. Le docteur pense, comme moi, que le crime n'a pas été commis ici.

— Dans ce cas, il s'agit vraisemblablement d'un règlement de comptes.

Le substitut était. péremptoire, satisfait d'avoir trouvé une solution adéquate au problème.

— Le crime aura été commis à Montmartre et les truands qui ont fait le coup se sont débarrassés du corps en le jetant ici...

Il se tourna vers Maigret.

— Je ne pense pas, monsieur le commis-

saire, que ce soit une affaire pour vous. Vous
devez avoir d'importantes enquêtes en cours.
Au fait! où en êtes-vous du hold-up du bureau
de poste du XIIIᵉ?

— Nulle part encore.

— Et des précédents hold-up? Combien en
avons-nous eus, rien qu'à Paris, en quinze
jours?

— Cinq.

— C'est le chiffre que j'avais en tête. Aussi
suis-je assez surpris de vous trouver ici à vous
occuper d'une affaire sans importance.

Ce n'était pas la première fois que Maigret
entendait cette chanson-là. Ces messieurs du
Parquet étaient effrayés par la vague de criminalité, comme ils disaient, et surtout par
les vols spectaculaires qui, ainsi que cela arrive périodiquement, se multipliaient depuis
un certain temps.

Cela signifiait qu'une nouvelle bande, un
nouveau gang, pour employer le mot cher
aux journaux, s'était formé récemment.

— Vous n'avez toujours aucun indice?

— Aucun.

Ce n'était pas tout à fait vrai. S'il ne possédait pas d'indices à proprement parler, il n'en
avait pas moins une théorie qui se tenait et
que les faits semblaient confirmer. Mais cela ne
regardait personne, surtout pas le Parquet.

— Ecoutez, Cajou. Vous allez prendre l'affaire en main. Si vous m'en croyez, faites en
sorte qu'on en parle le moins possible. C'est

un fait divers banal, un crime crapuleux et, ma foi, si les mauvais garçons se mettent à se tuer entre eux, tant mieux pour tout le monde. Vous me comprenez?

Il s'adressait à nouveau à Fumel.

— Vous êtes inspecteur dans le XVIe?

Fumel acquiesçait de la tête.

— Depuis combien de temps travaillez-vous dans la police?

— Trente ans... Vingt-neuf exactement...

A Maigret :

— Il est bien noté?

— C'est un homme qui connaît son métier.

Le substitut entraînait le juge à l'écart et lui parlait à voix basse. Quand les deux hommes revinrent, Cajou semblait un peu embarrassé.

— Eh! bien, monsieur le commissaire, je vous remercie de vous être dérangé. Je vais rester en rapport avec l'inspecteur Fumel, à qui je donnerai mes instructions. Si, à un moment donné, je juge qu'il a besoin d'aide, je vous enverrai des commissions rogatoires ou je vous convoquerai à mon cabinet. Vous avez une tâche trop importante et trop urgente à accomplir pour que je vous retienne plus longtemps.

Ce n'était pas seulement de froid que Maigret était pâle et il serra si fort sa pipe entre ses dents qu'il y eut un léger craquement de l'ébonite.

— Messieurs... prononça-t-il comme pour prendre congé.

— Vous avez un moyen de transport?

— Je trouverai un taxi à la porte Dauphine.

Le substitut hésita, faillit proposer de l'y conduire, mais déjà le commissaire s'éloignait après un petit salut de la main à l'adresse de Fumel.

Pourtant, une demi-heure plus tard, Maigret aurait sans doute pu leur en apprendre assez long sur le mort. Il n'en était pas encore sûr et c'est pourquoi il n'avait rien dit.

Dès l'instant où il s'était penché sur le corps, il avait eu une impression de déjà vu. Le visage avait beau avoir été réduit en bouillie, le commissaire aurait juré qu'il l'avait reconnu.

Il n'avait besoin que d'une petite preuve, que l'on découvrirait en déshabillant le cadavre.

Il est vrai que, s'il avait raison, on arriverait au même résultat par les empreintes digitales.

Il trouva, au stationnement, le même taxi qui l'avait amené.

— Déjà fini?

— Chez moi, boulevard Richard-Lenoir.

— Compris. N'empêche que, pour du travail rapide... Qui est-ce?

Un bar était ouvert, place de la République, et Maigret faillit faire arrêter la voiture pour y prendre un verre de n'importe quoi. Il ne le fit pas, par une sorte de pudeur.

Sa femme, qui s'était recouchée, ne l'entendit pas moins monter l'escalier et lui ouvrit la porte. Elle aussi s'étonna :

— Déjà?

Puis, tout de suite après, d'une voix inquiète :

— Que se passe-t-il?

— Rien. Ces messieurs n'ont pas besoin de moi.

Il lui en parlait le moins possible. C'était rare que, chez lui, il évoque les affaires du Quai des Orfèvres.

— Tu n'as pas mangé?

— Non.

— Je vais préparer ton petit déjeuner. Tu devrais vite prendre un bain pour te réchauffer.

Il n'avait plus froid. Sa colère avait fait place à de la mélancolie.

Il n'était pas le seul, à la P. J., à se sentir découragé, et le directeur avait parlé deux fois de donner sa démission. Il n'aurait pas l'occasion d'en reparler une troisième, car il était question de le remplacer.

On réorganisait, comme on disait. Des jeunes gens instruits, bien élevés, issus des meilleures familles de la République, étudiaient toutes les questions dans le silence de leur bureau, en quête d'efficacité. De leurs savantes cogitations, il sortait des plans mirifiques qui se tra-

duisaient, chaque semaine, par de nouveaux
règlements.

Et, d'abord, la police devait être un instrument au service de la justice. Un instrument.
Or, un instrument n'a pas de tête.

C'était le juge, de son cabinet, le procureur,
de son bureau prestigieux, qui menaient l'enquête et donnaient des ordres.

Encore, pour exécuter ces ordres, ne vou-
lait-on plus de policiers à l'ancienne mode, de
ces vieilles « chaussettes à clous » qui, comme
Aristide Fumel, ne savaient pas toujours
l'orthographe.

Que faire, lorsqu'il s'agissait surtout de remplir des paperasses, de ces gens qui avaient
appris leur métier dans la rue, passant de la
voie publique aux grands magasins et aux
gares, connaissant chaque bistrot de leur quartier, chaque mauvais garçon, chaque fille, et
capables, à l'occasion, de discuter le coup
avec eux en parlant leur langage?

Il leur fallait maintenant des diplômes, des
examens à chaque étape de leur carrière et,
quand il avait à commander une planque,
Maigret ne pouvait compter que sur les quelques anciens de son équipe.

On ne l'évinçait pas encore. On patientait,
sachant qu'il n'était qu'à deux ans de la retraite.

On n'en commençait pas moins à surveiller ses faits et gestes.

Il ne faisait pas jour et il prenait son petit

déjeuner tandis que des fenêtres de plus en
plus nombreuses s'éclairaient aux maisons d'en
face. A cause de ce coup de téléphone, il était
en avance, un peu engourdi, comme quand
on n'a pas assez dormi.

— Fumel, ce n'est pas celui qui louche?

— Oui.

— Et dont la femme est partie?

— Oui.

— On ne l'a jamais retrouvée?

— Il paraît qu'elle est mariée, en Amérique du Sud, et qu'elle a une ribambelle d'enfants.

— Il le sait?

— A quoi bon?

Au bureau aussi, il arriva en avance et,
bien que le jour fût enfin levé, il dut allu-
mer sa lampe à abat-jour vert.

— Donnez-moi la permanence de la Faisanderie, s'il vous plaît...

C'était lui qui avait tort. Il ne voulait pas
devenir sentimental.

— Allô!... L'inspecteur Fumel est-il là?...
Comment?... Il rédige son rapport?

Toujours du papier, des formulaires, du
temps perdu.

— C'est toi, Fumel?

Celui-ci parlait à nouveau d'une voix feu-
trée, comme s'il téléphonait en cachette.

— L'Identité Judiciaire a terminé son travail?

— Oui. Ils sont partis il y a une heure.

— Le médecin légiste est venu sur place?

— Oui. Le nouveau.

Car il y avait un nouveau médecin légiste aussi. Le vieux docteur Paul, qui pratiquait encore des autopsies à soixante-seize ans, était mort et avait été remplacé par un certain Lamalle.

— Qu'est-ce qu'il dit?

— Comme son confrère. L'homme n'a pas été tué sur place. Il n'y a pas de doute qu'il y ait eu une forte hémorragie. Les derniers coups au visage ont été portés alors que la victime était morte.

— On l'a déshabillé?

— En partie.

— Tu n'as pas remarqué un tatouage au bras gauche?

— Comment le savez-vous?

— Un poisson?... Une sorte d'hippocampe?

— Oui...

— On a relevé les empreintes digitales?

— A l'heure qu'il est, on s'en occupe aux Fichiers.

— Le corps est à l'institut médico-légal?

— Oui... Vous savez... J'étais très ennuyé, tout à l'heure... Je le suis encore. Mais je n'ai pas osé...

— Tu peux déjà écrire dans ton rapport que, selon toutes probabilités, la victime est un certain Honoré Cuendet, d'origine suisse, un Vaudois qui a passé jadis cinq ans dans la Légion Etrangère...

— Le nom me dit quelque chose... Vous savez où il habitait?

— Non. Mais je sais où sa mère habite, si elle vit encore. Je préférerais être le premier à lui parler.

— *Ils* le sauront.

— Cela m'est égal. Note toujours l'adresse, mais n'y va pas avant que je te fasse signe. C'est rue Mouffetard. Je ne connais pas le numéro. Elle occupe un entresol au-dessus d'une boulangerie, presque au coin de la rue Saint-Médard.

— Je vous remercie.

— De rien. Tu restes au bureau?

— J'en ai bien pour deux ou trois heures à rédiger ce sacré rapport.

Maigret ne s'était pas trompé et il en ressentait une certaine satisfaction en même temps qu'une pointe de tristesse. Il sortit de son bureau, gravit un escalier, entra au service des fiches où travaillaient des hommes en blouse grise.

— Qui s'occupe des empreintes du mort du bois de Boulogne?

— Moi, monsieur le commissaire.

— Tu as trouvé?

— A l'instant.

— Cuendet?

— Oui.

— Je te remercie.

Presque guilleret, maintenant, il franchis-

sait d'autres couloirs et atteignait les combles
du Palais de Justice. Dans les locaux de l'Identité Judiciaire, il retrouvait son vieil ami Moers
penché, lui aussi, sur des papiers. On n'avait
jamais accumulé autant de paperasses que
depuis six mois. Jadis, certes, le travail ad-
ministratif était assez important, mais Maigret avait calculé que, depuis peu, il prenait
à peu près quatre-vingts pour cent du temps
des policiers de tous les services.

— On t'a apporté les vêtements?

— Le type du bois de Boulogne?

— Oui.

Moers désignait deux de ses collaborateurs
qui agitaient de grands sacs de papier dans
lesquels les vêtements du mort avaient été en-
fermés. C'était la routine, la première opération technique. Il s'agissait de recueillir les
poussières de toutes sortes et de les analy-
ser ensuite, ce qui apportait parfois des indications précieuses, sur la profession d'un inconnu, par exemple, ou sur l'endroit où il
avait l'habitude de vivre, parfois sur le lieu
où le crime avait été réellement commis.

— Les poches?

— Rien. Pas de montre, de portefeuille, de
clés. Pas même un mouchoir. Ce qu'on appelle
rien.

— Et les marques sur le linge et les vêtements?

— Elles n'ont été ni arrachées, ni décousues. J'ai noté le nom du tailleur. Vous le voulez?

— Pas maintenant. L'homme est identifié.

— Qui est-ce?

— Une vieille connaissance à moi, un certain Cuendet.

— Un malfaiteur?

— Un homme tranquille, le plus tranquille, sans doute, des cambrioleurs.

— Vous croyez que c'est un complice qui a fait le coup?

— Cuendet n'a jamais eu de complices.

— Pourquoi a-t-il été tué?

— C'est bien ce que je me demande.

Ici aussi, on travaillait à la lumière artificielle, comme, aujourd'hui, dans la plupart des bureaux de Paris. Le ciel était couleur d'acier et, dans les rues, la chaussée si noire qu'elle semblait couverte d'une couche de glace.

Les gens marchaient vite, collés aux maisons, le visage précédé d'un petit nuage de vapeur.

Maigret retrouvait ses inspecteurs. Deux ou trois téléphonaient; la plupart écrivaient, eux aussi.

— Rien de neuf, Lucas?

— On cherche toujours le vieux Fernand. Quelqu'un croit l'avoir aperçu à Paris il y a trois semaines, mais ne peut rien affirmer.

Un cheval de retour. Dix ans plus tôt, ce Fer-

nand, dont on n'avait jamais connu l'identité
exacte, faisait partie d'une bande qui avait
commis, en quelques mois, un nombre impres-
sionnant de hold-up.

On avait arrêté la bande entière et le procès avait duré près de deux ans. Le chef était
mort en prison, de tuberculose. Quelques complices restaient sous les verrous, mais on en
arrivait à la période où, par le jeu des remises
de peine, on les relâchait l'un après l'autre.

Maigret n'en avait pas parlé tout à l'heure
au substitut affolé par la « recrudescence de
criminalité ». Il avait son idée. Certains détails des récents hold-up lui faisaient croire
que des anciens étaient dans le coup, avaient
sans doute reformé une nouvelle bande.

Il suffirait d'en retrouver un. Et, pour cela,
tous les hommes disponibles travaillaient patiemment depuis près de trois mois.

Les recherches avaient fini par se concentrer
sur Fernand. Il y avait un an qu'il avait été
remis en liberté et, depuis six mois, on avait
perdu sa trace.

— Sa femme?

— Elle jure toujours qu'elle ne l'a pas
revu. Les voisins confirment ses dires. Personne n'a aperçu Fernand dans le quartier.

— Continuez, mes enfants... Si on me demande... Si quelqu'un du Parquet me demande...

Il hésitait.

— Dites que je suis allé prendre un verre. Dites n'importe quoi...

On n'allait quand même pas l'empêcher de s'occuper d'un homme qu'il connaissait depuis trente ans et qui était presque un ami.

CHAPITRE

2

C'ETAIT RARE QU'IL parle de son métier, encore plus rare qu'il émette une opinion sur les hommes et leurs institutions. Il se méfiait des idées, toujours trop précises pour coller à la réalité qui, il le savait par expérience, est tellement fluide.

Avec son ami Pardon seulement, le docteur de la rue Popincourt, il lui arrivait, après dîner, de grommeler ce qui pouvait passer à la rigueur pour des confidences.

Quelques semaines plus tôt, justement, il s'était laissé aller à parler avec une certaine amertume.

— Les gens se figurent, Pardon, que nous sommes là pour découvrir les criminels et obtenir leurs aveux. C'est encore une de ces idées fausses comme il y en a tant en circulation et auxquelles on s'habitue si bien que personne ne songe à vérifier. En réalité, notre rôle principal est de protéger l'Etat, d'abord, le gouvernement, quel qu'il soit, les institutions, ensuite la monnaie et les biens publics, ceux des particuliers et enfin, tout à la fin, la vie des individus...

« Avez-vous eu la curiosité de feuilleter le Code pénal? Il faut arriver à la page 177 pour y trouver des textes visant les crimes contre les personnes. Un jour, je ferai le compte exact, plus tard, quand je serai à la retraite. Mettons que les trois quarts du Code, sinon les quatre cinquièmes, s'occupent des biens meubles et immeubles, de la fausse monnaie, des faux en écritures publiques ou privées, des captations d'héritages, etc., etc., bref, de tout ce qui se rapporte à l'argent... A tel titre que l'article 274, sur la mendicité sur la voie publique, passe avant l'article 295, lequel vise l'homicide volontaire... »

Ils avaient pourtant bien dîné, ce soir-là, et ils avaient bu un saint-émilion inoubliable.

— Dans les journaux, c'est de ma brigade, la Criminelle, selon le terme consacré, qu'on parle le plus, parce que c'est la plus spectaculaire. En réalité, nous avons moins d'importance, aux yeux du ministère de l'Intérieur, par exemple, que les Renseignements Généraux ou que la Section Financière...

« Nous sommes un peu comme les avocats d'assises. Nous constituons la façade et ce sont

les civilistes qui, dans l'ombre, font le travail
sérieux... »

Aurait-il parlé ainsi vingt ans plus tôt ? Ou
même six mois plus tôt, avant ces transforma-
tions auxquelles il assistait, mal à l'aise ?

Il grommelait entre ses dents en traversant,
le col du pardessus relevé, le pont Saint-
Michel, où la bise faisait pencher les passants
dans le même sens, dans le même angle.

Cela lui arrivait souvent de discourir ainsi
à mi-voix, l'air bougon, et un jour il avait surpris Lucas qui disait à Janvier, alors que celui-
ci était tout nouveau dans la maison :

— Il ne faut pas faire attention. Quand il
rumine, cela ne veut pas nécessairement dire
qu'il est de mauvaise humeur.

Ni qu'il était malheureux, en définitive.
Quelque chose le travaillait. Aujourd'hui,
c'était l'attitude du Parquet, au bois de Boulogne, et aussi cette fin stupide d'Honoré Cuendet à qui on avait écrabouillé le visage après
l'avoir assommé.

— *Qu'on dise que je suis allé prendre un
verre.*

Ils en étaient là. Ce qui intéressait ces messieurs, en haut lieu, c'était de mettre fin à la
série de hold-up qui causaient un préjudice
aux banques, aux assurances, aux caisses
d'épargne. Ils trouvaient aussi que les vols de
voitures devenaient trop nombreux.

— Et si les encaisseurs étaient mieux proté-
gés ? leur avait-il objecté. Si on ne confiait pas

à un seul homme, ou à deux hommes, le soin de transporter des millions sur un parcours que n'importe qui pouvait repérer?

Trop cher, évidemment!

Quant aux voitures, était-il normal de laisser au bord du trottoir, souvent sans en fermer la portière, voire en laissant la clé sur le tableau, un objet valant une fortune, parfois le prix d'un appartement moyen ou d'un pavillon en banlieue?

Autant laisser, à la portée du premier venu, un collier de diamants ou un portefeuille contenant deux ou trois millions...

A quoi bon? Cela ne le regardait pas. Il n'était qu'un instrument, plus que jamais, et ces questions-là n'étaient pas de son ressort.

Il ne s'en rendait pas moins rue Mouffetard où, malgré le froid, il trouvait l'animation habituelle autour des étals en plein vent et des petites charrettes. Il reconnaissait, deux maisons après la rue Saint-Médard, la boulangerie étroite, à la façade peinte en jaune, avec, au-dessus, les fenêtres basses de l'entresol.

La maison était vieille, étroite, toute en hauteur. Au fond de la cour, on entendait battre le fer.

Il s'engageait dans l'escalier où une corde tenait lieu de rampe, frappait à une porte et entendait bientôt des pas feutrés.

— C'est toi? demandait une voix, en même temps que le bouton tournait et que l'huis s'ouvrait.

La vieille femme avait encore grossi, du bas seulement, à partir de la taille. Son visage était plutôt mince, ses épaules étroites; les hanches, par contre, étaient devenues énormes, tellement énormes qu'elle marchait avec peine.

Elle le regardait, surprise, inquiète, d'un regard auquel il était habitué, celui des gens qui craignent toujours un malheur.

— Je vous connais, n'est-ce pas?... Vous êtes déjà venu... Attendez...

— Commissaire Maigret.. murmurait-il en pénétrant dans une pièce pleine de chaleur et d'odeur de ragoût.

— C'est ça, oui... Je me souviens... Qu'est-ce que vous lui reprochez, cette fois-ci?

On ne sentait pas d'hostilité, mais une sorte de résignation, d'acceptation de la fatalité.

Elle lui désignait une chaise. Sur le fauteuil recouvert de cuir usé, le seul fauteuil de l'appartement, un petit chien roussâtre montrait ses dents pointues et grondait sourdement tandis qu'un chat blanc, avec des taches café au lait, entrouvrait à peine ses yeux verts.

— Silence, Toto...

Et, au commissaire :

— Il grogne, comme ça, mais il n'est pas méchant... C'est le chien de mon fils... Je ne sais pas si c'est de vivre avec moi, mais il a fini par me ressembler...

L'animal, en effet, avait une tête minuscule, au museau pointu, des pattes grêles, mais un corps tout boudiné qui faisait plutôt penser à un cochon qu'à un chien. Il devait être très âgé. Ses dents étaient jaunes, espacées.

— Il y a au moins quinze ans de ça, Honoré l'a ramassé dans la rue, les deux pattes cassées par une auto... Il lui a fabriqué un appareil, avec des planches, et, deux mois après, la pauvre bête, que les voisins voulaient faire piquer, marchait comme les autres...

Le logement était bas de plafond, assez sombre, d'une propreté remarquable. La pièce servait à la fois de cuisine et de salle à manger, avec sa table ronde au milieu, son vieux buffet, sa cuisinière hollandaise d'un modèle qu'on ne voit presque plus.

Cuendet avait dû l'acheter aux Puces ou chez un brocanteur et l'avait remise à neuf, car il avait toujours été bricoleur. La fonte était presque rouge, les cuivres brillants et on entendait un ronflement.

Dans la rue, le marché battait son plein et Maigret se souvenait qu'à sa précédente visite, il avait trouvé la vieille accoudée à la fenêtre où, à la belle saison, elle passait le plus clair de son temps à regarder la foule.

— Je vous écoute, monsieur le commissaire.

Elle avait gardé l'accent traînant de son pays et, au lieu de s'asseoir en face de lui, elle restait debout, sur la défensive.

— Quand avez-vous vu votre fils pour la dernière fois?

— Dites-moi d'abord si vous l'avez encore arrêté.

Il n'hésita qu'une seconde et put répondre
sans mentir :

— Non.

— C'est donc que vous le recherchez? Dans
ce cas, je vous réponds tout de suite qu'il n'est
pas ici. Vous n'avez qu'à visiter le logement,
comme vous l'avez déjà fait. Vous ne trouverez rien de changé, bien qu'il y ait plus de dix
ans de ça...

Elle désignait une porte ouverte et il apercevait une salle à manger qui ne servait jamais,
encombrée de bibelots inutiles, de napperons,
de photos dans des cadres, comme on en voit
chez les petites gens qui tiennent, malgré tout,
à avoir une pièce d'apparat.

Deux chambres donnaient sur la cour, le
commissaire le savait, celle de la vieille, avec
un lit de fer auquel elle tenait, et celle qu'occupait parfois Honoré, presque aussi simple,
mais plus confortable.

Une odeur de pain chaud montait du rez-de-
chaussée et se mêlait à celle du ragoût.

Maigret était grave, un peu ému.

— Je ne le recherche pas non plus, madame Cuendet. J'aimerais seulement savoir...

Tout de suite, elle semblait comprendre, de-
viner, et son regard devenait plus aigu, avec
une lueur d'anxiété.

— Si vous ne le cherchez pas et si vous ne
l'avez pas arrêté, cela veut dire...

Elle avait les cheveux rares sur un crâne
qui paraissait dérisoirement étroit.

— Il lui est arrivé quelque chose, n'est-ce pas?

Il baissait la tête.

— J'ai préféré vous l'apprendre moi-même.

— La police lui a tiré dessus?

— Non... Je...

— Un accident?

— Votre fils est mort, madame Cuendet.

Elle le regardait durement, sans pleurer, et le chien roux, qui semblait avoir compris, sautait du fauteuil pour venir se frotter à ses grosses jambes.

— Qui a fait ça?

Elle sifflait ces mots entre ses dents aussi écartées que celles de l'animal qui se remettait à gronder.

— Je n'en sais rien. Il a été tué, on ignore encore où.

— Alors, comment pouvez-vous dire...

— On a retrouvé son corps, ce matin, dans une allée du bois de Boulogne.

Elle répétait, méfiante, comme si elle flairait toujours un piège :

— Du bois de Boulogne? Qu'est-ce qu'il serait allé faire au bois de Boulogne?

— C'est là qu'il a été découvert. On l'a tué ailleurs, transporté ensuite en auto.

— Pourquoi?

Patient, il évitait de la bousculer, prenait son temps.

— C'est une question que nous nous posons aussi.

Comment aurait-il expliqué au juge d'instruction, par exemple, ses relations avec
Cuendet? Ce n'était pas seulement dans son
bureau du Quai des Orfèvres qu'il avait appris
à le connaître. Et il n'avait pas suffi d'une
enquête plus ou moins bâclée.

Cela représentait trente ans de métier, plusieurs visites à ce logement où il ne se sentait
pas un étranger.

— Pour découvrir ses meurtriers, justement, j'ai besoin de savoir quand vous l'avez
vu pour la dernière fois. Il n'a pas dormi ici
depuis plusieurs jours, n'est-ce pas?

— A son âge, on a bien le droit...

Et s'interrompant, les paupières soudain
gonflées :

— Où est-il, à cette heure?

— Vous le verrez plus tard. Un inspecteur
viendra vous chercher.

— On l'a transporté à la morgue?

— A l'institut médico-légal, oui.

— Il a souffert?

— Non.

— On a tiré sur lui?

Des larmes coulaient sur ses joues, mais elle
n'avait pas de sanglots et regardait toujours
Maigret avec un reste de méfiance.

— On l'a frappé.

— Avec quoi?

On aurait dit qu'elle voulait reconstituer en
esprit la mort de son fils.

— On l'ignore. Un objet lourd.

Elle portait, d'instinct, la main à sa tête et faisait une grimace de douleur.

— Pourquoi?

— Nous le saurons, je vous le jure. C'est pour le découvrir que je suis ici et que j'ai besoin de vous. Asseyez-vous, madame Cuendet.

— Je ne peux pas.

Pourtant, ses genoux tremblaient.

— Vous n'avez rien à boire?

— Vous avez soif?

— Non. C'est pour vous. J'aimerais que vous preniez un petit verre.

Il se souvenait qu'elle buvait volontiers et, en effet, elle alla prendre dans le buffet de la salle à manger un flacon d'eau-de-vie blanche.

Même dans un moment comme celui-ci, elle éprouvait le besoin de tricher un peu.

— Je la gardais pour mon fils... Il lui arrivait d'en prendre une goutte, après le dîner...

Elle remplissait deux verres à fond épais.

— Je me demande, répétait-elle, pourquoi on l'a tué. Un garçon qui n'a jamais fait de mal à personne, l'homme le plus tranquille, le plus doux de la terre... N'est-ce pas, Toto?... Tu le sais mieux que n'importe qui, toi...

En pleurant, elle caressait le chien obèse qui remuait son bout de queue et la scène aurait sans doute paru grotesque au substitut et au juge Cajou.

Le fils dont elle parlait, n'était-il pas un repris de justice et, sans son habileté, ne serait-il pas encore en prison?

Il n'y était allé que deux fois, dont une comme prévenu seulement, et les deux fois, c'était Maigret qui l'avait arrêté.

Ils avaient passé des heures et des heures en tête à tête, Quai des Orfèvres, à ruser tous les deux, chacun, aurait-on dit, estimant l'autre à sa juste valeur.

— Depuis combien de temps...

Maigret revenait à charge, patiemment, d'une voix égale, sur un fond de bruits du marché.

— Il y a bien un mois, cédait-elle enfin.

— Il ne vous a rien dit?

— Il ne me parlait jamais de rien de ce qu'il faisait en dehors d'ici.

C'était vrai, Maigret en avait eu jadis la preuve.

— Il n'est pas venu vous voir une seule fois pendant ce temps?

— Non. Et pourtant, la semaine dernière, c'était mon anniversaire. Il m'a envoyé des fleurs.

— D'où les a-t-il envoyées?

— C'est un livreur qui les a apportées.

— Il n'y avait pas le nom du fleuriste?

— Peut-être. Je n'ai pas regardé.

— Vous n'avez pas reconnu le livreur? Ce n'était pas quelqu'un du quartier?

— Je ne l'avais jamais vu.

Il ne demandait pas à fouiller la chambre

d'Honoré Cuendet à la recherche d'un indice.
Il n'était pas ici officiellement. On ne l'avait
pas chargé de l'enquête.

L'inspecteur Fumel viendrait sans doute
tout à l'heure, muni de papiers en règle signés
du juge d'instruction. Il ne trouverait probablement rien. Les fois précédentes, Maigret
n'avait rien trouvé non plus, que des vêtements rangés avec soin, du linge dans l'armoire, quelques livres, des outils qui n'étaient
pas des outils de cambrioleur.

— Depuis combien de temps cela ne lui
était-il pas arrivé de disparaître de la sorte?

Elle cherchait dans sa mémoire. Elle n'était
plus tout à fait à la conversation et devait faire
un effort.

— Il a passé presque tout l'hiver ici.

— Et l'été?

— Je ne sais pas où il est allé.

— Il ne vous a pas proposé de vous emmener à la campagne ou à la mer?

— Je n'y serais pas allée. J'ai assez vécu à
la campagne pour ne pas avoir envie d'y retourner.

Elle devait avoir une cinquantaine d'années, ou un peu plus, quand elle avait découvert Paris et la seule ville qu'elle eût connue
jusqu'alors était Lausanne.

Elle était d'un petit village du canton de
Vaud, Sénarclens, près d'un bourg appelé Cos-
sonay où son mari, Gilles, travaillait comme
ouvrier agricole.

Maigret n'avait fait, jadis, en vacances, avec sa femme, que traverser le pays, dont il revoyait surtout les auberges.

C'étaient ces auberges, justement, propres et paisibles, qui avaient perdu Gilles Cuendet. Petit homme aux jambes tordues, il ne parlait pas volontiers et pouvait rester des heures, dans un coin, à boire des chopines de vin blanc.

D'ouvrier agricole, il était devenu taupier, allant poser ses pièges de ferme en ferme, et on prétendait qu'il sentait aussi fort que les animaux qu'il attrapait.

Ils avaient deux enfants, Honoré et sa sœur Laurence qui, envoyée comme fille de salle à Genève, avait fini par épouser quelqu'un de l'Unesco, un traducteur, si la mémoire de Maigret était exacte, et l'avait suivi en Amérique du Sud.

— Vous avez des nouvelles de votre fille?

— J'ai reçu des vœux au nouvel an. Elle a maintenant cinq enfants. Je peux vous montrer la carte.

Elle allait la chercher dans la pièce voisine, par besoin de bouger plutôt que pour convaincre.

— Tenez! C'est en couleur...

L'image représentait le port de Rio de Janeiro sous un coucher de soleil d'un rouge violacé.

— Elle ne vous en écrit jamais plus?

— A quoi bon? Avec l'océan entre nous,

on ne se reverra jamais. Elle a fait sa vie,
n'est-ce pas?

Honoré aussi avait fait la sienne, différemment. Dès l'âge de quinze ans, on l'avait envoyé travailler, lui aussi, comme apprenti chez
un serrurier de Lausanne.

C'était un garçon calme et secret, guère plus
bavard que son père. Il occupait une mansarde
dans une vieille maison près du marché et
c'est à la suite d'une dénonciation anonyme
que la police, un matin, avait fait irruption
dans cette pièce.

Honoré avait moins de dix-sept ans à l'époque. Chez lui, on avait trouvé de tout, les objets
les plus hétéroclites dont il n'avait même pas
essayé d'expliquer la provenance : réveils, outils, boîtes de conserves, vêtements d'enfant
avec encore leur étiquette, deux ou trois postes
de radio qu'il n'avait pas sortis de leur emballage original.

La police avait cru, d'abord, à ce qu'on
appelle des vols à la roulotte, c'est-à-dire des
vols accomplis sur des camions en stationnement.

Après enquête, on constatait qu'il n'en était
rien, que le jeune Cuendet s'introduisait dans
des magasins fermés, dans des dépôts, dans
des appartements inoccupés et emportait au
petit bonheur ce qui lui tombait sous la main.

A cause de son âge, on l'avait envoyé à la
maison de redressement de Vennes, au-dessus
de Lausanne, où, parmi les métiers qu'on lui

proposait d'apprendre, il avait choisi celui de chaudronnier.

Pendant un an, il avait été un pensionnaire modèle, calme et doux, travailleur, n'enfreignant jamais le règlement.

Puis, soudain, il avait disparu sans laisser de trace et dix ans devaient s'écouler avant que Maigret le retrouve à Paris.

Son premier soin, en quittant la Suisse, où il n'avait jamais remis les pieds, avait été de s'engager dans la Légion étrangère et il avait vécu cinq ans à Sidi-Bel-Abbès et en Indochine.

Le commissaire avait eu l'occasion de prendre connaissance de son dossier militaire et de bavarder avec un de ses chefs.

Là encore, Honoré Cuendet avait été, d'une façon générale, un soldat modèle. Tout au plus lui reprochait-on d'être un solitaire, de n'avoir aucun ami, de ne pas se mêler aux autres, même les soirs de baroud.

— Il était soldat comme d'autres sont ajusteurs ou cordonniers, disait son lieutenant.

Aucune punition en trois ans. Après quoi, sans raison connue, il désertait, pour être retrouvé, quelques jours plus tard, dans un atelier d'Alger où il s'était fait embaucher.

Il ne fournissait pas d'explication de ce départ soudain, qui pouvait lui coûter cher, se contentait de murmurer :

— Je ne pouvais plus.

— Pourquoi?

— Je ne sais pas.

Grâce à ses trois années de service impeccable, on l'avait traité avec indulgence et, six mois plus tard, il recommençait, se faisait pincer, cette fois, après seulement vingt-quatre heures de liberté, dans un camion de légumes où il s'était caché.

C'était à la Légion qu'on lui avait tatoué un poisson sur le bras gauche, à sa demande, et Maigret avait essayé de comprendre.

— Pourquoi un poisson? avait-il insisté. Et surtout pourquoi un hippocampe?

Les légionnaires, d'habitude, ont le goût d'images plus évocatrices.

C'était un homme de vingt-six ans que Maigret avait alors devant lui, les cheveux d'un blond roux, les épaules larges, la taille plutôt petite.

— Vous avez déjà vu des hippocampes?

— Pas vivants.

— Et des hippocampes morts?

— J'en ai vu un.

— Où?

— A Lausanne.

— Chez qui?

— Dans la chambre d'une femme.

Il fallait lui arracher les mots presque un à un.

— Quelle femme?

— Une femme chez qui je suis allé.

— Avant d'être enfermé à Vennes?

— Oui.

— Vous l'avez suivie?

— Oui.

— Dans la rue?

— Au bout de la rue Centrale, oui.

— Et, dans sa chambre, il y avait un hippo-campe séché?

— C'est cela. Elle m'a dit que c'était son porte-bonheur.

— Vous avez connu beaucoup d'autres femmes?

— Pas beaucoup.

Maigret croyait avoir compris.

— Qu'est-ce que vous avez fait lorsque, li-béré de la Légion, vous êtes arrivé à Paris?

— J'ai travaillé.

— Où?

— Chez un serrurier de la rue de la Ro-quette.

La police avait vérifié. C'était vrai. Il y avait travaillé deux ans et avait donné toute satis-faction. On se moquait bien de lui parce qu'il n'était pas « causant », mis on le considérait comme un ouvrier modèle.

— A quoi passiez-vous vos soirées?

— A rien.

— Vous alliez au cinéma?

— Presque jamais.

— Vous aviez des amis?

— Non.

— Des amies?

— Encore moins.

On aurait dit que les femmes lui faisaient

peur. Et pourtant, à cause de la première qu'il avait rencontrée, à seize ans, il s'était fait tatouer un hippocampe sur le bras.

L'enquête avait été minutieuse. A cette époque-là, on pouvait fignoler. Maigret n'était encore qu'inspecteur et n'avait guère que trois ans de plus que Cuendet.

Cela s'était passé un peu comme à Lausanne, sauf que, cette fois, il n'y avait pas eu de lettre anonyme.

Un matin, de très bonne heure, vers quatre heures du matin, au fait, comme pour la découverte du corps au bois de Boulogne, un agent en uniforme avait interpellé un homme chargé d'un paquet encombrant. C'était un hasard. Or, un instant, l'homme avait fait mine de fuir.

Dans le paquet, on avait trouvé de la pelleterie et Cuendet avait refusé d'expliquer cet étrange chargement.

— Où alliez-vous avec ça?

— Je ne sais pas.

— D'où venez-vous?

— Je n'ai rien à dire.

On avait fini par découvrir que les peaux provenaient de chez un fourreur en chambre de la rue des Francs-Bourgeois.

Cuendet vivait alors dans une maison meublée, rue Saint-Antoine, à cent mètres de la Bastille et, dans sa chambre, comme dans sa mansarde de Lausanne, on avait trouvé un assortiment de marchandises les plus diverses.

— A qui revendiez-vous votre butin?

— A personne.

Cela paraissait invraisemblable et pourtant il avait été impossible d'établir une connivence entre le Vaudois et les receleurs connus.

Il avait peu d'argent sur lui. Ses dépenses correspondaient avec ce qu'il gagnait chez son patron.

Le cas avait tellement intrigué Maigret qu'il avait obtenu de son chef d'alors, le commissaire Guillaume, que le prisonnier soit examiné par un médecin.

— C'est certainement ce que nous appelons un associal, mais je lui trouve une intelligence plutôt au-dessus de la moyenne et une affectivité normale.

Cuendet avait eu la chance d'être défendu par un jeune avocat qui devait par la suite devenir un des ténors des assises, maître Gambier, et celui-ci avait obtenu pour son client le minimum.

D'abord incarcéré à la Santé, Cuendet avait passé un peu plus d'un an à Fresnes où, une fois de plus, il s'était montré un prisonnier modèle, ce qui lui avait valu une remise de quelques mois de sa peine.

Son père était mort, entre-temps, écrasé par une auto un samedi soir qu'il rentrait chez lui, ivre mort, sur un vélo non éclairé.

Honoré avait fait venir sa mère de Sénarclens et cette femme, qui n'avait connu que la campagne la plus paisible d'Europe, s'était

trouvée transplantée dans la cohue grouil-
lante de la rue Mouffetard.

N'était-elle pas une sorte de phénomène,
elle aussi? Au lieu de s'effrayer et de prendre
la grande ville en grippe, elle s'était si bien
incrustée dans son quartier, dans sa rue,
qu'elle en était devenue un des personnages
les plus populaires.

Elle s'appelait Justine et, d'un bout à l'autre
de la rue Mouffetard, tout le monde connaissait maintenant la vieille Justine au parler
lent et aux yeux malicieux.

Que son fils ait fait de la prison ne la gênait
point.

— Chacun ses goûts et ses opinions, disait-
elle.

Deux fois encore, Maigret s'était occupé
d'Honoré Cuendet, la seconde à la suite d'un
important vol de bijoux rue de la Pompe, à
Passy.

Le cambriolage avait eu lieu dans un appartement luxueux où, en plus des maîtres, vivaient trois domestiques. Les bijoux avaient
été déposés, le soir, sur une coiffeuse, dans le
boudoir attenant à la chambre à coucher dont
la porte était restée ouverte toute la nuit.

Ni monsieur ni madame D, qui avaient
dormi dans leur lit, n'avaient rien entendu. La
femme de chambre, qui couchait au même
étage, était sûre d'avoir fermé la porte à clé
et de l'avoir trouvée, le matin, fermée de la

même façon. Aucune trace d'effraction. Aucune empreinte.

Comme l'appartement se trouvait au troisième étage, il n'était pas question d'escalade. Pas de balcon, non plus, permettant d'atteindre le boudoir par un appartement voisin.

C'était le cinquième ou le sixième vol de cette espèce en trois ans et les journaux commençaient à parler d'un cambrioleur-fantôme.

Maigret se souvenait de ce printemps-là, des aspects de la rue de la Pompe à toutes les heures du jour, car il allait de porte en porte, questionnant inlassablement les gens, non seulement les concierges et les commerçants, mais les locataires des immeubles et les domestiques.

C'est ainsi, par hasard, par opiniâtreté plutôt, qu'il était tombé sur Cuendet. Dans l'immeuble situé en face de la maison du vol, une chambre de bonne, donnant sur la rue, s'était trouvée à louer six semaines auparavant.

— C'est un monsieur bien gentil, bien calme qui l'occupe, disait la concierge. Il sort peu, jamais le soir, et ne reçoit pas de femmes. Il ne reçoit d'ailleurs personne.

— Il fait son ménage lui-même?

— Bien sûr. Et je vous jure que c'est propre!

Cuendet était-il si sûr de lui qu'il ne s'était pas donné la peine de déménager après le vol? Ou bien avait-il craint d'éveiller les soupçons en quittant le logement?

Maigret l'avait trouvé chez lui, occupé à lire. En se penchant à la fenêtre, il avait pu suivre les allées et venues des locataires dans les appartements d'en face.

— Il faut que je vous prie de me suivre à la P. J.

Le Vaudois n'avait pas protesté. Il avait laissé fouiller son logement sans mot dire. On n'avait rien trouvé, pas un bijou, pas une fausse clé, pas un outil de monte-en-l'air.

L'interrogatoire, Quai des Orfèvres, avait duré près de vingt-quatre heures, entrecoupé de verres de bière et de sandwiches.

— Pourquoi avez-vous loué cette chambre?

— Parce qu'elle me plaisait.

— Vous vous êtes disputé avec votre mère?

— Non.

— Vous ne vivez plus chez elle?

— J'y retournerai un jour ou l'autre.

— Vous y avez laissé presque toutes vos affaires.

— Justement.

— Etes-vous allé la voir ces derniers temps?

— Non.

— Qui avez-vous rencontré?

— La concierge, les voisins, les gens qui passent dans la rue.

Son accent mettait dans ses réponses une ironie peut-être involontaire, car son visage restait calme et sérieux, il avait l'air de faire son possible pour satisfaire le commissaire.

L'interrogatoire n'avait rien donné, mais

l'enquête, rue Mouffetard, avait fourni des
présomptions. On apprenait en effet que ce
n'était pas la première fois qu'Honoré dis-
paraissait de la sorte pour un temps plus ou
moins long, de trois semaines à deux mois en
général, après quoi il revenait vivre chez sa
mère.

— Quels sont vos moyens d'existence?

— Je bricole. J'ai un peu d'argent de côté.

— A la banque?

— Non. Je me méfie des banques.

— Où se trouve cet argent?

Il se taisait. Depuis sa première arrestation,
il avait étudié le Code pénal qu'il connaissait
par cœur.

— Ce n'est pas à moi de prouver mon in-
nocence. C'est à vous d'établir que je suis
coupable.

Une seule fois, Maigret s'était fâché et, devant l'air doucement réprobateur de Cuendet,
il l'avait regretté tout de suite.

— Vous vous êtes débarrassé des bijoux
d'une façon ou d'une autre. Il est probable
que vous les avez revendus. A qui?

On avait fait le tour, bien entendu, des recé-
leurs connus, alerté Anvers, Amsterdam et
Londres. On avait aussi passé le mot aux indi-
cateurs.

Personne ne connaissait Cuendet. Personne
ne l'avait vu. Personne n'avait été en rapport
avec lui.

— Qu'est-ce que je vous disais? triomphait

sa mère. Je sais bien que vous êtes malins,
mais mon fils, voyez-vous, c'est quelqu'un!

Malgré son casier judiciaire, malgré la
chambre de bonne, malgré tous les indices,
force avait été de le relâcher.

Cuendet n'avait pas triomphé. Il avait pris la
chose tranquillement. Le commissaire le revoyait encore, cherchant son chapeau, s'ar-
rêtant devant la porte, tendant une main hé-
sitante.

— Au revoir, monsieur le commissaire...

Comme s'il s'attendait à revenir!

3

LES CHAISES ETAIENT
à fond de paille tressée et avaient, dans la
pénombre, des reflets dorés. Le plancher, de
vulgaire sapin pourtant, très vieux, était si
bien encaustiqué qu'on y voyait comme dans
un miroir le rectangle de la fenêtre. Le balan-
cier de cuivre d'une horloge, au mur, battait
à un rythme paisible.

On aurait dit que le moindre objet, le tison-
nier, les bols à grandes fleurs roses et jusqu'au
balai où le chat se frottait le dos avait sa vie
propre, comme dans les anciens tableaux hol-
landais ou dans les sacristies.

La vieille ouvrait le poêle pour y verser
deux pelletées de charbon luisant et un instant les flammes venaient lui lécher la figure.

— Vous permettez que j'enlève mon pardessus?

— Cela veut dire que vous allez rester longtemps?

— Il y a moins cinq degrés dehors et, chez vous, il fait plutôt chaud.

— On prétend que les vieux deviennent frileux, grommelait-elle, plutôt pour elle-même, pour occuper son esprit, que pour lui. Moi, mon poêle me tient compagnie. Tout jeune, mon fils était déjà comme ça. Je le vois encore, chez nous, à Sénarclens, collé contre le poêle pour étudier ses leçons.

Elle regardait le fauteuil vide, au bois poli, au cuir usé.

— Ici aussi, il le rapprochait du feu et pouvait passer des journées à lire sans rien entendre.

— Qu'est-ce qu'il lisait?

Elle levait les bras en signe d'impuissance.

— Est-ce que je sais, moi? Des livres qu'il allait chercher au cabinet de lecture de la rue Monge. Tenez! Voici le dernier. Il les échangeait au fur et à mesure. Il avait une sorte d'abonnement. Vous devez connaître ça...

Relié d'une toile noire et lustrée qui faisait penser à une vieille soutane, c'était un ouvrage de Lenotre sur un épisode de la Révolution.

— Il savait beaucoup de choses, Honoré. Il ne parlait pas beaucoup, mais sa tête n'ar-

rêtait pas de travailler. Il lisait des journaux
aussi, quatre ou cinq chaque jour, et de gros
illustrés qui coûtent cher, avec des images en
couleur...

Maigret aimait l'odeur du logement, faite
de maintes odeurs différentes. Il avait toujours eu un faible pour les habitations qui ont
une odeur caractéristique et il hésitait à al-
lumer sa pipe qu'il avait bourrée machinale-
ment.

— Vous pouvez fumer. Il fumait la pipe
aussi. Il tenait même tellement à ses vieilles
pipes qu'il lui arrivait de les réparer avec du
fil de fer.

— Je voudrais vous poser une question,
madame Cuendet.

— Cela me fait un drôle d'effet que vous
m'appeliez comme ça. Il y a tellement longtemps que tout le monde m'appelle Justine!
Je crois bien qu'à part le maire, quand il m'a
félicitée le jour de mon mariage, personne ne
m'a appelée autrement. Dites toujours! Je
vous répondrai si j'en ai envie.

— Vous ne travaillez pas. Votre mari était
pauvre.

— Vous avez rencontré un taupier riche,
vous? Surtout un taupier qui boit du matin
au soir?

— Vous vivez donc de l'argent que vous remettait votre fils.

— Il y a du mal à ça?

— Un ouvrier remet sa paie à sa femme ou

à sa mère chaque semaine, un employé tous
les mois. Je suppose qu'Honoré vous donnait
de l'argent au fur et à mesure de vos besoins?

Elle le regardait avec attention, comme si
elle comprenait la portée de la question.

— Et alors?

— Il aurait aussi pu vous remettre une
somme importante au retour de ses absences,
par exemple.

— Il n'y a jamais eu de somme importante
ici. Qu'est-ce que j'en aurais fait?

— Ces absences duraient plus ou moins
longtemps, parfois des semaines, n'est-ce pas?
Si, pendant ce temps-là, vous aviez besoin
d'argent, que faisiez-vous?

— Je n'en avais pas besoin.

— Il vous en donnait donc suffisamment
avant de partir?

— Sans compter que j'ai un compte chez
le boucher, chez l'épicier, que je peux acheter
à crédit chez n'importe quel commerçant du
quartier et même aux petites charrettes. Tout
le monde, dans la rue, connaît la vieille Justine.

— Il ne vous a jamais envoyé de mandat?

— Je ne sais pas comment j'aurais fait pour
le toucher.

— Ecoutez, madame Cuendet...

— J'aime encore mieux que vous disiez Justine...

Elle était toujours debout et remettait un
peu d'eau chaude dans son ragoût, reposait le

couvercle en laissant une légère ouverture
pour la vapeur.

— Je ne peux plus lui causer d'ennuis et je
n'ai aucune intention de vous en causer à
vous. Ce que je cherche, c'est à retrouver ceux
qui l'ont tué.

— Quand est-ce que je pourrai le voir?

— Cet après-midi, sans doute. Un inspecteur viendra vous chercher.

— Et on me le rendra?

— Je pense que oui. Pour retrouver son ou
ses assassins, j'ai besoin de comprendre certaines choses.

— Qu'est-ce que vous voulez comprendre?

Elle se méfiait encore, en paysanne qu'elle
était restée, en vieille femme à peu près illet-
trée qui flaire partout des pièges. C'était plus
fort qu'elle.

— Votre fils vous quittait plusieurs fois par
an, restait absent pendant plusieurs semaines...

— Quelquefois trois semaines, quelquefois
deux mois.

— Comment était-il à son retour?

— Comme un homme satisfait de retrouver
ses pantoufles au coin du feu.

— Vous avertissait-il de ses départs ou
quittait-il la maison sans rien dire?

— Qui est-ce qui aurait préparé sa valise?

— Donc, il vous en parlait. Il emportait des
vêtements de rechange, du linge...

— Il emportait tout ce qu'il faut.

— Il avait plusieurs costumes?

— Quatre ou cinq. Il aimait être bien habillé.

— Avez-vous l'impression qu'à son retour il cachait quelque chose dans l'appartement?

— Ce ne serait pas facile de trouver une cachette dans les quatre pièces. D'ailleurs, vous les avez fouillées, et pas seulement une fois. Je me souviens que vos hommes ont fouiné partout et qu'ils ont même démonté des meubles. Ils sont allés dans la cave, qui est pourtant commune à tous les locataires, et dans le coin de grenier auquel nous avons droit.

C'était vrai. On n'avait rien trouvé.

— Votre fils n'a pas de compte en banque, nous nous en sommes assurés, ni de carnet de caisse d'épargne. Or, il fallait bien qu'il dépose son argent quelque part. Savez-vous s'il lui arrivait de se rendre à l'étranger, en Belgique, par exemple, ou en Suisse, en Espagne?

— En Suisse, il se serait fait arrêter.

— C'est exact.

— Il ne m'a jamais parlé des autres pays que vous dites.

On avait plusieurs fois alerté les frontières. Pendant des années, la photographie d'Honoré Cuendet avait figuré parmi celle des personnes à surveiller dans les gares et aux différentes sorties du pays.

Maigret pensait à voix haute.

— Il a dû forcément, revendre des bijoux, des objets. Il ne s'est pas adressé à des receleurs professionnels. Et, comme il dépensait peu, il avait forcément quelque part une somme importante.

Il regardait la vieille avec plus d'attention.

— S'il ne vous remettait l'argent du ménage qu'au fur et à mesure, qu'est-ce que vous allez devenir?

Cette idée la frappa et elle tressaillit. Il vit une inquiétude passer dans ses yeux.

— Je n'ai pas peur, n'en répondit-elle pas moins avec fierté. Honoré est un bon fils.

Elle ne disait pas « était », cette fois. Et elle continuait, comme s'il était toujours en vie :

— Je suis sûre qu'il ne me laissera pas sans rien.

Il enchaîna :

— Il n'a pas été tué par un rôdeur. Il ne s'agit pas d'un crime crapuleux. Il n'a pas non plus été abattu par un complice.

Elle ne lui demandait pas pourquoi et il ne le lui expliquait pas. Un rôdeur n'aurait eu aucune raison de défigurer le cadavre en s'acharnant sur le visage et en vidant les poches des moindres objets, y compris les papiers sans valeur, la pipe, les allumettes.

Un complice ne l'aurait pas fait non plus, sachant que Cuendet avait fait de la prison et serait par conséquent identifié par ses empreintes digitales.

— Celui qui l'a tué ne le connaissait pas.

Pourtant, il avait une raison importante de le supprimer. Vous comprenez?

— Qu'est-ce que je dois comprendre?

— Que, quand nous saurons quel coup Honoré préparait, dans quelle maison, dans quel appartement il s'est introduit, nous serons bien près de connaître son assassin.

— Cela ne le fera pas revivre.

— Vous permettez que je jette un coup d'œil dans sa chambre?

— Je ne peux pas vous en empêcher.

— Je préfère que vous y veniez avec moi.

Elle le suivait, haussant ses maigres épaules, balançant ses hanches presque monstrueuses et le petit chien roux marchait sur leurs talons, prêt à gronder à nouveau.

La salle à manger était neutre, sans vie, presque sans odeur. Une courtepointe très blanche recouvrait le lit de fer de la vieille et la chambre d'Honoré, mal éclairée par la fenêtre donnant sur la cour, prenait déjà un aspect mortuaire.

Maigret ouvrait la porte d'une armoire à glace, trouvait trois complets qui pendaient à des cintres, deux gris et un bleu marine, des souliers rangés dans le fond et, sur une tablette, des chemises sur lesquelles était posé un bouquet de lavande séchée.

Des livres, sur une étagère : un exemplaire rouge du Code pénal, tout usé, qui avait dû être acheté sur les quais ou chez un bouquiniste du boulevard Saint-Michel; quelques ro-

mans datant du début du siècle, plus un Zola
et un Tolstoï; un plan de Paris qu'on avait
dû souvent consulter...

Dans un coin, sur une console à deux étages,
des magazines dont les titres firent froncer
les sourcils du commissaire. Ils ne cadraient
pas avec le reste. C'étaient des magazines
épais, luxueux, sur papier couché, qui pu-
bliaient des photographies en couleur des
plus beaux châteaux de France et des inté-
rieurs somptueux de Paris.

Il en feuilleta quelques-uns, espérant y trouver des notes, des coups de crayon.

A Lausanne, le jeune Cuendet, apprenti serrurier, vivant dans un galetas, s'appropriait
tout ce qui lui tombait sous la main, y compris des objets sans valeur.

Plus tard, rue Saint-Antoine, il devait montrer un peu plus de discernement, mais il ne
cambriolait encore, au petit bonheur, que les
boutiques et les appartements du quartier.

Il allait gravir un nouvel échelon, s'en
prendre à des maisons bourgeoises où il
trouvait à la fois de l'argent et des bijoux.

Il en était arrivé, enfin, patiemment, aux
beaux quartiers. La vieille, tout à l'heure, sans
le vouloir, avait prononcé une phrase importante. Elle avait parlé des quatre ou cinq
journaux que son fils lisait chaque jour.

Maigret aurait parié que ce n'étaient pas les
faits divers qu'il y cherchait, moins encore les
nouvelles politiques, mais les rubriques mon-

daines, mariages, comptes rendus de réceptions, de répétitions générales.

N'y décrivait-on pas les bijoux des femmes en vue?

Les magazines que Maigret avait sous les yeux apportaient à Honoré des renseignements aussi précieux : non seulement la description minutieuse des hôtels particuliers et des appartements, mais encore des photographies des différentes pièces.

Assis au coin du feu, le Vaudois méditait, pesait le pour et le contre, faisait son choix.

Puis il allait rôder dans le quartier, louait une chambre dans un hôtel ou, s'il s'en trouvait une de libre, dans une maison particulière, comme ça avait été le cas rue de la Pompe.

Lors de la dernière enquête, qui remontait à plusieurs années, on avait aussi retrouvé sa trace dans un certain nombre de cafés dont, du jour au lendemain, il était devenu, pour un temps, un habitué.

— Un homme bien tranquille, qui passait des heures dans son coin, à boire du vin blanc, à lire les journaux et à regarder dans la rue...

En fait, il observait les allées et venues d'une maison, patrons et domestiques, étudiait leurs habitudes, leur emploi du temps et, de sa fenêtre, il les épiait ensuite dans leur intérieur.

Ainsi, après quelque temps, un immeuble entier n'avait-il plus de secrets pour lui.

— Je vous remercie, madame Cuendet.

— Justine!

— Pardon : Justine. J'avais beaucoup de...

Il cherchait le mot. Amitié était trop fort. Attirance n'aurait pas eu de sens pour elle.

— ... J'avais beaucoup d'estime pour votre fils...

Le mot n'était pas exact non plus, mais ni le substitut ni le juge d'instruction n'étaient là pour l'entendre.

— L'inspecteur Fumel viendra vous voir. Si vous avez besoin de quoi que ce soit, adressez-vous à moi.

— Je n'aurai besoin de rien.

— Au cas où vous apprendriez dans quel quartier Honoré a passé ces dernières semaines...

Il remettait son lourd pardessus, descendait avec précaution l'escalier aux marches usées. Il était repris par le vacarme de la rue et par le froid. Il y avait maintenant dans l'air un peu de poudre blanche comme en suspens mais il ne neigeait pas et on ne voyait aucune trace sur le sol.

Quand il pénétra dans le bureau des inspecteurs, Lucas lui annonça :

— Moers vous a demandé au téléphone.

— Il n'a pas dit pourquoi?

— Il a demandé que vous l'appeliez.

— Toujours pas de nouvelles de Fernand?

Il n'oubliait pas que sa tâche principale était de découvrir les auteurs des hold-up. Cela pouvait durer des semaines, sinon des mois. Des centaines, des milliers de policiers et de gendarmes avaient en poche la photographie du prisonnier libéré. Des inspecteurs faisaient du porte à porte, comme des marchands d'aspirateurs électriques.

— Pardon, madame. Avez-vous vu récemment cet homme?

La brigade des meublés s'occupait des hôtels. Celle des mœurs, la « mondaine », interrogeait les filles. Dans les gares, les voyageurs ne se doutaient pas que des yeux anonymes les examinaient au passage.

Il n'était pas chargé de l'enquête au sujet de Cuendet. Il n'avait pas le droit de détourner ses hommes de leur service. Il n'en trouva pas moins un moyen de concilier son devoir et sa curiosité.

— Tu vas demander là-haut une photographie, la plus récente possible, de Cuendet. Tu en feras remettre une copie à tous ceux qui recherchent Fernand, surtout ceux qui visitent les bistrots et les meublés.

— Dans tous les quartiers?

Il hésita, faillit répondre :

— Seulement dans les quartiers riches.

Mais il se souvint qu'on trouve des hôtels particuliers et des immeubles de luxe dans les vieux quartiers aussi.

Une fois dans son bureau, il appela Moers.

— Tu as trouvé quelque chose?

— Je ne sais pas si cela peut vous servir.

En examinant les vêtements à la loupe, mes hommes ont mis la main sur trois ou quatre poils qu'ils ont étudiés au microscope. Delage, qui s'y connaît, affirme que ce sont des poils de chat sauvage.

— Sur quelle partie des vêtements se trouvaient-ils?

— Dans le dos, vers l'épaule gauche. Il y a aussi des traces de poudre de riz. Nous arriverons peut-être à en déterminer la marque, mais ce sera plus long.

— Je te remercie. Fumel ne t'a pas appelé?

— Il vient de passer. Je lui ai donné le tuyau.

— Où est-il?

— Aux Sommiers, plongé dans le dossier Cuendet.

Maigret se demanda un moment pourquoi ses paupières picotaient et il se souvint qu'il avait été tiré du lit à quatre heures du matin.

Il dut donner des signatures, remplir plusieurs formulaires, recevoir deux personnes qui l'attendaient et qu'il écouta d'une oreille distraite. Une fois seul, il appela un important fourreur de la rue La Boétie, dut insister longtemps pour l'avoir en personne au bout du fil.

— Commissaire Maigret, de la P. J. Je vous demande pardon de vous déranger, mais je voudrais que vous me donniez un renseignement. Pouvez-vous me dire combien il y a à

peu près de manteaux de chat sauvage à
Paris?

— De chat sauvage?

On aurait dit que l'homme était vexé par la
question.

— Ici, nous n'en avons pas. Il fut un temps,
à l'époque héroïque des premières automobiles, où notre maison en faisait pour certaines clientes et surtout pour certains clients.

Maigret revoyait de vieilles photographies
d'automobilistes qui ressemblaient à des ours.

— C'était du chat sauvage?

— Pas toujours, mais les plus beaux. On en
porte encore dans les pays très froids, au Ca-
nada, en Suède, en Norvège, dans le nord des
Etats-Unis...

— Il n'y en a plus à Paris?

— Je pense que certaines maisons en ven-
dent parfois, mais très peu. Il m'est difficile
de vous citer un chiffre exact. Je parierais
pourtant qu'il n'existe pas cinq cents manteaux de ce genre dans tout Paris et la plupart doivent être assez vieux. Maintenant...

Une idée lui venait.

— Vous ne vous intéressez qu'aux manteaux?

— Pourquoi?

— Parce qu'il nous arrive, de loin en loin,
de traiter le chat sauvage à des fins non ves-
timentaires. On en fait par exemple des couvertures à jeter sur un divan. Ces couvertures
servent aussi dans les autos...

— Il en existe beaucoup?

— En cherchant dans nos livres, je pourrais vous dire combien sont sorties de chez nous ces dernières années. Trois ou quatre douzaines, à vue de nez. Mais des fourreurs les fabriquent en série, d'une qualité plus ordinaire, bien entendu. Un instant. Je pense à autre chose. Tout en vous parlant, je viens de revoir la vitrine d'une pharmacie, non loin d'ici, avec une peau de chat sauvage que l'on vend comme remède contre les rhumatismes...

— Je vous remercie.

— Vous voulez que je vous fasse préparer une liste des...

— Si cela ne vous dérange pas trop.

C'était assez décourageant. Depuis des semaines, on recherchait Fernand sans avoir la certitude qu'il était mêlé aux récents hold-up. Cela représentait un travail presque aussi considérable que, par exemple, l'élaboration d'un dictionnaire ou même d'une encyclopédie.

Or, on connaissait Fernand, ses goûts, ses habitudes, ses manies. Par exemple, un détail tout bête pourrait aider à le faire retrouver : il ne buvait jamais que du mandarin-curaçao.

Maintenant, pour obtenir éventuellement une indication sur les assassins de Cuendet, on possédait quelques poils de chat sauvage.

Moers avait dit que ces poils avaient été trouvés dans le dos du veston, près de la manche gauche. S'ils provenaient d'un man-

teau, n'auraient-ils pas plutôt été découverts
sur le devant du complet?

Une femme avait-elle aidé à le porter, en le
tenant par les épaules?

Maigret préférait l'hypothèse de la couverture, surtout d'une couverture d'auto. Et, dans
ce cas, ce n'était pas une petite voiture quelconque, car on n'utilise guère de couvertures
de fourrure dans une 4 CV.

Depuis quelques années, Cuendet ne s'en
prenait-il pas exclusivement aux maisons
riches?

Il aurait fallu faire le tour des garages de
Paris, poser inlassablement la même question.

On frappait à la porte. C'était l'inspecteur
Fumel, le sang à la tête, les paupières rou-
geâtres. Il avait encore moins dormi que Maigret. De service la nuit précédente, il n'avait
même pas dormi du tout.

— Je ne vous dérange pas?

— Entre.

Ils étaient quelques-uns, comme ça, que le
commissaire tutoyait, des anciens d'abord,
avec qui il avait débuté et qui, à l'époque, le
tutoyaient aussi, qui n'osaient plus, qui l'ap-
pelaient maintenant monsieur le commissaire
ou, quelquefois, patron. Il y avait aussi Lucas.
Pas Janvier, il ignorait pourquoi. Et enfin les
très jeunes, comme le petit Lapointe.

— Assieds-toi.

— J'ai tout lu. En fin de compte, je ne sais
plus par quel bout commencer. Une équipe de

vingt hommes n'y suffirait pas. Je me suis rendu compte, par les procès-verbaux, que vous le connaissiez bien.

— Assez bien. Ce matin, je suis allé voir sa mère, officieusement. Je lui ai annoncé la nouvelle et je lui ai dit que tu irais la chercher tout à l'heure pour la conduire à l'institut médico-légal. Tu as des indications sur les résultats de l'autopsie?

— Rien. J'ai téléphoné au docteur Lamalle. Il m'a fait dire par son assistant qu'il enverrait son rapport, ce soir ou demain, au juge d'instruction.

Le docteur Paul, lui, n'attendait pas que Maigret l'appelle. Il lui arrivait même de grommeler :

— Qu'est-ce que je dis au juge?

Il est vrai qu'à cette époque-là la police menait l'enquête et que, la plupart du temps, le magistrat ne s'en occupait qu'une fois que le coupable avait avoué.

Il y avait alors trois étapes distinctes : l'enquête, qui était, à Paris, l'affaire du Quai des Orfèvres; l'instruction; et enfin, plus tard, après l'examen du dossier par la chambre des mises en accusation, le procès aux assises.

— Moers t'a parlé des poils?

— Oui. Du chat sauvage.

— Je viens de téléphoner à un fourreur. Tu ferais bien de te renseigner sur les couvertures

en chat sauvage qui ont été vendues à Paris.
Et, en questionnant les garagistes...

— Je suis seul là-dessus.

— Je sais, vieux.

— J'ai envoyé un premier rapport. Le juge
Cajou m'a convoqué cet après-midi, à cinq
heures. Cela va faire un drame. Comme j'étais
de service la nuit dernière, je devais être
libre aujourd'hui et quelqu'un m'attend. Je
téléphonerai, mais je sais qu'on ne me croira
pas et cela créera des complications à n'en
plus finir...

Une femme, bien sûr!

— Si je trouve quelque chose, je te passerai
un coup de fil. Surtout, ne dis pas au juge
que je m'en occupe.

— Compris!

Maigret rentra déjeuner chez lui. L'appartement était aussi propre, les parquets et les
meubles aussi bien astiqués que chez la vieille
Cuendet.

Il faisait chaud aussi et il y avait un poêle,
malgré les radiateurs, car Maigret avait toujours aimé les poêles et il avait obtenu longtemps de l'administration qu'on lui en laisse
un dans son bureau.

Il régnait une bonne odeur de cuisine. Pourtant, il lui semblait soudain qu'il manquait
quelque chose, il n'aurait pu dire quoi.

Chez la mère d'Honoré, l'atmosphère était
encore plus calme et plus enveloppante, peut-
être par contraste avec l'animation de la rue.

Par la fenêtre, on touchait presque les échoppes et on entendait les appels des marchands.

Le logement était plus bas de plafond, plus petit, plus replié sur lui-même. La vieille y vivait du matin au soir, du soir au matin. Et, Honoré absent, on n'en sentait pas moins où était sa place.

Il se demanda un instant s'il n'achèterait pas un chien et un chat, lui aussi.

C'était stupide. Il n'était pas une vieille femme, ni un gamin de la campagne venu vivre en solitaire dans la rue la plus populeuse de Paris.

— A quoi penses-tu?

Il sourit.

— A un chien.

— Tu as l'intention d'acheter un chien?

— Non. D'ailleurs ce ne serait pas la même chose. Celui-là a été trouvé dans la rue, les deux pattes cassées...

— Tu ne fais pas la sieste?

— Pas le temps, hélas!

— On dirait que tes préoccupations sont à la fois agréables et déplaisantes...

Il fut frappé par la justesse de l'observation. La mort de Cuendet le rendait mélancolique et chagrin. Il en voulait personnellement à ses assassins, comme si le Vaudois eût été un ami, un camarade, en tout cas une vieille relation.

Il leur en voulait aussi de l'avoir défiguré et de l'avoir jeté, comme une bête morte, dans une allée du bois de Boulogne, sur la terre gelée où le corps avait dû rebondir.

En même temps, il ne pouvait s'empêcher de sourire en pensant à la vie de Cuendet et, à ses manies qu'il s'efforçait de comprendre. Chose curieuse, alors qu'ils étaient si différents l'un de l'autre, il avait l'impression d'y parvenir.

Certes, au début de sa carrière, si l'on peut dire, quand il n'était qu'un maigre apprenti, Honoré s'était fait la main de la façon la plus banale qui soit, celle de tous les mauvais garçons nés dans des quartiers pauvres, chipant sans distinction ce qui se trouvait à sa portée.

Il ne revendait même pas les objets acquis de la sorte, les entassait dans sa mansarde, comme un jeune chien entasse des croûtons et de vieux os sous sa paillasse.

Pourquoi, considéré comme un soldat modèle, avait-il déserté par deux fois? Gauchement! Bêtement! Les deux fois, il s'était laissé reprendre sans tenter de fuir ou de résister.

A Paris, dans le quartier de la Bastille, il se perfectionnait et on commençait à voir se dessiner sa manière. Il n'appartenait à aucune bande. Il n'avait pas d'amis. Il travaillait seul.

Serrurier, chaudronnier, bricoleur, habile de ses mains, méticuleux, il apprenait à pénétrer dans des magasins, dans des ateliers, dans des entrepôts.

Il n'était pas armé. Il n'avait jamais possédé une arme, fût-ce un couteau à cran d'arrêt.

Pas une fois il n'avait provoqué l'alarme, laissé une trace. C'était l'homme silencieux par excellence, dans sa vie comme dans son travail.

Quels étaient ses rapports avec les femmes? On n'en trouvait pas dans sa vie. Il n'avait jamais cohabité qu'avec sa mère et, s'il s'offrait des amours de passage, il devait le faire discrètement, dans des quartiers éloignés où nul ne le remarquait.

Il pouvait rester des heures assis dans un café, près de la vitre, devant une chopine de vin blanc. Il pouvait aussi guetter, pendant des journées entières, à la fenêtre d'une chambre meublée, tout comme, rue Mouffetard, il lisait au coin du feu.

Il n'avait presque pas de besoins. Or, la liste des bijoux volés, pour ne parler que des vols qu'on pouvait raisonnablement lui attribuer, représentait une fortune.

Lui arrivait-il d'aller, ailleurs qu'à Paris, mener une autre vie et dépenser son argent?

— Je pense, expliquait Maigret à sa femme, à un drôle de type, un cambrioleur...

— Celui qui a été assassiné ce matin?

— Comment le sais-tu?

— C'est dans le journal de midi qu'on vient de me monter.

— Laisse voir.

— Il n'y a que quelques lignes. Je suis tombée dessus par hasard.

Un cadavre au bois de Boulogne.

La nuit dernière vers trois heures, deux agents cyclistes du XVI° arrondissement ont découvert, dans une allée du bois de Boulogne, le corps d'un homme au crâne défoncé. Il s'agit d'Honoré Cuendet, d'origine suisse, 50 ans, repris de justice. Selon le juge d'instruction Cajou, qui a été chargé de l'affaire et qui s'est transporté sur les lieux en compagnie du substitut Kernavel et du médecin légiste, il s'agirait d'un règlement de comptes.

— Qu'est-ce que tu disais?

Le « règlement de comptes » le mettait en boule, car cela signifiait que, pour ces messieurs du Palais de Justice, l'affaire était pratiquement enterrée. Comme disait un procureur :

« Qu'ils s'entretuent donc jusqu'au dernier. C'est autant de besogne en moins pour le bourreau et autant de gagné pour le contribuable. »

— Je disais... Ah! oui... Imagine un cambrioleur qui choisirait, exprès, des maisons ou des appartements occupés...

— Pour y pénétrer?

— Oui. Chaque année, à Paris, et pour ainsi dire à chaque saison, des appartements restent vides pendant plusieurs semaines tandis

que les locataires sont à la mer, à la mon-
tagne, dans leur château ou à l'étranger.

— On les cambriole, non?

— On les cambriole, c'est vrai. Des spécialistes, qui ne s'attaqueront jamais à une habi-
tation où ils risquent de rencontrer des gens.

— Où veux-tu en venir?

— A mon Cuendet qui, lui, ne s'intéresse
qu'aux appartements occupés. Souvent, il attend, pour y pénétrer, que les maîtres soient
rentrés du théâtre ou d'ailleurs, que la femme
ait déposé ses bijoux dans une pièce voisine
ou même, parfois, sur un meuble de la chambre à coucher.

Mme Maigret répliqua avec logique :

— S'il opérait quand la femme se trouve à
une soirée, il ne trouverait pas les bijoux,
puisque tu dis qu'elle les porte.

— Il en trouverait probablement d'autres,
en tout cas, des objets de valeur, des tableaux,
de l'argent liquide.

— Tu veux dire que, chez lui, c'est une
sorte de vice?

— Le mot est peut-être trop fort, mais je
soupçonne que c'était une manie, qu'il ressentait un certain plaisir à s'introduire dans la
vie toute chaude des gens. Une fois, il a pris
un chronomètre sur la table de nuit d'un
homme qui dormait et qui n'a rien entendu.

Elle souriait aussi.

— Combien de fois l'as-tu attrapé?

— Il n'a été condamné qu'une fois, et en-

core n'avait-il pas alors adopté cette technique et volait-il comme tout le monde. Nous
n'en possédons pas moins, au bureau, une
liste des cambriolages qui peuvent lui être
attribués à coup presque sûr. Dans certains
cas, il a loué une chambre pendant plusieurs
semaines en face des locaux cambriolés et il ne
fournit aucune explication plausible.

— Pourquoi l'a-t-on assassiné?

— C'est ce que je me demande. Pour le
savoir, j'ai besoin de découvrir à quelle maison il s'est attaqué, la nuit dernière probablement...

Il en avait rarement autant dit à sa femme
sur une affaire en cours sans doute parce que,
pour lui, ce n'était pas une affaire comme les
autres et il n'en était même pas chargé.

Cuendet l'intéressait en tant qu'homme et
en tant que spécialiste, le fascinait presque,
tout comme la vieille Justine.

— *Je suis sûre qu'il ne me laissera pas
sans rien...* avait-elle dit avec confiance.

Pourtant, Maigret en était persuadé, elle
ignorait où son fils cachait l'argent.

Elle avait confiance, la foi du charbon-
nier : Honoré était incapable de la laisser sans
ressources.

Comment cet argent parviendrait-il jusqu'à
elle? Quelles mesures son fils avait-il prises,
lui qui, pas une fois dans sa vie, n'avait eu de
complices?

Et pouvait-il prévoir qu'un jour il serait assassiné?

Le plus curieux, c'est que Maigret en arrivait à partager la confiance de la vieille, à croire, lui aussi, que Cuendet avait envisagé toutes les éventualités.

Il buvait son café à petites gorgées. Allumant sa pipe, il jetait un coup d'œil au buffet. Comme rue Mouffetard, il y avait là un carafon, avec une eau-de-vie blanche qui, ici, était de l'eau-de-vie de prunes.

Mme Maigret avait compris et lui en servait un petit verre.

A QUATRE HEURES
moins cinq, penché sur le rond de lumière de
sa lampe qui éclairait un dossier annoté, Maigret hésitait entre deux pipes quand le téléphone sonna. C'était le central de Police-Se-
cours, boulevard du Palais.

— Hold-up rue La Fayette, entre la rue
Taitbout et la Chaussée d'Antin. On a tiré. Il
y a des morts.

Cela s'était passé à quatre heures moins dix
et déjà l'alerte générale était donnée, les voitures radio alertées, un car d'agents en uniforme quittait la cour de la police municipale
tandis que, dans son bureau paisible du Palais de Justice, le procureur général, selon des
ordres qu'il avait donnés, recevait la nouvelle
à son tour.

Maigret ouvrait la porte, faisait signe à Jan-

vier, grommelait quelques mots plus ou moins
distincts et les deux hommes descendaient l'escalier en enfilant leur pardessus, s'engouf-
fraient dans une voiture-pie.

A cause du brouillard qui avait commencé
à descendre sur la ville, jaunâtre, un peu
après le déjeuner, il faisait aussi sombre qu'à
six heures du soir et le froid, au lieu de dimi-
nuer, était devenu plus pénétrant.

— Demain matin, il vaudra mieux faire
attention au verglas, remarqua le chauffeur.

Il faisait fonctionner sa sirène, son feu cli-
gnotant. Taxis et autobus se rangeaient au
bord du trottoir et les passants suivaient la
police des yeux. Dès l'Opéra, la circulation
était perturbée. Des bouchons s'étaient formés.
Des agents arrivés en renfort sifflaient et ges-
ticulaient.

Rue La Fayette, du côté des Galeries et du
Printemps, c'était l'heure de pointe, une foule
dense, surtout composée de femmes, sur les
trottoirs; c'était aussi l'endroit le plus illu-
miné de Paris.

On avait canalisé la foule, établi des bar-
rages. Un tronçon de la rue était désert, avec
seulement quelques silhouettes sombres d'of-
ficiels qui allaient et venaient.

Le commissaire de police du IX⁰ était arrivé avec plusieurs de ses hommes. Des spécialistes prenaient des mesures et faisaient
des marques à la craie. Une auto, ses deux
roues avant sur le trottoir, avait son pare-

brise en éclats et, à deux ou trois mètres, on
voyait une tache sombre autour de laquelle
des gens discutaient à mi-voix.

Un petit monsieur à cheveux gris, vêtu de
noir, un foulard de laine tricotée autour du
cou, tenait encore à la main le verre de rhum
qu'on était allé lui chercher à la brasserie
d'en face. C'était le caissier d'un grand magasin d'articles de ménage de la rue de Châ-
teaudun.

Il recommençait son récit pour la troisième
ou la quatrième fois, en évitant de se tourner
vers une forme humaine, recouverte d'un
tissu râpeux, étendue à quelques mètres.

Derrière les barrières mobiles, comme
celles dont la ville se sert pour les cortèges,
la foule poussait et les femmes, excitées, parlaient d'une voix aiguë.

— Comme toutes les fins de mois...

Maigret avait oublié qu'on était le 31.

— ... j'étais allé chercher à la banque, derrière l'Opéra, l'argent nécessaire à la paie du
personnel...

Maigret, en passant, avait vu le magasin
sans soupçonner son importance. Il comportait trois étages de rayons, deux sous-sols et
trois cents personnes y étaient occupées.

— J'avais à peine six cents mètres à parcourir. Je tenais ma mallette de la main gauche.

— Elle n'était pas attachée à votre poignet
par une chaîne?

Ce n'était pas un encaisseur professionnel et aucun dispositif d'alarme n'était prévu. Le caissier avait seulement un automatique dans la poche droite de son pardessus.

Il avait traversé la rue entre les lignes jaunes. Il se dirigeait vers la rue Taitbout, dans une foule si dense qu'aucun attentat ne paraissait possible. Soudain, il avait remarqué qu'un homme marchait très près de lui, à sa hauteur, puis, tournant la tête, il en avait vu un autre sur ses talons.

La suite avait été si rapide que l'employé s'était mal rendu compte du déroulement des événements. Il se souvenait surtout des mots murmurés à son oreille :

— Si tu tiens à ta peau, fais pas le mariole !

Au même moment, on lui arrachait violemment sa mallette. Un des hommes se précipitait vers une auto qui venait en sens inverse, rasant le trottoir au ralenti. Entendant une détonation le caissier avait d'abord cru que c'était sur lui qu'on tirait. Des femmes criaient, se bousculaient. Un second coup de feu avait été suivi d'un bruit de verre brisé.

Il y en avait eu d'autres, certains disaient trois, certains quatre ou cinq.

Un personnage rougeaud se tenait à l'écart avec le commissaire de police. Il était assez ému, ne sachant pas encore si on allait le traiter en héros ou lui réclamer des comptes.

C'était l'agent Margeret, du 1er arrondissement. N'étant pas de service cet après-midi-là, il ne portait pas son uniforme. Pourquoi avait-il néanmoins son automatique en poche? Il aurait à s'en expliquer plus tard.

— J'allais rechercher ma femme qui faisait des courses... J'ai assisté au hold-up... Quand les trois hommes se sont précipités vers l'auto...

— Ils étaient trois?

— Un de chaque côté du caissier, un autre derrière...

L'agent Margeret avait tiré. Un des bandits était tombé à genoux, puis s'était étendu lentement sur le trottoir parmi les jambes des femmes qui se mettaient à courir.

L'auto fonçait dans la direction de Saint-Augustin. L'agent de la circulation sifflait. On tirait, de la voiture, qui avait bientôt disparu dans le trafic.

Pendant deux jours, Maigret n'allait guère avoir le temps de penser à son Vaudois paisible et, deux fois, l'inspecteur Fumel l'appela au téléphone alors qu'il était trop occupé pour répondre.

On avait relevé le nom et l'adresse d'une cinquantaine de témoins, y compris la marchande de gaufres dont le stand était tout proche, un infirme au violon qui mendiait à quelques pas et deux des garçons de café qui travaillaient en face, ainsi que la caissière qui prétendait avoir tout vu, bien que les vitres fussent embuées.

Il y avait un second mort, un passant de

trente-cinq ans, père de famille, tué sur le coup sans se douter de ce qui lui arrivait.

Pour la première fois depuis que cette série de hold-up avait commencé, on tenait un membre de la bande, celui que l'agent Margeret, qui se trouvait miraculeusement sur place, avait abattu.

— Mon idée était de lui tirer dans les jambes pour l'empêcher de fuir...

La balle n'en avait pas moins atteint l'homme à la nuque et, à l'hôpital Beaujon où une ambulance l'avait transporté, il restait dans le coma.

Lucas, Janvier, Torrence se relayaient à la porte de sa chambre, guettant l'instant où il pourrait enfin parler, car on ne désespérait pas de le sauver.

Le lendemain, comme le chauffeur de la voiture-pie l'avait prévu, les rues de Paris étaient couvertes de verglas. Il faisait sombre. Les autos n'avançaient qu'au pas. Des camions de la municipalité répandaient du sable dans les principales artères.

Le grand couloir de la P. J. était plein de gens qui attendaient en silence et Maigret, avec chacun, reprenait patiemment les mêmes questions en traçant des signes cabalistiques sur un plan des lieux dressé par les services compétents.

Dès le soir du hold-up, il s'était rendu à Fontenay-aux-Roses, au domicile du gangster abattu, un nommé Joseph Raison, que sa carte d'identité donnait comme ajusteur.

Dans un immeuble neuf, il avait trouvé un appartement clair et coquet, une jeune femme blonde, deux petites filles de six et neuf ans occupées à leurs devoirs.

Joseph Raison, qui avait quarante-deux ans, était vraiment ajusteur et travaillait dans une usine du quai de Javel. Il possédait une 2 CV et, chaque dimanche, emmenait sa famille à la campagne.

Sa femme prétendait n'y rien comprendre et Maigret la croyait sincère.

— Je ne vois pas pourquoi il aurait fait ça, monsieur le commissaire. Nous étions heureux. Nous avions acheté cet appartement il y a à peine deux ans. Joseph gagnait bien sa vie. Il ne buvait pas, ne sortait presque jamais seul...

Le commissaire l'avait conduite à Beaujon pendant qu'une voisine gardait les enfants. Elle avait pu voir son mari pendant quelques instants puis, malgré son insistance, sur l'ordre des médecins, on l'avait ramenée chez elle.

Il fallait maintenant s'y retrouver dans le fouillis de témoignages confus et contradictoires. Certains en avaient trop vu, d'autres pas assez.

— Si je parle, ces gens-là sauront bien me retrouver...

Il en ressortait malgré tout une description

à peu près plausible des deux hommes qui avaient encadré le caissier, surtout de celui qui avait arraché la serviette.

Mais c'est seulement en fin d'après-midi qu'un des garçons de café crut reconnaître Fernand sur une des photographies qu'on lui montrait.

— Il est entré dans l'établissement dix ou quinze minutes avant le hold-up et m'a commandé un café-crème. Il était assis à un guéridon près de la porte, tout contre la vitre...

Le deuxième jour après le drame, Maigret obtenait un autre témoignage au sujet de Fernand qui était vêtu, le 31 janvier, d'un épais manteau brun.

Ce n'était pas grand-chose, mais cela indiquait que le commissaire ne s'était pas trompé en pensant que l'ancien prisonnier de Saint-Martin-de-Ré était la tête de la bande.

Le blessé, à Beaujon, avait repris connaissance pendant quelques instants mais n'avait fait que murmurer :

— Monique...

C'était le prénom de sa plus jeune fille.

Maigret était fort intéressé par une autre découverte : c'est que Fernand ne recrutait plus exclusivement ses hommes parmi les mauvais garçons.

Le Parquet lui téléphonait d'heure en heure et il envoyait rapport sur rapport. Il ne pouvait sortir de son bureau sans être entouré d'une grappe de journalistes.

A onze heures, le vendredi, le couloir était
enfin vide. Maigret discutait avec Lucas qui
venait de Beaujon, lui parlait de l'opération
qu'un chirurgien connu allait tenter sur le
blessé. On frappa à la porte. Il cria, impatient :

— Entrez!

C'était Fumel qui, sentant le moment mal
choisi, se faisait tout petit. Il devait avoir
attrapé un rhume de cerveau, car il avait le
nez rouge, les yeux humides.

— Je peux revenir...

— Entre!

— Je crois que j'ai trouvé une piste... Ou
plutôt c'est la brigade des garnis qui l'a trouvée
pour moi... Je sais où Cuendet a vécu pendant
les cinq dernières semaines...

— C'était un soulagement, un délassement
presque, pour Maigret, d'entendre parler de
son Vaudois tranquille.

— Dans quel quartier?

— Son ancien quartier... Il occupait une
chambre dans un petit hôtel de la rue Neuve-
Saint-Pierre...

— Derrière l'église Saint-Paul?

Une rue étroite, vieillotte, entre la rue Saint-
Antoine et les quais. C'était rare d'y voir passer une auto et il n'y avait que quelques boutiques.

— Raconte.

— Il paraît que c'est surtout un hôtel de
passe. Ils ont pourtant quelques chambres au

mois. Cuendet y vivait sans se faire remarquer, ne sortant guère de chez lui que pour aller manger dans un petit restaurant qu'on appelle le Petit Saint-Paul.

— Qu'est-ce qu'il y a en face de l'hôtel?

— Une maison du XVIIIe siècle, avec une cour d'honneur et de hautes fenêtres, qu'on a entièrement restaurée il y a quelques années...

— Qui l'habite?

— Une dame seule, avec ses domestiques, bien entendu. Une certaine Mme Wilton.

— Tu t'es renseigné sur elle?

— J'ai commencé mais, dans le quartier, on ne sait à peu près rien.

C'était la mode, depuis une dizaine d'années, pour les gens fort riches, de racheter un vieil immeuble du Marais, rue des Francs-Bourgeois, par exemple, et de le remettre plus ou moins dans son état primitif.

Cela avait commencé par l'île Saint-Louis et, maintenant, on cherchait les anciens hôtels particuliers partout où il s'en trouvait encore, fût-ce dans les rues les plus populeuses.

— Il y a même un arbre dans la cour... On ne voit pas beaucoup d'arbres dans le quartier...

— La dame est veuve?

— Divorcée. Je suis allé voir un journaliste à qui je donne parfois des tuyaux, quand cela ne peut pas nuire... C'est lui qui, cette fois, m'a renseigné... Bien que divorcée, elle voit

encore assez souvent son ancien mari et il leur
arrive de sortir ensemble...

— Comment s'appelle-t-il?

— Wilton. Stuart Wilton. Avec son autorisation, paraît-il, elle a conservé son nom. Son
nom de jeune fille, que j'ai trouvé au commissariat du quartier, est Florence Lenoir.
Sa mère était repasseuse rue de Rennes et
son père, qui est mort depuis longtemps, agent
de police. Elle a fait du théâtre. D'après mon
journaliste, elle dansait avec une troupe de
girls au Casino de Paris et Stuart Wilton,
déjà marié, a divorcé pour l'épouser...

— Il y a combien de temps?

Maigret crayonnait sur son buvard, évo-
quant Honoré Cuendet à la fenêtre du petit
hôtel louche.

— Une dizaine d'années à peine... L'hôtel
particulier appartenait à Wilton. Il en possède
un autre, qu'il habite actuellement, à Au-
teuil, et le château de Besse, près de Maisons-
Laffitte...

— Il fait courir?

— Pas d'après mes renseignements, c'est
un assidu des courses, mais il ne possède pas
d'écurie.

— Il est américain?

— Anglais. Il vit en France depuis très
longtemps.

— D'où vient sa fortune?

— Je ne fais toujours que vous répéter ce
qu'on m'a raconté. Il appartient à une famille

de gros industriels et a hérité d'un certain
nombre de brevets. Cela rapporte beaucoup
d'argent sans qu'il ait à s'en occuper. Il voyage
une partie de l'année, loue, chaque été, une
villa au Cap-d'Antibes ou au Cap-Ferrat et appartient à un certain nombre de clubs. Mon
journaliste affirme que c'est un homme fort
connu, mais seulement dans un milieu fermé
dont on parle rarement dans les journaux...

Maigret se leva en soupirant, alla décrocher
son manteau, s'entoura le cou de son écharpe.

— Allons! dit-il.

Et, à Lucas :

— Si on me demande, je serai ici dans
une heure.

A cause du gel, du verglas, les rues étaient
presque aussi désertes qu'au mois d'août et
il n'y avait pas un seul enfant à jouer dans
l'étroite rue Neuve-Saint-Pierre. La porte en-
trouverte de l'hôtel Lambert était surmontée
d'un globe laiteux et, dans le bureau qui sentait le renfermé, un homme, le dos collé au
radiateur, lisait le journal.

Il reconnut l'inspecteur Fumel et grogna en
se levant :

— Les ennuis commencent, à ce que je
vois!

— Il n'y aura aucun ennui pour vous si
vous vous taisez. La chambre de Cuendet est-
elle occupée?

— Pas encore. Il avait payé le mois d'avance.
J'aurais pu en disposer le 31 janvier mais,

comme il y a encore ses affaires, j'ai préféré
attendre.

— Quand a-t-il disparu?

— Je ne sais pas. Attendez que je compte.
Si je ne me trompe pas, cela doit être samedi
dernier... samedi ou vendredi... On pourra le
demander à la femme de chambre...

— Il vous a prévenu qu'il s'absentait?

— Il n'a rien dit du tout. D'ailleurs, il ne disait jamais rien.

— Le soir de sa disparition, il est sorti
tard?

— C'est ma femme qui l'a vu. La nuit,
les clients qui entrent avec une femme n'aiment pas être reçus par un homme. Cela
les gêne. Alors...

— Elle ne vous en a pas parlé?

— Bien sûr que si. D'ailleurs, vous pourrez
la questionner tout à l'heure. Elle ne tardera
pas à descendre.

L'air était stagnant, surchauffé, et il régnait
une odeur équivoque, avec comme un fond
de désinfectant qui rappelait le métro.

— A ce qu'elle m'a dit, il n'est pas allé
dîner ce soir-là.

— C'était exceptionnel?

— Cela lui est arrivé quelquefois. Il s'ache-
tait de quoi manger. On le voyait monter avec
des petits paquets et des journaux. Il disait
bonsoir et on ne l'entendait plus jusqu'au lendemain.

— Ce soir-là, il est ressorti?

— Il faut bien qu'il soit sorti, puisqu'il n'était plus chez lui le lendemain matin. Mais, pour ce qui est de l'avoir vu, ma femme ne l'a pas vu. Elle était montée avec un couple, au fond du couloir du premier. Elle est allée chercher des serviettes et c'est alors qu'elle a entendu quelqu'un qui descendait l'escalier.

— Quelle heure était-il?

— Passé minuit. Elle a bien eu l'intention de voir qui c'était mais, le temps de refermer le placard à linge et de parcourir le corridor et l'homme était déjà en bas...

— Quand avez-vous su qu'il n'était plus dans sa chambre?

— Le lendemain. Sans doute vers dix ou onze heures, quand la bonne a frappé pour faire le ménage. Elle est entrée et a remarqué que le lit n'était pas défait.

— Vous n'avez pas signalé la disparition de votre locataire à la police?

— Pourquoi? Il était libre, non? Il avait payé. Je fais toujours payer d'avance. Il arrive que des gens s'en aillent comme ça sans rien dire...

— En laissant leurs affaires?

— Pour ce qu'il a laissé!

— Conduisez-nous dans sa chambre.

Le patron traîna ses pantoufles sur le plancher, sortit du bureau derrière les policiers, tourna la clé dans la serrure et la mit dans sa poche. Il n'était pas très âgé, mais il marchait

avec peine et, dans l'escalier, on l'entendait
souffler.

— C'est au troisième... soupira-t-il.

Il y avait une pile de draps sur le palier du
premier et plusieurs portes qui donnaient sur
le couloir étaient ouvertes; une domestique
s'affairait quelque part.

— C'est moi, Rose! Je monte avec des messieurs...

L'odeur devenait plus fade à mesure qu'on
avançait et, au troisième, il n'y avait plus de
tapis dans le couloir. Quelqu'un, dans sa
chambre, jouait de l'harmonica.

— C'est ici...

On voyait le chiffre 33, gauchement peint,
sur le panneau. La chambre sentait déjà le
renfermé.

— J'ai tout laissé en place.

— Pourquoi?

— Je pensais qu'il reviendrait... Il avait une
bonne tête... Je me suis demandé ce qu'il venait faire ici, surtout qu'il était bien habillé
et qu'il ne paraissait pas manquer d'argent...

— Comment savez-vous qu'il avait de l'argent?

— Les deux fois qu'il a payé, j'ai vu des
gros billets dans son portefeuille...

— Il n'a jamais reçu personne?

— Pas à ma connaissance, ni à celle de ma
femme. Un de nous deux est toujours au bureau.

— Pas pour le moment.

— Bien sûr, il nous arrive de le quitter pour quelques minutes, mais on tend l'oreille et vous avez remarqué que j'ai prévenu la bonne...

— Il ne recevait pas de courrier?

— Jamais.

— Qui occupe la chambre voisine?

Il n'y en avait qu'une, car le 33 était au bout du couloir.

— Olga. Une fille.

L'homme savait que c'était inutile de tricher, qu'on n'ignorait rien, à la police, de ce qui se trafiquait dans sa maison.

— Elle est chez elle?

— A cette heure, elle doit dormir.

— Vous pouvez nous laisser.

Il s'éloignait, maussade, traînant la jambe. Maigret refermait la porte, commençait par ouvrir une armoire bon marché, en sapin verni, avec une serrure qui ne tenait pas.

Il ne découvrit pas grand-chose : une paire de souliers noirs bien cirés, des pantoufles du type charentaises, presque neuves, et un complet gris pendu à un cintre. Il y avait aussi un chapeau de feutre sombre d'une marque courante.

Dans un tiroir, six chemises blanches, une bleu clair, des caleçons, des mouchoirs et des chaussettes de laine. Dans le tiroir voisin, deux pyjamas et des livres : *Impressions de voyage en Italie, la Médecine pour Tous* (éditée en 1899) et un roman d'aventures.

Le lit était en fer, la table ronde recouverte d'un tapis en velours vert sombre, l'unique fauteuil à moitié défoncé. Les rideaux, coincés sur leur tringle, ne fermaient plus, mais des brise-bise tamisaient la lumière.

Maigret, debout, regardait la maison d'en face, la cour d'abord, où on apercevait une grosse voiture noire de marque anglaise, le perron de plusieurs marches, la porte vitrée à deux battants.

On avait nettoyé la pierre de la façade, qui était devenue d'un gris clair très doux et, autour des fenêtres, il y avait de délicates moulures.

Une lumière brillait au rez-de-chaussée, éclairant un tapis à dessins compliqués, un fauteuil Louis XV, le coin d'un guéridon.

Les fenêtres du premier étage étaient très hautes, celles du second mansardées.

L'hôtel particulier, plus large que haut, ne devait pas comporter, en définitive, autant de pièces qu'on aurait pu le croire à première vue.

Deux des fenêtres du premier étaient ouvertes et un valet de chambre en gilet rayé passait l'aspirateur dans une pièce qui avait l'air d'un salon.

— Tu as dormi, la nuit dernière?

— Oui, patron. J'ai eu presque mes huit heures.

— Tu as faim?

— Cela ne presse pas encore.

— J'enverrai quelqu'un, tout à l'heure, pour te relayer. Tu n'as qu'à t'installer dans le fauteuil et rester devant la fenêtre. Du moment que tu n'allumes pas, on ne peut pas te voir d'en face.

N'était-ce pas ce que Cuendet avait fait pendant près de six semaines?

— Note les allées et venues et, s'il vient des voitures, essaie d'en relever le numéro.

L'instant d'après, Maigret frappait de petits coups à la porte voisine. Il devait attendre un certain temps avant d'entendre le grincement d'un sommier, puis des pas sur le plancher. La porte ne faisait que s'entrouvrir.

— Qu'est-ce que c'est?

— Police.

— Encore?

Résignée, la femme ajoutait :

— Entrez!

Elle était en chemise, les yeux bouffis. Son maquillage, qu'elle n'avait pas enlevé avant de se coucher, s'était étendu, lui déformant les traits.

— Je peux me recoucher?

— Pourquoi avez-vous dit : encore? La police est venue récemment?

— Pas ici, mais dans la rue. Depuis quelques semaines, elle ne cesse de nous houspiller et, en un mois, j'ai couché au moins six fois au dépôt. Qu'est-ce que j'ai fait, ce coup-ci?

— Rien, je l'espère. Et je vous demande de ne pas parler de ma visite.

— Vous n'êtes pas des mœurs, vous?

— Non.

— Il me semble que j'ai vu votre photographie quelque part.

Sans son maquillage fondu, ses cheveux mal teints, elle n'aurait pas été laide; un peu grasse, mais drue, les yeux encore vifs.

— Commissaire Maigret.

— Qu'est-ce qui s'est passé?

— Je n'en sais encore rien. Il y a longtemps que vous habitez ici?

— Depuis mon retour de Cannes, en octobre. Je fais toujours Cannes l'été.

— Vous connaissez votre voisin?

— Lequel?

— Celui du 33.

— Le Suisse?

— Comment savez-vous qu'il est suisse?

— A cause de son accent. J'ai travaillé en Suisse aussi, il y a trois ans. J'étais entraîneuse dans un cabaret de Genève, mais on ne m'a pas renouvelé mon permis de séjour. Je suppose que, là-bas, ils n'aiment pas la concurrence.

— Il vous a parlé? Il est venu chez vous?

— C'est moi qui suis allée chez lui. Un après-midi, en me levant, je me suis aperçue que je n'avais plus de cigarettes. Je l'avais déjà rencontré dans le couloir et il me faisait chaque fois un gentil bonjour.

— Qu'est-il arrivé?

Elle eut une mimique expressive en répliquant :

— Justement : rien! J'ai frappé. Il a mis un temps à ouvrir. Je me demandais ce qu'il fricotait. Pourtant, il était habillé et il n'y avait personne chez lui, pas de désordre. J'ai vu qu'il fumait la pipe. Il en avait une à la bouche. Je lui ai dit :

« — Je suppose que vous n'avez pas de cigarettes?

« Il m'a répondu que non, qu'il le regrettait, puis, après une hésitation, il a proposé d'aller m'en acheter.

« J'étais comme quand je vous ai ouvert la porte, avec seulement ma chemise sur le corps. Il y avait du chocolat sur la table et, quand il a vu que je le regardais, il m'en a offert un morceau.

« J'ai cru que ça y était. Entre voisins, on se doit bien ça. Je me suis mise à manger un morceau de chocolat et j'ai jeté un coup d'œil sur le livre qu'il était en train de lire, quelque chose sur l'Italie, avec de vieilles gravures.

« — Vous ne vous ennuyez pas, tout seul? lui ai-je demandé?

« Je suis sûre qu'il en avait envie. Et je ne crois pas que je sois bien impressionnante. A certain moment, j'ai compris qu'il hésitait, puis il a soudain bafouillé :

« — Il faut que je sorte. On m'attend... »

— C'est tout?

— Je crois bien que oui. Les murs ne sont

pas épais, ici. On entend les bruits d'une chambre à l'autre. Et, la nuit, il ne devait pas avoir
beaucoup de chances de dormir, si vous voyez
ce que je veux dire.

« Il ne s'en est jamais plaint. Les lavabos,
vous l'avez peut-être remarqué en montant,
sont à l'autre bout du couloir, au-dessus de
l'escalier. Il y a une chose que je peux dire,
c'est qu'il ne se couchait pas de bonne heure,
car je l'ai rencontré au moins deux fois, au
milieu de la nuit, allant aux toilettes, tout habillé. »

— Il ne vous arrive pas de jeter un coup
d'œil à la maison d'en face?

— Chez la folle?

— Pourquoi l'appelez-vous là folle?

— Pour rien. Parce que je trouve qu'elle a
l'air d'une folle. Vous savez, d'ici, on voit très
bien. L'après-midi, je n'ai rien à faire et je
regarde parfois par la fenêtre. C'est rare, en
face, qu'ils tirent les rideaux et ça vaut le coup,
le soir, d'admirer leurs lustres. D'énormes lustres de cristal, avec des douzaines de lampes...

« Sa chambre est juste devant la mienne.
C'est à peu près la seule pièce où on tire les
rideaux vers la fin de l'après-midi, mais on
les ouvre le matin et alors on dirait qu'elle ne
se rend pas compte qu'on la voit se promener
toute nue. Peut-être qu'elle le fait exprès? Il
y a des femmes qui ont ce vice-là.

« Elle a deux femmes de chambre pour s'occuper d'elle, mais elle sonne aussi bien le valet quand elle est dans cette tenue.

« Certains jours, le coiffeur vient au milieu de l'après-midi, des fois plus tard quand elle se met en grand tralala.

« Elle n'est pas mal, pour son âge, je dois l'avouer... »

— Quel âge lui donnez-vous?

— Dans les quarante-cinq piges. Seulement avec les femmes qui se soignent comme elle, on ne peut pas savoir.

— Elle reçoit beaucoup?

— Quelquefois, il y a deux ou trois voitures dans la cour, rarement plus. C'est plus souvent elle qui sort. A part le gigolo, bien entendu!

— Quel gigolo?

— Je ne prétends pas que ce soit un vrai gigolo. Il est pourtant un peu jeunet pour elle, dans les trente ans à peine. Un beau garçon, grand, brun, habillé comme un mannequin, qui conduit une magnifique voiture.

— Il vient souvent la voir?

— Je ne suis pas toujours à la fenêtre, hein! J'ai mon boulot aussi. Des jours, je commence à cinq heures de l'après-midi et cela ne me donne guère le temps de regarder chez les gens. Mettons qu'il vienne une ou deux fois par semaine? Trois fois?

« Ce dont je suis sûre, c'est qu'il lui arrive d'y coucher. D'habitude, je me lève tard mais, les jours de visite, je suis obligée de sortir au

petit matin. A croire que vos collègues le font
exprès de choisir ces heures-là! Eh! bien, deux
ou trois fois, la voiture du gigolo, comme je
l'appelle, était encore dans la cour à neuf heures.

« Quant à l'autre... »

— Il y en a un autre?

— Le vieux, quoi! Le sérieux.

Maigret ne pouvait s'empêcher de sourire
en écoutant cette interprétation des faits par
Olga.

— Qu'est-ce qu'il y a? J'ai dit une bêtise?

— Continuez.

— Il y a un type très chic, aux cheveux ar-
gentés, qui vient parfois en Rolls Royce et qui
a le plus beau chauffeur que j'aie jamais vu.

— Il lui arrive de coucher en face, lui aussi?

— Je ne crois pas. Il ne reste jamais longtemps. Autant que mes souvenirs sont exacts,
je ne l'ai jamais vu tard le soir. Plutôt vers
les cinq heures. Sans doute pour le thé...

Elle semblait tout heureuse de montrer ainsi
qu'elle savait que certaines gens, dans un univers fort éloigné du sien, prennent le thé à
cinq heures.

— Je suppose que vous ne pouvez pas me
dire pourquoi vous me posez ces questions?

— En effet.

— Et je dois me taire?

— J'y tiens énormément.

— Cela vaudra mieux pour moi, n'est-ce

pas? N'ayez pas peur. J'avais entendu parler de vous par des copines, mais je vous imaginais plus vieux.

Elle lui souriait, le corps légèrement arqué sous la couverture.

Après un court silence, elle murmura :

— Non?

Et il répondit en souriant :

— Non.

Alors, elle éclata de rire.

— Comme mon voisin, quoi!

Puis, soudain sérieuse :

— Qu'est-ce qu'il a fait?

Il fut sur le point de lui dire la vérité. Il en était tenté. Il savait qu'il pouvait compter sur elle. Il savait aussi qu'elle était capable de comprendre plus de choses que le juge d'instruction Cajou, par exemple. Peut-être certains indices qui ne lui revenaient pas à l'esprit la frapperaient-ils si elle était mise au courant?

Plus tard, si cela devenait nécessaire.

Il se dirigeait vers la porte.

— Vous reviendrez?

— C'est probable. Comment mange-t-on, au Petit Saint-Paul?

— La patronne fait la cuisine et, si vous aimez les andouillettes, vous n'en trouverez pas de meilleures dans le quartier. Seulement, les nappes sont en papier et la fille de salle est une garce.

Il était midi quand il se dirigea vers le Petit

Saint-Paul où il demanda d'abord un jeton afin de téléphoner à sa femme qu'il ne rentrerait pas déjeuner.

Il n'en oubliait pas Fernand et ses gangsters, mais c'était plus fort que lui.

5

EN REALITE, C'ETAIT
une récréation qu'il s'était offerte, comme à
la sauvette, et il en avait un peu de remords.
Pas trop cependant parce que, d'abord, Olga
n'avait pas exagéré quant à l'andouillette, ensuite parce que le beaujolais, encore qu'un
peu épais, n'en était pas moins fruité, enfin
parce que, dans un coin, devant une table sur
laquelle du papier rugueux tenait lieu de
nappe, il avait pu ruminer à son aise.

La patronne, courte et grosse, un chignon
gris sur le sommet de la tête, entrouvrait parfois la porte de la cuisine pour jeter un coup
d'œil dans la salle et portait un tablier du
même bleu qu'autrefois la mère de Maigret,
un bleu qui restait plus sombre sur les bords
et devenait plus pâle vers le milieu où on
avait frotté davantage au lavage.

C'était vrai aussi que la fille de salle, une

grande brune au teint décoloré, avait la mine
revêche, l'expression méfiante. De temps en
temps, ses traits se crispaient, au passage d'une
douleur, et le commissaire aurait juré qu'elle
venait de faire une fausse-couche.

Il y avait des ouvriers en tenue de travail,
quelques Nord-Africains, une vendeuse de
journaux vêtue d'un veston d'homme et coif-
fée d'une casquette.

A quoi bon montrer la photographie de
Cuendet à la servante ou au patron à mous-
taches qui s'occupait du vin? De la place que
Maigret occupait et qui avait sans doute été la
sienne, le Vaudois pouvait, à condition d'es-
suyer la buée sur la vitre toutes les trois minutes, surveiller la rue et l'hôtel particulier.

Il n'avait sûrement fait de confidences à
personne. On l'avait pris, comme partout,
pour un petit monsieur tranquille et, dans un
certain sens, c'était vrai.

Cuendet, dans son genre, était un artisan et,
parce que Maigret pensait en même temps aux
types de la rue La Fayette — c'était ça qu'il
appelait ruminer — il le trouvait un tantinet
démodé, comme ce restaurant, d'ailleurs, qui
ne tarderait pas à faire place à un établissement plus clair où les clients se serviraient
eux-mêmes.

Maigret avait connu d'autres solitaires, en
particulier le fameux Commodore, portant
monocle, œillet rouge à la boutonnière, des-
cendant dans les plus grands palaces, impec-

cable et digne sous ses cheveux blancs, qu'on n'avait jamais pu prendre la main dans le sac.

Celui-là n'avait jamais mis les pieds en prison et nul ne savait comment il avait fini. S'était-il retiré à la campagne sous une nouvelle identité ou bien avait-il filé ses vieux jours au soleil d'une île du Pacifique? Avait-il été assassiné par un truand qui en voulait à son magot?

Il existait des bandes organisées à cette époque-là aussi, mais elles ne travaillaient pas de la même manière et surtout leur recrutement était différent.

Vingt ans plus tôt encore, par exemple, dans une affaire comme celle de la rue La Fayette, Maigret aurait su immédiatement où chercher, dans quel quartier, pour ainsi dire dans quel bistrot fréquenté par les mauvais garçons.

Alors, ils savaient à peine lire et écrire et ils portaient leur profession sur leur visage.

Maintenant, c'étaient des techniciens. Le hold-up de la rue La Fayette, comme les précédents, avait été monté minutieusement, et il avait fallu un hasard improbable pour qu'un des hommes reste sur le carreau, la présence, dans la foule, d'un sergent de ville en congé qui, contre les règlements, était armé et, perdant son sang-froid, risquant d'atteindre un innocent dans la foule, avait tiré.

Cuendet aussi, il est vrai, s'était modernisé. Une phrase de la fille qui habitait la chambre voisine revenait à l'esprit de Maigret. Elle avait parlé des gens qui prennent le thé à cinq heures. Pour elle, c'était un monde à part. Pour le commissaire également. Le Vaudois, lui, avait pris la peine d'étudier avec soin les faits et gestes quotidiens de ces gens-là.

Il ne cassait pas de carreaux, n'utilisait pas de pince-monseigneur, n'abîmait rien.

Dehors, les passants marchaient vite, les mains dans les poches, le visage raide de froid, chacun avec ses petites affaires, ses petites préoccupations dans la tête, chacun avec son drame personnel et la nécessité, pour tous, de faire quelque chose.

— L'addition, mademoiselle...

Elle crayonnait les chiffres sur la nappe en papier gaufré en remuant les lèvres et en regardant parfois l'ardoise sur laquelle étaient écrits les prix des plats.

Il retourna au bureau à pied et, dès qu'il s'assit à sa place, devant ses dossiers et ses pipes, la porte livra passage à Lucas. Ils ouvrirent la bouche en même temps. Le commissaire parla le premier.

— Il faudrait envoyer quelqu'un relayer Fumel, rue Neuve-Saint-Pierre, à l'hôtel Lambert.

Pas quelqu'un appartenant à ce qu'on aurait pu appeler son équipe personnelle, mais un homme comme Lourtie, par exemple, ou comme Lesueur. Ni l'un ni l'autre n'était libre et c'est Baron qui quitta un peu plus tard le Quai des Orfèvres avec des instructions.

— Et toi ? Que voulais-tu me dire ?

— Il y a du nouveau. L'inspecteur Nicolas a peut-être mis le doigt sur quelque chose.

— Il est ici ?

— Il vous attend.

— Fais-le entrer.

C'était un homme qui passait inaperçu et, pour cette raison, on l'avait envoyé rôder à Fontenay-aux-Roses. Sa mission était de faire parler, sans en avoir l'air, les voisins du ménage Raison, les fournisseurs, les ouvriers du garage où le gangster blessé laissait sa voiture.

— Je ne sais pas encore, patron, si ça nous conduira quelque part, mais j'ai l'impression qu'on tient peut-être un bout du fil. Hier soir, déjà, j'ai appris que Raison et sa femme fréquentaient un autre ménage qui habite l'immeuble. Ils étaient même très amis. Le soir, il leur arrivait de regarder la télévision ensemble. Quand ils allaient au cinéma, une des deux femmes gardait les enfants de l'autre en même temps que les siens.

« Ces gens-là s'appellent Lussac. Ils sont plus jeunes que les Raison. René Lussac n'a que trente et un ans et sa femme deux ou trois ans de moins. Elle est très jolie et ils ont un petit garçon de deux ans et demi.

« Selon vos instructions, je me suis donc attaché à René Lussac, qui est représentant de commerce pour une maison d'instruments de musique. Il a une voiture, lui aussi, une Floride.

« Hier soir, je l'ai suivi quand il est sorti de chez lui après le dîner. Je disposais d'une bagnole. Il ne se doutait pas que j'étais derrière lui, sinon il m'aurait semé sans peine.

« Il s'est rendu dans un café de la porte de Versailles, le café des Amis, un endroit calme, fréquenté par des commerçants du quartier qui viennent y faire leur partie de cartes.

« Deux personnages l'y attendaient et ils ont joué à la belote comme des gens qui ont l'habitude d'occuper la même table.

« Cela m'a paru bizarre. Lussac n'a jamais habité le quartier de la porte de Versailles. Je me suis demandé pourquoi il venait de si loin pour faire sa partie dans un établissement assez peu attrayant. »

— Tu étais à l'intérieur du café?

— Oui. J'étais sûr qu'il ne m'avait pas repéré à Fontenay-aux-Roses et je ne risquais rien en me montrant. Il ne s'est pas occupé de moi. Tous les trois jouaient normalement, mais il leur arrivait assez souvent de regarder l'heure.

« A neuf heures et demie, exactement, Lussac a demandé un jeton à la caisse et s'est enfermé dans la cabine téléphonique, où il est resté environ dix minutes. Je pouvais le voir à travers la vitre. Il ne téléphonait pas à Paris car, après avoir décroché une première fois, il n'a dit que quelques mots et a raccroché. Sans sortir de la cabine, il a attendu et la sonnerie a retenti quelques instants plus

tard. Autrement dit, la communication a passé
par l'inter ou par le régional.

« Quand il est retourné à sa table, il semblait
soucieux. Il leur a dit quelques mots, puis a
regardé autour de lui d'un air méfiant et leur
a fait signe de reprendre la partie. »

— Comment sont les deux autres?

— Je suis sorti avant eux et j'ai attendu
dans ma voiture. Ce n'était plus la peine, ai-
je pensé, de suivre Lussac, qui retournerait
sans doute à Fontenay-aux-Roses. J'ai choisi
un de ses compagnons, au petit bonheur. Chacun avait son auto. Celui qui m'a paru le plus
âgé est monté le premier dans la sienne et je
l'ai suivi jusqu'à un garage de la rue La Boétie.
Il y a laissé sa voiture et s'est ensuite dirigé
vers un immeuble de la rue de Ponthieu, derrière les Champs-Elysées, où il occupe un stu-
dio meublé.

« Il s'agit d'un nommé Georges Macagne.
J'ai fait vérifier ce matin par le service des
garnis. Ensuite, je suis monté aux Sommiers et
j'ai trouvé son casier judiciaire. Il a été
condamné deux fois pour vol de voitures et
une fois pour coups et blessures... »

C'était peut-être enfin la fissure, qu'on attendait depuis si longtemps.

— J'ai préféré ne pas interroger les patrons
du café.

— Tu as bien fait. Je vais demander une
commission rogatoire au juge d'instruction et
tu iras au central téléphonique afin qu'ils re-

cherchent à qui René Lussac a téléphoné hier soir. Ils ne feront rien sans un ordre écrit.

Comme l'inspecteur quittait son bureau, Maigret appela l'hôpital Beaujon, eut quelque peine à obtenir au bout du fil l'inspecteur en fonction à la porte de Raison.

— Où en est-il?

— J'attendais justement quelques minutes pour vous téléphoner. On est allé chercher sa femme. Elle vient d'arriver. Je l'entends qui pleure dans sa chambre. Attendez. L'infirmière-chef sort à l'instant. Vous restez à l'appareil?

Maigret continuait à entendre les bruits assourdis d'un couloir d'hôpital.

— Allô! C'est bien ce que je pensais. Il est mort.

— Il n'a pas parlé?

— Il n'a même pas repris connaissance. Sa femme est couchée de tout son long au milieu de la chambre, le visage sur le plancher, et sanglote.

— Elle t'a remarqué?

— Certainement pas dans l'état où elle est.

— Elle est arrivée en taxi?

— Je ne sais pas.

— Descends jusqu'à la grande porte et attends. Suis-la à tout hasard, pour le cas où elle aurait envie de prendre contact avec quelqu'un ou de téléphoner.

— Compris, patron.

Peut-être était-ce une affaire à peu près ter-

minée et allait-on, grâce à un coup de téléphone, arriver enfin à Fernand. C'était assez
logique qu'il soit terré quelque part dans la
campagne, pas loin de Paris, probablement
dans une de ces auberges tenues par d'an-
ciennes filles ou par d'anciens truands.

Si le téléphone ne donnait rien, on pourrait toujours faire le tour de ces endroits-là,
mais cela risquait d'être long et rien ne prou-
vait que Fernand, qui était le cerveau de la
bande, ne changeait pas de refuge chaque jour.

Il appela le juge d'instruction qui s'occupait de l'affaire, le mit au courant, promit un
rapport qu'il se mit tout de suite à rédiger,
car le magistrat voulait en parler le soir
même au procureur.

Il signalait entre autres choses que l'auto
qui avait servi au hold-up avait été retrouvée
près de la porte d'Italie; comme on s'y attendait, c'était une voiture volée et, bien entendu, on n'y avait trouvé aucun indice, à
plus forte raison aucune empreinte digitale
intéressante.

Il était en plein travail quand l'huissier, le
vieux Joseph, vint lui annoncer que le directeur de la P. J. le priait de le rejoindre dans
son bureau. Il crut un instant qu'il s'agissait
de l'affaire Cuendet, que son chef avait eu,
Dieu sait comment, des échos de son activité,
et il s'attendit à se faire taper sur les doigts.

Il fut question, en réalité, d'une nouvelle
affaire, la disparition, depuis trois jours, de

la fille d'un personnage important. Elle avait
dix-sept ans et on avait découvert qu'elle suivait en cachette des cours d'art dramatique et
qu'elle avait fait de la figuration dans des
films qui n'étaient pas encore sortis.

— Les parents veulent éviter que cela arrive
jusqu'aux journaux. Il y a toutes les chances
pour qu'elle soit partie de son plein gré...

Il mit Lapointe sur cette affaire-là et, tandis que les vitres devenaient de plus en plus
sombres, se replongea dans son rapport.

A cinq heures, il frappait à la porte de son
collègue des Renseignements Généraux, qui
avait l'air d'un officier de cavalerie. Ici, pas
de bousculades, d'allées et venues comme à la
Criminelle. Les murs étaient tapissés de dossiers verts et la serrure était aussi compliquée
qu'une serrure de coffre-fort.

— Dites-moi, Danet, connaîtriez-vous par
hasard un certain Wilton?

— Pourquoi me demandez-vous ça?

— C'est encore assez vague. On m'a parlé
de lui et j'aimerais en savoir un peu plus sur
son compte.

— Il est mêlé à une histoire?

— Je ne crois pas.

— Vous parlez de Stuart Wilton?

— Oui.

Danet le connaissait donc, comme il connaissait toute personnalité étrangère habitant
Paris ou y faisant de longs séjours. Peut-être
même y avait-il, dans les classeurs verts, un

dossier au nom de Wilton, mais le chef des
Renseignements Généraux ne fit pas un geste
pour s'en saisir.

— C'est un homme très important.

— Je sais. Très riche aussi, m'a-t-on dit.

— Très riche, oui, et un grand ami de la
France. Il a d'ailleurs choisi d'y vivre la plus
grande partie de l'année.

— Pourquoi?

— Parce qu'il aime la vie ici, d'abord...

— Ensuite?

— Peut-être parce qu'il se sent plus libre
dans notre pays que de l'autre côté de la Manche. Ce qui m'intrigue, c'est que vous veniez
me poser des questions, car je ne vois pas le
rapport qui peut exister entre Stuart Wilton
et vos services.

— Il n'y en a pas encore.

— C'est à cause d'une femme que vous vous
occupez de lui?

— On ne peut même pas dire que je m'en
occupe. Il y a certainement une femme qui...

— Laquelle?

— Il a été marié plusieurs fois, n'est-ce pas?

— Trois fois. Et il se remariera sans doute
un jour ou l'autre, bien qu'il approche des
soixante-dix ans.

— Il est très porté sur les femmes?

— Très.

Danet ne répondait qu'à regret, comme si
on touchait indûment à un milieu qui ne concernait que lui.

— Je suppose qu'il n'y a pas que celles qu'il épouse?

— Bien entendu.

— Dans quels termes est-il avec sa dernière femme?

— Vous parlez de la Française?

— Florence, oui, celle qui, à ce qu'on m'a raconté, a appartenu à une troupe de girls.

— Il est resté en excellents termes avec elle, comme, d'ailleurs, avec ses deux précédentes épouses. La première était la fille d'un riche brasseur anglais et il en a eu un fils. Elle s'est remariée et vit à présent aux Bahamas.

« La seconde était une jeune actrice. Il n'en a pas eu d'enfant. Il n'a vécu que deux ou trois ans avec elle et il met à sa disposition une villa, sur la Côte d'Azur, où elle vit paisiblement. »

— Et, à Florence, grommela Maigret, il a donné un hôtel particulier.

Danet fronçait les sourcils, inquiet.

— C'est elle qui vous intéresse?

— Je ne sais pas encore.

— Elle ne fait pourtant pas parler d'elle. Remarquez que je n'ai jamais eu l'occasion d'étudier Wilton sous cet angle-là. Ce que j'en sais, c'est ce que chacun raconte dans un certain milieu de Paris.

« Florence, en effet, habite un des hôtels particuliers qui ont appartenu à son ex-mari... »

— Rue Neuve-Saint-Pierre...

— C'est exact. Je ne suis d'ailleurs pas certain que cet hôtel soit à elle. Comme je vous l'ai dit, Wilton, lorsqu'il divorce, reste en relations amicales avec ses épouses. Il leur abandonne leurs bijoux, leurs fourrures, mais je doute qu'il leur laisse en bien propre un hôtel particulier comme celui dont vous parlez.

— Et le fils?

— Il passe, lui aussi, une partie de son temps à Paris, mais moins que son père. Il fait beaucoup de ski en Suisse et en Autriche, participe à des rallyes automobiles, à des régates, sur la Côte d'Azur, en Angleterre et en Italie, joue au polo...

— Donc, sans profession.

— Définitivement.

— Marié?

— Il l'a été pendant un an, à un mannequin, et a divorcé. Ecoutez, Maigret, je ne veux pas jouer au plus fin avec vous. Je ne sais pas où vous essayez d'en venir, ni ce que vous avez dans la tête. Je vous demande seulement de ne rien faire sans m'en parler. Quand je dis que Stuart Wilton est un grand ami de la France, c'est vrai, et ce n'est pas pour rien qu'il est commandeur de la Légion d'honneur.

« Il possède, chez nous, d'énormes intérêts et c'est un homme à ménager.

« Sa vie privée ne nous regarde pas, à moins qu'il n'ait enfreint gravement les lois, ce qui me surprendrait.

« C'est un homme à femmes. Je ne serais

pas surpris, pour être tout à fait franc, d'apprendre qu'il a quelque manie cachée. Laquelle, je ne tiens pas à le savoir.

« Pour ce qui est de son fils et du divorce de celui-ci, je peux vous répéter ce qui a été une rumeur à l'époque, car vous l'apprendrez de toute façon.

« Lida, le mannequin que le jeune Wilton avait épousé, était une fille exceptionnellement belle, d'origine hongroise, si je ne me trompe... Stuart Wilton était opposé au mariage. Le fils a passé outre et, un beau jour, il se serait aperçu que sa femme était la maîtresse de son père.

« Il n'y a pas eu d'éclat. Dans ce milieu-là, les éclats sont rares et on s'arrange entre gens du monde.

« Le fils a donc demandé le divorce. »

— Et Lida?

— Ce que je vous raconte s'est passé il y a environ trois ans. On a vu, depuis, sa photographie dans les journaux, car elle a été tour à tour l'amie de plusieurs personnalités internationales et, si je ne me trompe, elle vit aujourd'hui à Rome avec un prince italien. C'est ce que vous vouliez savoir?

— Je l'ignore.

C'était vrai. Maigret était tenté de jouer cartes sur table, de tout raconter à son collègue. Mais les deux hommes voyaient les choses d'un point de vue trop différent.

Pour en revenir à la petite phrase du matin,

le commissaire Danet, lui, devait parfois prendre le thé à cinq heures tandis que Maigret, à midi, avait déjeuné dans un bistrot aux nappes en papier avec des ouvriers et des Nord-Africains.

— Je viendrai vous en reparler quand j'aurai une idée. Au fait, Stuart Wilton est à Paris en ce moment?

— A moins qu'il se trouve sur la Côte d'Azur. Je peux m'en assurer. Il vaut mieux que ce soit moi qui m'informe.

— Et le fils?

— Il habite le George-V, dans la partie résidence, où il a un appartement à l'année.

— Je vous remercie, Danet.

— Soyez prudent, Maigret.

— Promis!

Il n'était pas question, pour le commissaire, d'aller sonner à la porte de Stuart Wilton et de lui poser des questions. Au George-V, d'autre part, on lui répondrait d'une façon polie, mais vague.

Le juge Cajou savait ce qu'il faisait en remettant son communiqué à la presse : l'affaire du bois de Boulogne était un règlement de comptes. Ce qui signifiait qu'il n'y avait pas lieu de s'émouvoir, ni de trop chercher à savoir.

Certains crimes soulèvent l'émotion publique. Cela tient parfois à peu de choses, à la personnalité de la victime, à la façon dont elle a été tuée, ou encore à l'endroit où cela s'est passé.

Par exemple, si Cuendet avait été assassiné dans un cabaret des Champs-Elysées, il aurait eu droit à un gros titre en première page.

Mais c'était un mort presque anonyme, sans rien pour retenir l'attention des gens qui lisent leur journal dans le métro.

Un repris de justice qui n'avait jamais commis de crime sensationnel et qu'on aurait aussi bien pu repêcher n'importe où dans la Seine.

Or, c'était lui, justement, bien plus que Fernand et sa bande, qui intéressait Maigret, alors qu'il n'avait pas le droit de s'occuper officiellement de l'affaire.

Pour les gangsters de la rue La Fayette, on mettait toute la police en alerte. Pour Cuendet, le pauvre Fumel, sans voiture à sa disposition, pas sûr de se voir rembourser ses frais de taxi s'il avait le malheur d'en prendre, était seul chargé des recherches.

Il avait dû se rendre rue Mouffetard, fouiller l'appartement de Justine, lui poser des questions auxquelles elle n'avait répondu qu'à sa façon.

De son bureau, Maigret appela quand même l'institut médico-légal. Au lieu de s'adresser au Dr Lamalle ou à un de ses assistants, il préféra parler à un garçon de laboratoire qu'il connaissait depuis longtemps et à qui il avait eu l'occasion de rendre un service.

— Dites-moi, François, vous avez assisté à

l'autopsie d'Honoré Cuendet, le type du bois
de Boulogne?

— J'y étais, oui. Vous n'avez pas eu le rapport?

— Ce n'est pas moi qui suis chargé de l'enquête; j'aimerais pourtant savoir.

— Je comprends. Le docteur Lamalle pense
que le client a reçu une dizaine de coups. Il
a d'abord été frappé par-derrière, avec tant
de force que le crâne a été défoncé et que la
mort a été instantanée. Vous savez que le
docteur Lamalle est très bien? Ce n'est pas encore notre brave docteur Paul, certes, mais,
ici, tout le monde l'aime déjà.

— Les autres coups?

— Ils ont atteint le visage alors que l'homme
était couché sur le dos.

— Avec quel genre d'instrument suppose-
t-on qu'il a été frappé?

— Ces messieurs en ont longuement discuté
et ont même fait plusieurs expériences. Ce
n'est, paraît-il, ni avec un couteau, ni avec une
clé anglaise ou un outil de ce genre, comme
d'habitude. Pas avec une pince-monseigneur
non plus, ni un casse-tête. L'objet employé
présentait, ai-je entendu dire, plusieurs aspé-
rités. En outre, il était lourd et massif.

— Une statue?

— C'est la supposition qu'ils ont émise dans
leur rapport.

— Ils ont pu déterminer à peu près l'heure
de la mort?

— Selon eux, il était environ deux heures
du matin. Entre une heure et demie et trois
heures, mais plutôt vers deux heures.

— Il a beaucoup saigné?

— Non seulement il a saigné, mais de la
matière cervicale a été répandue. Il lui en
collait encore dans les cheveux.

— On a analysé le contenu de l'estomac?

— Vous savez ce qu'il contenait? Du chocolat pas encore digéré. Il y avait aussi de l'alcool, pas beaucoup, qui avait à peine commencé à pénétrer dans le sang.

— Je vous remercie, François. Si on ne vous
demande rien, ne dites pas que je vous ai téléphoné.

— Cela vaut mieux pour moi aussi.

Fumel téléphonait un peu plus tard, au
commissaire.

— Je suis allé chez la vieille, patron, et elle
m'a accompagné à l'institut médico-légal. C'est
bien lui.

— Comment cela s'est-il passé?

— Elle a été plus calme que je ne le crai-
gnais. Quand j'ai proposé de la reconduire,
elle a refusé et est partie toute seule vers la
station de métro.

— Tu as fouillé l'appartement?

— Je n'ai rien trouvé, que des livres et des
revues.

— Pas de photographies?

— Une mauvaise photo du père, en soldat
suisse, et un portrait d'Honoré bébé.

— Pas de notes? Tu as fouillé les livres?

— Rien. Cet homme-là n'écrivait pas, ne recevait pas de lettres. A plus forte raison sa mère.

— Il y a une piste que tu pourrais suivre, à condition d'être très prudent. Un certain Stuart Wilton habite rue de Lonchamp, où il possède un hôtel particulier à je ne sais quel numéro. Il a une Rolls Royce et un chauffeur. Il doit bien leur arriver de laisser l'auto au bord du trottoir ou de la confier à un garage. Essaie de voir si, à l'intérieur, il n'y a pas une couverture en chat sauvage.

« Le fils Wilton habite le George-V et a une auto aussi. »

— J'ai compris, patron.

— Ce n'est pas tout. Il serait intéressant d'avoir une photo des deux hommes.

— Je connais un photographe qui travaille sur les Champs-Elysées.

— Bonne chance!

Maigret passa une demi-heure à donner des signatures et, quand il quitta la P. J., au lieu de se diriger vers son autobus habituel, il marcha en direction du quartier Saint-Paul.

Il faisait toujours aussi froid, aussi sombre et les lumières de la ville avaient un éclat différent de leur éclat habituel, les silhouettes des passants étaient plus noires, comme si on avait gommé les demi-teintes.

Alors qu'il tournait le coin de la rue Saint-

Paul, une voix, sortant de l'obscurité, prononça :

— Alors, commissaire ?

C'était Olga, vêtue d'un manteau de lapin, qui se tenait sur un seuil. Cela lui donna l'idée de demander à la fille un renseignement qu'il allait justement chercher ailleurs, d'autant plus qu'elle était la mieux placée pour lui répondre.

— Dites-moi, quand vous avez besoin de boire un verre ou de vous réchauffer après minuit, qu'est-ce qu'il y a d'ouvert dans le quartier ?

— Chez Léon.

— Un bar ?

— Oui. Rue Saint-Antoine, juste devant le métro.

— Vous y avez parfois rencontré votre voisin ?

— Le Suisse ? Pas la nuit, non. Une fois ou deux, l'après-midi.

— Il buvait ?

— Du vin blanc.

— Je vous remercie.

Ce fut elle qui lui lança, avant de battre à nouveau la semelle :

— Bonne chance !

Il avait une photo de Cuendet en poche et il pénétra dans le bar plein de vapeurs, commanda un verre de cognac, le regretta en voyant sur la bouteille six ou sept étoiles.

— Vous connaissez cet homme ?

Le patron s'essuyait les mains à son tablier avant de saisir la photographie qu'il examinait d'un air réfléchi :

— Qu'est-ce qu'il a fait? demandait-il alors prudent.

— Il est mort.

— Comment? Il s'est suicidé?

— Qu'est-ce qui vous fait penser ça?

— Je ne sais pas... Je ne l'ai pas vu souvent. Trois ou quatre fois... Il ne parlait à personne... Le dernier soir...

— Quand était-ce?

— Je ne pourrais pas vous dire au juste... Jeudi ou vendredi dernier... Peut-être samedi... Les autres fois, il était venu boire un coup sur le zinc dans l'après-midi comme un homme qui a soif...

— Un seul?

— Mettons deux... Pas plus... Ce n'était pas ce qu'on appelle un buveur... Je les reconnais du premier coup d'œil...

— Quelle heure était-il, le dernier soir?

— Passé minuit... Attendez... Ma femme était montée... Il devait donc être entre minuit et demi et une heure du matin...

— Qu'est-ce qui fait que vous vous en souveniez?

— D'abord, la nuit, il n'y a guère que des habitués et des habituées, parfois un chauffeur de taxi en maraude... ou encore des flics qui viennent avaler un coup en fraude... Il y avait

un couple, je me le rappelle, qui parlait bas,
au guéridon du coin... A part ça, la salle était
vide... J'étais occupé avec mon percolateur...
Je n'ai pas entendu de pas... Et, quand je me
suis retourné, il était accoudé au zinc... J'ai
été tout saisi...

— C'est pour cela que vous vous en souve-
nez?

— Et aussi parce qu'il m'a demandé si
j'avais du vrai kirsch, pas du kirsch de fantai-
sie... On n'en sert pas souvent... J'ai pris une
bouteille de la seconde rangée, celle-ci, tenez,
avec des mots écrits en allemand sur l'étiquette, et cela a paru lui faire plaisir. Il a dit :

« — C'est du bon!

« Il a pris le temps de réchauffer le verre
dans le creux de sa main et a bu lentement,
en regardant l'heure à l'horloge. J'ai compris
qu'il hésitait à en commander un second et,
quand j'ai tendu la bouteille, il n'a pas résisté.

« Il ne buvait pas pour boire, mais parce
qu'il aimait le kirsch. »

— Il n'a parlé à personne?

— Sauf à moi.

— Les consommateurs du coin n'ont pas
fait attention à lui?

— C'étaient des amoureux. Je les connais.
Ils viennent deux fois la semaine et chuchotent
pendant des heures en se regardant dans les
yeux.

— Ils sont sortis peu après lui?

— Sûrement pas.

— Vous n'avez remarqué personne qui aurait pu le guetter du trottoir?

L'homme haussa les épaules, comme si on lui faisait une injure.

— Il y a quinze ans que je suis dans le coin... soupira-t-il.

Sous-entendu : rien ne pouvait s'y passer d'anormal sans qu'il s'en aperçoive.

Un peu plus tard, Maigret pénétrait à l'hôtel Lambert et c'était la patronne qui, cette fois, occupait le bureau. Elle était plus jeune, plus appétissante que le commissaire l'aurait pensé après avoir vu son mari.

— Vous venez pour le 33, n'est-ce pas? Le monsieur est là-haut.

— Je vous remercie.

Il dut se ranger contre le mur, dans l'escalier, pour laisser descendre un couple. La femme était très parfumée et l'homme détourna la tête d'un air gêné.

La chambre était dans l'obscurité, Baron assis dans le fauteuil qu'il avait tiré près de la fenêtre. Il avait dû fumer tout un paquet de cigarettes, car l'air était suffocant.

— Rien de neuf?

— Elle est sortie il y a une demi-heure. Avant cela, une femme est venue la voir, portant un grand carton, une lingère ou une couturière, je suppose. Elles sont passées toutes les deux dans la chambre à coucher et je

voyais seulement des ombres aller et venir,
puis rester immobiles, avec une des silhouettes
à genoux, comme pour un essayage.

Au rez-de-chaussée, il n'y avait de lumière
que dans le hall d'entrée. L'escalier était
éclairé jusqu'au second étage et, à gauche,
deux lampes restaient allumées dans le salon,
mais pas le grand lustre.

A droite, une femme de chambre en noir et
blanc, un bonnet de dentelle sur la tête, mettait de l'ordre dans le boudoir.

— La cuisine et la salle à manger doivent
donner sur le derrière. A les regarder vivre,
on se demande ce que ces gens-là font toute la
journée. J'ai compté au moins trois domestiques qui vont et viennent sans qu'on puisse
savoir à quoi ils s'occupent. En dehors de la
couturière ou de la lingère, il n'y a pas eu
d'autre visite. Cette femme est venue en taxi
et est repartie à pied, sans son carton. Un garçon livreur, en triporteur, a apporté des paquets. C'est le valet de chambre qui les a pris,
sans le faire entrer dans la maison. Je reste?

— Tu as faim?

— Cela commence, mais je peux attendre

— Va.

— Je ne reste pas jusqu'à la relève?

Maigret haussa les épaules. A quoi bon?

Il ferma la porte à clé, glissa celle-ci dans
sa poche. En bas, il dit à la patronne :

— Ne louez pas le 33 avant que je vous

fasse signe. Personne ne doit y entrer, vous entendez?

Dans la rue, il aperçut de loin Olga qui s'en venait au bras d'un homme et il fut content pour elle.

CHAPITRE

Il NE SAVAIT PAS, EN
se mettant à table, qu'un coup de téléphone,
tout à l'heure, l'arracherait à la tranquillité
un peu sirupeuse de son appartement, ni que
des dizaines de gens qui, en ce moment, faisaient des projets pour la soirée, allaient passer une nuit différente de celle qu'ils avaient
prévue, enfin que, jusqu'au matin, toutes les
fenêtres du Quai des Orfèvres resteraient éclairées comme les nuits de grand branle-bas.

Ce dîner était bien agréable pourtant, plein
d'intimité, de compréhension subtile entre sa
femme et lui. Il lui avait parlé de l'andouillette de midi, dans le bistrot du quartier
Saint-Antoine. Ils avaient souvent fréquenté
ensemble ce genre de restaurants-là, autrefois
plus nombreux. Typiques de Paris, on en trouvait presque dans chaque rue et on les appelait des restaurants de chauffeurs.

— Au fond, si on y mangeait si bien, c'est que les patrons venaient tous de leur province, Auvergnats, Bretons, Normands, Bourguignons et qu'ils avaient gardé, non seulement les traditions de chez eux, mais des contacts, faisant venir de leur pays, jambons et charcuterie, parfois même le pain de campagne...

Il pensait à Cuendet et à sa mère qui, eux, avaient apporté rue Mouffetard l'accent traînant du pays de Vaud, un certain calme, un certain immobilisme où il y avait comme de la paresse.

— Tu n'as pas de nouvelles de la vieille?

Mme Maigret avait suivi sa pensée dans ses yeux.

— Tu oublies qu'officiellement je ne m'occupe en ce moment que des hold-up. Ça, c'est plus grave, car ça menace les banques, les compagnies d'assurances, les grosses affaires. Les gangsters se sont modernisés plus vite que nous.

Un petit coup de cafard, en passant. Plus exactement de la nostalgie, sa femme le savait, sachant aussi que cela ne durait jamais longtemps.

A ces moments-là, d'ailleurs, il s'effrayait moins de la retraite, qui l'attendait dans deux ans. Le monde changeait, Paris changeait, tout changeait, hommes et méthodes. Sans cette retraite, qui lui apparaissait parfois comme un épouvantail, ne se sentirait-il pas dépaysé dans un univers qu'il ne comprendrait plus?

Il n'en mangeait pas moins de bon appétit, lentement.

— C'est un drôle de type! Rien ne laissait prévoir ce qui lui est arrivé et pourtant sa mère s'est contentée de murmurer, quand je me suis inquiété de son avenir :

— *Je suis sûre qu'il ne me laissera pas sans rien...*

Si c'était vrai, comment Cuendet s'y était-il pris; quelle combinaison avait-il fini par échafauder dans sa grosse tête rougeaude?

C'est alors, comme Maigret commençait son dessert, que le téléphone sonna.

— Tu veux que je réponde?

Il était déjà debout, sa serviette à la main. On l'appelait du Quai. C'était Janvier.

— Une nouvelle qui pourrait être importante, patron. L'inspecteur Nicolas vient de m'appeler. On a pu retrouver l'appel téléphonique fait par René Lussac du café de la porte de Versailles.

« Il s'agit d'un numéro des environs de Corbeil, une villa au bord de la Seine, qui appartient à quelqu'un que vous connaissez, Rosalie Bourdon. »

— La belle Rosalie?

— Oui. J'ai appelé la brigade mobile de Corbeil. La femme est chez elle.

Encore une qui avait, maintes fois, passé des heures entières dans le bureau de Maigret. A présent, elle approchait de la cinquantaine, mais c'était encore une créature appétissante, bien en chair, haute en couleur, au langage vert et pittoresque.

Elle avait débuté, très jeune, sur le trottoir, aux alentours de la place des Ternes et, à vingt-cinq ans, elle dirigeait une maison de rendez-vous fréquentée par les hommes les plus distingués de Paris.

Elle avait tenu ensuite, rue Notre-Dame-de-Lorette, un cabaret de nuit d'un genre spécial à l'enseigne de *La Cravache.*

Son dernier amant, l'homme de sa vie, était un certain Pierre Sabatini, de la bande des Corses, condamné à vingt ans de travaux forcés après avoir abattu deux membres du gang des Marseillais, dans un bar de la rue de Douai.

Sabatini était encore à Saint-Martin-de-Ré pour plusieurs années. L'attitude de Rosalie, au procès, avait été pathétique et, la condamnation prononcée, elle avait remué ciel et terre pour obtenir l'autorisation d'épouser son amant.

Toute la presse en avait parlé, à l'époque. Elle s'était prétendue enceinte. Certains avaient imaginé qu'elle s'était fait faire un enfant par le premier venu dans l'espoir de ce mariage.

Lorsque le ministère avait refusé, d'ailleurs, il n'avait plus été question de maternité et Rosalie avait disparu de la circulation, s'était

retirée dans sa villa des environs de Corbeil
d'où elle envoyait régulièrement lettres et colis
au prisonnier. Chaque mois, elle faisait le
voyage de l'île de Ré et on la tenait à l'œil,
là-bas, craignant qu'elle prépare l'évasion de
son amant.

Or, à Saint-Martin, Sabatini partageait la
cellule de Fernand.

Janvier continuait :

— J'ai demandé à Corbeil de surveiller la
villa. Plusieurs hommes sont autour en ce
moment.

— Et Nicolas?

— Il vous fait dire qu'il se rend à la porte
de Versailles. D'après ce qu'il a vu hier, son
impression est que Lussac et ses deux amis s'y
réunissent chaque soir. Il préfère s'installer
dans le café avant eux, afin de moins attirer
leur attention.

— Lucas est encore au bureau?

— Il vient de rentrer.

— Dis-lui de garder, cette nuit, un certain
nombre d'hommes sous la main. Je te rappel-
lerai dans quelques minutes.

Il se mit en communication avec le Parquet,
n'eut au bout du fil qu'un substitut de garde.

— Je désire parler au procureur Dupont
d'Hastier.

— Il n'est pas ici.

— Je sais. J'ai pourtant besoin de lui parler
d'urgence. Il s'agit des derniers hold-up et,
sans doute, de Fernand.

— Je vais essayer de l'atteindre. Vous êtes au Quai?

— Chez moi.

Il donna son numéro et, dès lors, les événements s'enchaînèrent avec rapidité. Il avait à peine fini son dessert que la sonnerie retentissait à nouveau. C'était le procureur.

— On m'apprend que vous avez arrêté Fernand?

— Pas encore, monsieur le procureur, mais nous avons peut-être une chance de l'arrêter, cette nuit.

Il le mettait au courant, en quelques phrases.

— Venez me rejoindre à mon bureau d'ici un quart d'heure. Je suis à table chez des amis, mais je les quitte immédiatement. Vous avez pris contact avec Corbeil?

Mme Maigret lui préparait du café très noir et sortait la bouteille de framboise du buffet.

— Fais attention de ne pas prendre froid. Tu crois que tu iras à Corbeil?

— Cela m'étonnerait qu'ils m'en laissent une chance.

Il ne se trompait pas. Au Palais de Justice, dans un des vastes bureaux du Parquet, il trouvait, non seulement le procureur Dupont d'Hastier, en smoking, mais le juge d'instruction Legaille, chargé du dossier des hold-up, ainsi qu'un de ses vieux camarades de l'autre maison, c'est-à-dire de la rue des Saussaies, le commissaire Buffet.

Buffet était plus grand, plus large, plus

épais que lui, le teint rouge, les yeux toujours comme endormis, ce qui ne l'empêchait pas d'être un des policiers les plus redoutables.

— Asseyez-vous, Maigret, et dites-nous où vous en êtes exactement.

Avant de quitter le boulevard Richard-Lenoir, il avait eu une nouvelle conversation téléphonique avec Janvier.

— J'attends des nouvelles, ici, d'un instant à l'autre. Je peux déjà vous affirmer qu'il y a un homme depuis quelques jours, dans la villa de Rosalie Bourdon, à Corbeil.

— Nos policiers l'ont vu? questionna Buffet, qui avait une toute petite voix pour un si gros corps, presque une voix de fille.

— Pas encore. Des voisins leur en ont parlé, et le signalement correspond assez bien avec celui de Fernand.

— Ils cernent la villa?

— D'assez loin, pour ne pas donner l'alarme.

— Il existe plusieurs issues?

— Bien entendu, mais la situation se développe par ailleurs aussi. Comme je l'ai dit tout à l'heure par téléphone au procureur, Lussac est un ami de Joseph Raison, le gangster qui a été tué rue La Fayette, et qui habitait le même immeuble que lui, à Fontenay-aux-Roses. Or, Lussac fréquente, avec au moins deux camarades, un café de la porte de Versailles, le café des Amis.

« Ils y jouaient aux cartes hier soir et, à

neuf heures et demie, Lussac s'est enfermé dans la cabine pour appeler Corbeil.

« Il apparaît donc que c'est de cette façon que les trois hommes restent en contact avec leur chef. J'attends un coup de fil d'un moment à l'autre.

« Maintenant, si, ce soir, ils se réunissent au même endroit, ce que nous ne tarderons pas à savoir, nous aurons une décision à prendre. »

Autrefois, il l'aurait prise seul, et cette sorte de conseil de guerre, dans les bureaux du Parquet, n'aurait pas eu lieu. Elle aurait même été impensable, à moins d'une affaire politique.

— Selon un témoin, Fernand se trouvait, au moment du hold-up, dans une brasserie située juste en face de l'endroit où le caissier a été assailli et où ses attaquants, moins un, ont sauté en voiture.

« Ces hommes emportaient la mallette contenant les millions.

« Il est improbable que, depuis, étant donné surtout l'accident qui s'est produit, Fernand ait pu les rencontrer.

« Si c'est lui qui se cache chez la belle Rosalie, il s'y est planqué le soir même et chaque soir, par téléphone, il donne ses instructions au café des Amis...

Buffet écoutait, l'air endormi. Maigret savait que son collègue de la Sûreté voyait les choses de la même façon que lui, envisageait les mêmes possibilités, les mêmes dangers. Ce

n'était que pour ces messieurs du Parquet
qu'il fournissait tant de détails.

— Tôt ou tard, un des complices sera
chargé de porter à Fernand tout ou une partie
du magot. Dans ce cas-là, évidemment, nous
disposerions d'une preuve absolue. L'attente
peut durer plusieurs jours. D'ici là, il est possible que Fernand cherche une autre retraite
et, même avec la villa cernée, il est capable
de nous glisser entre les doigts.

« D'un autre côté, si la réunion a lieu ce
soir, comme hier, au café des Amis, nous
avons la possibilité d'arrêter les trois hommes
en même temps qu'à Corbeil on mettrait la
main sur Fernand. »

Le téléphone sonnait. Le greffier tendait
l'appareil à Maigret.

— C'est pour vous.

C'était Janvier, qui faisait en quelque sorte
la liaison.

— Ils y sont, patron. Qu'est-ce que vous
avez décidé?

— Je te le dirai dans quelques minutes.
Envoie un de nos hommes, avec une Assistante sociale, à Fontenay-aux-Roses. Une fois
arrivé, qu'il t'appelle au téléphone.

— Compris.

Maigret raccrocha.

— Quelle est votre décision, messieurs?

— De ne pas courir de risques, prononça
le procureur. Des preuves, on finira par en
trouver, n'est-ce pas?

— Ils retiendront les meilleurs avocats, refuseront de parler et sans doute se sont-ils fabriqués d'excellents alibis.

— Par contre, si on ne les arrête pas ce soir, nous risquons de ne jamais les arrêter.

— Je me charge de Corbeil, annonça Buffet.

Maigret n'avait pas à protester. C'était en dehors de son secteur et regardait la Sûreté nationale.

Le juge d'instruction questionna :

— Vous croyez qu'ils tireront?

— S'ils en ont l'occasion, c'est à peu près certain, mais nous essayerons de ne pas leur laisser le choix.

Quelques minutes plus tard, Maigret et le gros commissaire de la rue des Saussaies passaient d'un monde à un autre en franchissant la simple porte séparant le Palais de Justice de la Police judiciaire.

Ici, on sentait déjà l'animation des grands jours.

— Il vaut mieux, avant d'attaquer la villa, attendre de savoir si, à neuf heures et demie, il y a un coup de téléphone...

— D'accord. Je préfère néanmoins être là-bas en avance, pour tout préparer. Je vous téléphonerai afin de savoir où vous en êtes.

Dans la cour obscure et froide, il y avait déjà une voiture radio dont on chauffait le moteur et un car plein de policiers. Le commissaire de police du XVIe devait se trouver quelque part aux alentours du café des Amis, avec tous ses hommes disponibles.

De paisibles commerçants y discutaient de leurs affaires, jouaient aux cartes sans se douter de rien et nul ne remarquait l'inspecteur Nicolas plongé dans la lecture d'un journal.

Il venait de téléphoner, laconique :

— C'est fait.

Cela signifiait que les trois hommes étaient là, comme la veille, René Lussac regardant parfois l'heure afin, sans doute, à neuf heures et demie, de ne pas rater son coup de fil à Corbeil.

Là-bas, autour de la villa, où deux fenêtres du rez-de-chaussée étaient éclairées, des hommes étaient figés un peu partout dans le noir, parmi les flaques de glace.

Le standard téléphonique, alerté, attendait. A neuf heures trente-cinq, il annonçait :

— On vient de demander Corbeil.

Et un inspecteur, à la table d'écoute, enregistrait l'entretien.

— Ça va? demandait Lussac.

Ce n'était pas un homme qui répondait, mais Rosalie.

— Ça va, rien de nouveau.

— Jules est impatient.

— Pourquoi?

— Il voudrait partir en voyage.

— Garde l'appareil.

Elle devait s'entretenir avec quelqu'un, revenait au téléphone.

— Il dit qu'il faut encore attendre.

— Pourquoi?

— Parce que!

— Ici, on commence à nous regarder de travers.

— Un instant.

Nouveau silence, puis :

— Demain, il y aura sans doute du nouveau.

Buffet appelait, de Corbeil :

— Ça y est?

— Oui. Lussac a téléphoné. C'est la femme qui a répondu, mais il y a quelqu'un près d'elle. Il paraît qu'un certain Jules, qui appartient à la bande, commence à s'impatienter.

— On y va?

— Dix heures un quart.

Il fallait que les deux actions soient simultanées afin d'éviter que si, avenue de Versailles, un des hommes échappait par miracle au coup de filet, il puisse donner l'alerte à Corbeil.

— Dix heures un quart.

Maigret donnait ses dernières instructions à Janvier.

— Quand Fontenay-aux-Roses appellera, fais arrêter Mme Lussac, mandat ou pas mandat. Qu'on l'amène ici et qu'on laisse l'Assistante sociale s'occuper de l'enfant.

— Et Mme Raison?

— Pas elle. Pas tout de suite.

Maigret prenait place dans la voiture radio. Le car était parti. Quelques passants, à la porte de Versailles, froncèrent les sourcils en voyant une animation inhabituelle, des hommes qui frôlaient les maisons et parlaient bas, d'autres qui disparaissaient comme par magie dans des coins obscurs.

Maigret prenait contact avec le commissaire de police, mettait au point avec lui la marche à suivre.

Une fois encore, on avait le choix entre deux méthodes. On pouvait attendre la sortie des trois joueurs de cartes qu'on apercevait de loin, derrière les vitres du café, chacun ayant, comme la veille, sa voiture à proximité.

Cela paraissait la solution la plus simple. C'était pourtant la plus dangereuse car, dehors, ces hommes auraient toute liberté de mouvement et peut-être le temps de tirer. A la faveur de la bagarre, l'un d'eux ne risquait-il pas de sauter dans son auto et de s'échapper?

— Il y a une seconde sortie?

— Une porte donne sur la cour, mais les murs sont hauts et la seule issue est le couloir de l'immeuble.

La mise en place ne dura pas un quart d'heure et n'éveilla pas l'attention des consommateurs du café des Amis.

Des hommes, qui pouvaient passer pour des locataires, entrèrent dans la maison et certains d'entre eux se postèrent dans la cour.

Trois autres, bons vivants, un verre dans le nez, poussèrent la porte du café et s'assirent à la table voisine des joueurs de cartes.

Maigret regardait sa montre, comme un chef d'état-major qui attend l'heure H et, à dix heures quatorze, il poussa, seul, la porte du café. Il avait son écharpe tricotée autour du cou, la main droite dans la poche de son pardessus.

Il n'avait que deux mètres à parcourir et les gangsters n'eurent pas le temps de se lever. Debout, tout près d'eux, il prononçait à mi-voix :

— Ne bougez pas. Vous êtes cernés. Gardez les mains sur la table.

L'inspecteur Nicolas s'était rapproché.

— Passe-leur les menottes. Vous autres aussi.

D'un mouvement brusque, un des hommes parvint à renverser la table et on entendit un bruit de verre brisé, mais deux inspecteurs lui tenaient déjà les poignets.

— Dehors...

Maigret se retournait vers les consommateurs.

— Ne craignez rien, messieurs-dames... Simple opération de police...

Quinze minutes plus tard, on débarquait les trois hommes du car et on les conduisait chacun dans un bureau du Quai des Orfèvres.

Corbeil était au bout du fil, la voix fluette du gros Buffet.

— Maigret? C'est fait.

— Sans anicroches?

— Il est quand même parvenu à tirer et un de mes hommes a une balle dans l'épaule.

— La femme?

— J'ai le visage couvert d'égratignures. Je vous les amène dès que j'en ai fini avec les formalités.

Le téléphone n'arrêtait pas de sonner.

— Oui, monsieur le procureur. Nous les tenons tous... Non. Je ne leur ai pas posé une seule question. Je les ai mis séparément dans des bureaux et j'attends l'homme et la femme que Buffet va m'amener de Corbeil...

— Soyez prudent. N'oubliez pas qu'ils prétendront que la police les a brutalisés.

— Je sais.

— Ni qu'ils ont le droit strict de ne rien dire en dehors de la présence de leur avocat.

— Oui, monsieur le procureur...

Maigret n'avait d'ailleurs pas l'intention de les interroger tout de suite, préférant les laisser mariner chacun dans son jus. Il attendait Mme Lussac.

Elle n'arriva qu'à onze heures, car l'inspecteur l'avait trouvée couchée et elle avait dû prendre le temps de s'habiller, d'expliquer à l'Assistante sociale les soins à donner éventuellement à son fils.

C'était une petite brune, maigre, assez jolie,

qui n'avait guère plus de vingt-cinq ans. Elle était pâle, les narines pincées. Elle ne disait rien, évitait de jouer la comédie de l'indignation.

Maigret la fit asseoir en face de lui tandis que Janvier s'installait au bout du bureau avec du papier et un crayon.

— Votre mari s'appelle René Lussac et exerce la profession de représentant de commerce.

— Oui, monsieur.

— Il est âgé de trente et un ans. Depuis combien de temps êtes-vous mariés?

— Quatre ans.

— Quel est votre nom de jeune fille?

— Jacqueline Beaudet.

— Originaire de Paris?

— D'Orléans. Je suis venue vivre à Paris, chez ma tante, à l'âge de seize ans.

— Que fait votre tante?

— Sage-femme. Elle habite rue Notre-Dame-de-Lorette.

— Où avez-vous rencontré René Lussac?

— Dans une maison de disques et d'instruments de musique où je travaillais comme vendeuse. Où est-il, monsieur le commissaire? Dites-moi ce qui lui est arrivé. Depuis que Joseph...

— Vous parlez de Joseph Raison?

— Oui. Joseph et sa femme étaient nos amis. Nous habitons le même immeuble.

— Les deux hommes sortaient beaucoup ensemble?

— Cela leur arrivait. Pas souvent. Depuis que Joseph est mort...

— Vous avez peur que le même accident arrive à votre mari, n'est-ce pas?

— Où est-il? Il a disparu?

— Non. Il est ici.

— Vivant?

— Oui.

— Blessé?

— Il a failli l'être, mais il ne l'est pas.

— Je peux le voir?

— Pas tout de suite.

— Pourquoi?

Elle eut un sourire amer.

— Je suis bête de vous poser cette question! Je devine ce que vous cherchez, pourquoi vous m'interrogez. Vous vous dites que ce sera plus facile de faire parler une femme qu'un homme, n'est-ce pas vrai?

— Fernand est arrêté.

— Qui est-ce?

— Vous ne le savez vraiment pas?

Elle le regarda dans les yeux.

— Non. Mon mari ne m'en a jamais parlé. Je sais seulement que quelqu'un donne des ordres.

Si elle avait tiré un mouchoir de son sac, par contenance, elle ne pleurait pas.

— Vous voyez que c'est plus facile que vous ne l'imaginiez. Il y a assez longtemps que j'ai

peur et que je supplie René de ne plus fré-
quenter ces gens-là. Il a un bon métier. Nous
étions heureux. Si nous n'étions pas riches,
nous n'avions pas une mauvaise vie. Je ne
sais pas qui il a rencontré...

— Il y a combien de temps?

— Environ six mois... C'était l'hiver dernier... Vers la fin de l'été... J'aime encore
mieux que ce soit fini, car je n'aurai plus à
trembler... Vous êtes sûr que cette femme
saura s'occuper de mon fils?

— Vous n'avez rien à craindre de ce côté.

— Il est nerveux, comme son père. Il
s'agite, la nuit...

On la sentait lasse, un peu perdue, s'effor-
çant de mettre ses pensées en ordre.

— Ce que je peux vous affirmer, c'est que
René n'a pas tiré.

— Comment le savez-vous?

— D'abord, parce qu'il en serait incapable.
Il s'est laissé entraîner par ces gens-là, sans se
figurer que cela deviendrait aussi grave.

— Il vous en parlait?

— Je voyais bien, depuis quelque temps,
qu'il rapportait plus d'argent qu'il n'aurait
dû. Il sortait davantage aussi, presque toujours avec Joseph Raison. Un jour, j'ai trouvé
son automatique.

— Qu'est-ce qu'il a dit?

— Que je n'avais pas à avoir peur, que
dans quelques mois nous pourrions aller vivre
tranquillement dans le Midi. Il avait envie

d'ouvrir un commerce à son compte, à Cannes ou à Nice...

Elle pleurait enfin, sans bruit, à petits coups.

— Au fond, c'est la faute à la voiture... Il tenait absolument à une Floride... Il a signé des traites... Puis le moment est venu de les payer... Quand il saura que j'ai parlé, il m'en voudra... Peut-être n'acceptera-t-il plus de vivre avec moi...

On entendait du bruit dans le couloir et Maigret fit signe à Janvier d'emmener la jeune femme dans le bureau voisin. Il avait reconnu la voix de Buffet.

Ils étaient trois à pousser devant eux un homme qui avait les menottes aux poignets et qui regarda tout de suite Maigret d'un air de défi.

— La femme! questionna le commissaire.

— A l'autre bout du couloir. Elle est plus dangereuse que lui, car elle griffe et elle mord.

C'était vrai que Buffet avait le visage égratigné, du sang sur le nez.

— Entre, Fernand.

Buffet entrait aussi, cependant que les deux inspecteurs restaient dehors. L'ancien bagnard inspectait les lieux autour de lui et remarquait :

— Il me semble que je suis déjà venu ici.

Il redevenait goguenard, sûr de lui.

— Je suppose que vous allez m'abrutir de questions, comme la dernière fois. J'aime mieux vous prévenir tout de suite que je ne répondrai pas.

— Quel est ton avocat?

— Toujours le même. Maître Gambier.

— Tu veux qu'on l'appelle?

— Personnellement, je n'ai rien à lui dire. Si cela vous amuse, vous, de tirer cet homme de son lit...

Toute la nuit, Quai des Orfèvres, il y eut des allées et venues dans les couloirs et de bureau à bureau. On entendait crépiter les machines à écrire. Le téléphone sonnait sans cesse, car le Parquet tenait à garder le contact et le juge d'instruction ne s'était pas couché.

Un inspecteur passait le plus clair de son temps à préparer du café et, parfois, Maigret rencontrait un de ses collaborateurs entre deux portes.

— Toujours rien?

— Il se tait.

Aucun des trois hommes du café des Amis ne reconnaissait Fernand. Chacun jouait la même comédie.

— Qui est-ce?

Et, quand on leur faisait entendre l'enregistrement de la communication avec Corbeil, ils répondaient :

— Cela regarde René. Ses affaires de cœur ne nous intéressent pas.

Celui-ci répondait :

— J'ai le droit d'avoir une maîtresse, non?

On mettait Mme Lussac en présence de Fernand.

— Vous le reconnaissez?

— Non.

— Qu'est-ce que je vous disais? triomphait l'ancien prisonnier. Ces gens-là ne m'ont jamais vu. Je suis sorti de Saint-Martin-de-Ré sans un, et un copain m'a fourni l'adresse de son amie en me disant qu'elle me donnerait à croûter. J'étais chez elle, peinard...

Maître Gambier arrivait à une heure du matin et soulevait tout de suite des points de droit.

Selon le nouveau code de procédure criminelle, la police ne pouvait détenir ces hommes plus de vingt-quatre heures, après quoi, l'affaire dépendait du Parquet et du juge d'instruction qui auraient à prendre leurs responsabilités.

Déjà, du côté du Palais, on commençait à sentir des doutes.

La confrontation entre Mme Lussac et son mari ne donnait rien.

— Dis-leur la vérité.

— Quelle vérité? Que j'ai une maîtresse?

— L'automatique...

— Un copain m'a refilé un automatique. Et après? Je suis souvent en voyage, seul sur les routes au volant de ma voiture...

Dès le matin, on irait chercher les témoins, tous ceux qui avaient déjà défilé Quai des Orfèvres, les garçons de café de la rue La

Fayette, la caissière, le mendiant, les passants, l'agent de police en civil qui avait tiré.

Dès le matin aussi, on fouillerait le logement des trois hommes arrêtés à la porte de Versailles et peut-être, chez l'un d'eux, retrouverait-on la mallette.

Ce n'était plus que de la routine, une routine un peu écœurante, harassante.

— Vous pouvez retourner à Fontenay-aux-Roses, mais l'Assistante sociale restera avec vous jusqu'à nouvel ordre...

Il la fit reconduire. Elle ne tenait plus debout et écarquillait les yeux en regardant autour d'elle comme si elle ne savait plus où elle en était.

Pendant que ses hommes continuaient à harceler les prisonniers, Maigret alla faire un tour, à pied, recevant sur son chapeau et ses épaules les premiers flocons de neige. Un bar ouvrait ses portes, boulevard du Palais, et il s'accouda au zinc, mangea des croissants chauds en buvant deux ou trois tasses de café.

Quand, à sept heures, il revint au bureau, le pas pesant, les paupières clignotantes, il fut surpris d'y trouver Fumel.

— Tu as du nouveau, aussi, toi?

Et l'inspecteur, très excité, se mettait à parler avec volubilité.

— J'étais de service, cette nuit. On m'a tenu au courant de ce que vous faisiez avenue de Versailles, mais je n'étais pas dans le coup et j'en ai profité pour appeler au téléphone des copains des autres arrondissements. Ils ont tous, à présent, la photographie de Cuendet.

« Je me disais qu'un jour ou l'autre cela donnerait peut-être quelque chose...

« Alors, comme je bavardais avec Duffieux, du XVIIIᵉ, je lui ai parlé de mon zèbre. Et Duffieux m'a dit qu'il allait justement m'appeler à ce sujet.

« Il travaille avec l'inspecteur Lognon, un de vos amis. Quand Lognon a vu la photographie, hier matin, il a tout de suite tiqué et l'a fourrée dans sa poche sans rien dire.

« La tête de Cuendet lui rappelait quelqu'un. Il s'est mis, paraît-il, à poser des questions dans les bars et les petits restaurants de la rue Caulaincourt et de la place Constantin-Pecqueur.

« Vous savez que quand Lognon a une idée en tête, il y tient. Il a fini par frapper à la bonne porte, tout en haut de la rue Caulaincourt, une brasserie à l'enseigne de La Régence.

« Ils ont reconnu Cuendet sans hésiter et ont affirmé à Lognon qu'il venait assez souvent chez eux en compagnie d'une femme. »

Maigret questionna :

— Depuis longtemps ?

— Justement, c'est le plus intéressant. Depuis des années, selon eux.

— On connaît la femme ?

— Le garçon ne sait pas son nom, mais

jure qu'elle habite dans une des maisons voisines, car il la voit passer chaque matin quand elle va faire son marché.

La P. J. tout entière s'occupait de Fernand et de ses gangsters. Dans deux heures, les couloirs déborderaient à nouveau de témoins à qui on présenterait successivement les quatre hommes. On en avait pour toute la journée et les machines à écrire n'arrêtaient pas de taper des dépositions.

Seul au milieu de cette agitation qui ne le concernait pas, l'inspecteur Fumel, les doigts brunis par la nicotine des cigarettes qu'il fumait jusqu'à l'extrême bout au point d'en avoir une marque indélébile au-dessus de la lèvre, seul Fumel venait entretenir Maigret du Vaudois tranquille dont personne ne parlait plus.

N'était-ce pas une affaire enterrée? Le juge d'instruction Cajou n'était-il pas persuadé qu'il n'aurait plus à s'en soucier?

Il avait tranché la question, dès le premier jour :

— *Règlement de comptes...*

Il ne connaissait ni la vieille Justine, ni le logement de la rue Mouffetard, encore moins l'hôtel Lambert et la somptueuse maison d'en face.

— Tu es fatigué?

— Pas trop.

— On y va, tous les deux?

C'était presque en complice que Maigret

parlait à Fumel, comme il lui eût proposé de faire l'école buissonnière.

— Quand nous arriverons là-bas, il fera jour...

Il laissa des instructions à ses hommes, s'arrêta au coin du quai pour acheter du tabac et, flanqué de l'inspecteur qui grelottait, attendit l'autobus pour Montmartre.

CHAPITRE

7

LOGNON SOUPÇON-
nait-il que Maigret attachait plus d'importance
au mort quasi anonyme du bois de Boulogne
qu'au hold-up de la rue La Fayette et à la
bande de gangsters dont les journaux seraient
pleins le lendemain?

Si oui, n'aurait-il pas suivi le fil dont il
avait saisi un bout? Dieu sait alors jusqu'où
il serait allé dans la découverte de la vérité,
car c'était sans doute le policier qui avait le
plus de flair de Paris, le plus obstiné aussi,
et celui qui aurait le plus désespérément voulu
réussir.

Etait-ce la malchance qui le poursuivait, ou
la conviction que le destin était définitivement
contre lui, qu'il n'était en somme qu'une victime désignée?

Toujours est-il qu'il finirait sa carrière comme inspecteur au commissariat du XVIII*, comme Aristide Fumel à celui du XVI*. La femme de Fumel était partie sans laisser d'adresse; celle de Lognon, malade, geignait depuis quinze ans.

Pour ce qui est de Cuendet, cela s'était sans doute passé bêtement. Lognon, occupé par autre chose, avait passé le tuyau à un collègue qui, lui-même, n'y avait pas attaché d'importance pour n'en parler à Fumel, au téléphone, qu'incidemment.

La neige tombait assez épaisse et commençait à tenir sur les toits, pas dans les rues, malheureusement. Maigret était toujours déçu de voir fondre la neige sur le trottoir.

L'autobus était surchauffé. La plupart des voyageurs se taisaient et regardaient droit devant eux, les têtes se balançant de gauche à droite et de droite à gauche, avec une expression figée.

— Tu n'as pas de nouvelles de la couverture?

Fumel, plongé dans ses pensées, sursauta, répéta comme s'il ne comprenait pas tout de suite :

— La couverture?

Il manquait de sommeil, lui aussi.

— La couverture en chat sauvage.

— J'ai regardé dans l'auto de Stuart Wilton. Je n'ai pas vu de couverture. Non seulement la voiture a le chauffage, mais encore l'air conditionné. Elle comporte même un petit bar, c'est un mécanicien du garage qui me l'a dit.

— Et celle du fils?

— Il la range d'habitude devant le Geor`ge-V. J'y ai jeté un coup d'œil. Je n'ai pas vu de couverture non plus.

— Tu sais où il prend son essence?

— La plupart du temps, chez un pompiste de la rue Marbeuf.

— Tu y es allé?

— Je n'ai pas eu le temps.

L'autobus s'arrêtait au coin de la place Constantin-Pecqueur. Les trottoirs étaient à peu près vides. Il n'était pas huit heures du matin.

— Cela doit être cette brasserie.

Elle était éclairée et un garçon balayait la sciure sur le plancher. C'était encore une brasserie à l'ancienne mode, comme on en trouve de moins en moins, à Paris, avec des boules de métal pour les torchons, un comptoir de marbre où une caissière devait prendre place devant la caisse enregistreuse et des glaces tout autour des murs. Des pancartes recommandaient la choucroute garnie et le cassoulet.

Les deux hommes entrèrent.

— Tu as mangé?

— Pas encore.

Fumel commanda du café et des brioches tandis que Maigret, qui avait déjà bu trop de café pendant la nuit et qui en avait la bouche pâteuse, commandait un petit verre d'alcool.

On aurait dit que la vie, dehors, avait du mal à embrayer. Ce n'était ni la nuit ni le jour. Des enfants se dirigeaient vers l'école en essayant de happer des flocons de neige qui devaient avoir le goût de poussière.

— Dites-moi, garçon...

— Oui, monsieur?

— Vous connaissez cet homme?

Le garçon de café regardait le commissaire d'un air entendu.

— Vous êtes M. Maigret, n'est-ce pas? Je vous reconnais. Vous êtes venu ici il y a deux ans avec l'inspecteur Lognon.

Il examinait la photographie avec complaisance.

— C'est un client, oui. Il vient toujours avec la petite dame aux chapeaux.

— Pourquoi l'appelez-vous la petite dame aux chapeaux?

— Parce qu'elle porte presque chaque fois des chapeaux différents, des bibis amusants. Le plus souvent, ils viennent pour dîner et s'installent dans le coin, là-bas, au fond. Ils sont gentils. Elle adore la choucroute. Ils ne se pressent pas, boivent ensuite leur café, dégustent un petit verre en se tenant par la main.

— Il y a longtemps qu'ils fréquentent l'établissement?

— Des années. Je ne sais pas combien.

— Il paraît qu'elle habite le quartier?

— On m'a déjà posé la question. Elle doit avoir un appartement dans une des maisons voisines, car je la vois passer presque chaque matin avec son filet à provisions.

Pourquoi cela enchantait-il Maigret de découvrir une femme dans la vie d'Honoré Cuendet?

Un peu plus tard, il pénétrait avec Fumel, dans une première loge de concierge où on triait le courrier.

— Vous connaissez cet homme?

Elle regardait avec attention, hochait la tête.

— Je pense que je l'ai déjà vu, mais je ne peux pas dire que je le connais. En tout cas, il n'est jamais venu dans la maison.

— Vous n'avez pas, parmi vos locataires, une femme qui change souvent de chapeau?

Elle regarda Maigret, ahurie, haussa les épaules en grommelant quelque chose qu'il ne comprit pas.

Ils n'eurent pas plus de succès dans le second immeuble, ni dans le troisième. Dans le quatrième, la concierge faisait un pansement à la main de son mari qui s'était coupé en sortant les poubelles.

— Vous le connaissez?

— Et après?

— Il habite la maison?

— Il habite sans l'habiter. C'est l'ami de la petite dame du cinquième.

— Quelle petite dame?

— Mlle Eveline, la modiste.

— Il y a longtemps qu'elle est dans la maison?

— Au moins douze ans. C'était avant que j'y sois moi-même.

— Il était déjà son ami?

— Peut-être bien que oui. Je ne m'en souviens pas.

— Vous l'avez vu ces derniers temps?

— Qui? Elle? Je la vois tous les jours, parbleu!

— Lui?

— Tu te rappelles la dernière fois qu'il est venu, Désiré?

— Non, mais cela fait un bout de temps.

-- Il lui arrivait de passer la nuit?

Elle semblait trouver le commissaire naïf.

— Et alors? Ils sont majeurs, non?

— Il vivait ici plusieurs jours de suite?

— Même des semaines.

— Mlle Eveline est chez elle? Quel est son nom de famille?

— Schneider.

— Elle reçoit beaucoup de courrier.

Le paquet de lettres, devant les casiers, n'était pas défait.

— Pour ainsi dire pas.

— Cinquième à gauche?

— A droite.

Maigret alla voir dans la rue s'il y avait de la lumière aux fenêtres et, comme il y en avait, s'engagea dans l'escalier avec Fumel. Il n'y avait pas d'ascenseur. L'escalier était bien entretenu, la maison propre et calme, avec des paillassons devant les portes et une plaque de cuivre ou d'émail par-ci, par-là.

Ils notèrent un dentiste au second étage, une sage-femme au troisième. Maigret s'arrêtait de temps en temps pour souffler, entendait de la radio.

Au cinquième, il hésitait presque à pousser le timbre électrique. Il y avait de la radio dans l'appartement aussi, mais on la coupa, des pas se rapprochèrent de la porte qui s'ouvrit. Une femme assez petite, aux cheveux blond clair, vêtue, non d'une robe de chambre, mais d'une sorte de blouse d'intérieur, les regardait de ses yeux bleus, un torchon à la main.

Maigret et Fumel étaient aussi embarrassés qu'elle, car ils voyaient l'étonnement, puis la crainte croître dans son regard, ses lèvres qui frémissaient et murmuraient enfin :

— Vous m'apportez une mauvaise nouvelle?

Elle leur faisait signe d'entrer dans un living-room dont elle était occupée à faire le ménage et elle repoussa l'aspirateur électrique qui se trouvait dans le chemin.

— Pourquoi demandez-vous ça?

— Je ne sais pas... Une visite, à cette heure-ci, quand Honoré est absent depuis si long-temps...

Agée d'environ quarante-cinq ans, elle fai-

sait encore très jeune. Sa peau était fraîche,
ses formes arrondies et fermes.

— Vous êtes de la police?

— Commissaire Maigret. Mon compagnon
est l'inspecteur Fumel.

— Honoré a eu un accident?

— Je vous apporte, en effet, une mauvaise
nouvelle.

Elle ne pleurait pas encore et on sentait
qu'elle essayait de se raccrocher à des mots
sans importance.

— Asseyez-vous. Débarrassez-vous de votre
pardessus, car il fait très chaud ici. Honoré
aime la chaleur. Ne faites pas attention au
désordre...

— Vous l'aimez beaucoup?

Elle se mordait les lèvres, essayant de de-
viner la gravité de la nouvelle.

— Il est blessé?

Puis, presque tout de suite :

— Il est mort?

Elle pleurait enfin, la bouche ouverte, à la
façon des enfants, sans craindre de s'enlaidir.
En même temps, elle se prenait les cheveux à
deux mains et regardait autour d'elle comme
pour chercher un coin où se réfugier.

— J'en ai toujours eu le pressentiment...

— Pourquoi?

— Je ne sais pas... Nous étions trop heureux...

La pièce était confortable, intime, avec des
meubles massifs, de bonne qualité, quelques

bibelots qui n'étaient pas de trop mauvais goût. Par une porte ouverte, on apercevait la cuisine claire où le couvert du petit déjeuner était encore mis.

— Ne faites pas attention... répétait-elle. Excusez-moi...

Elle ouvrait une autre porte, celle de la chambre à coucher non éclairée et où elle se jetait en travers du lit, à plat ventre, pour pleurer à son aise.

Maigret et Fumel se regardaient en silence et l'inspecteur était le plus ému des deux, peut-être parce qu'il n'avait jamais su résister aux femmes, malgré les ennuis qu'elles lui avaient causés.

Cela dura moins longtemps qu'on aurait pu le craindre et elle passa dans la salle de bains, fit couler l'eau, revint, le visage presque détendu, en murmurant :

— Je vous demande pardon. Comment est-ce arrivé?

— On l'a retrouvé mort au bois de Boulogne. Vous n'avez pas lu les journaux des derniers jours?

— Je ne lis pas les journaux. Mais pourquoi le bois de Boulogne? Que serait-il allé y faire?

— Il a été assassiné ailleurs.

— Assassiné? Pour quelle raison?

Elle s'efforçait de ne pas éclater à nouveau en sanglots.

— Il était votre ami depuis longtemps?

— Plus de dix ans.

— Où l'avez-vous connu?

— Tout près d'ici, dans une brasserie.

— *La Régence?*

— Oui. J'y prenais déjà un repas de temps en temps. Je l'ai remarqué, seul dans son coin.

Cela n'indiquait-il pas que, vers cette époque, Cuendet avait préparé un cambriolage dans le quartier? Probablement. En étudiant la liste des vols dont on n'avait pas retrouvé les auteurs, on en trouverait sans doute un commis rue Caulaincourt.

— Je ne me rappelle pas comment nous avons engagé la conversation. Toujours est-il qu'un soir nous avons dîné à la même table. Il m'a demandé si j'étais allemande et je lui ai répondu que j'étais alsacienne. Je suis née à Strasbourg.

Elle souriait d'un sourire pâle.

— Nous nous amusions chacun de l'accent de l'autre, car il avait gardé l'accent vaudois comme j'ai gardé le mien.

C'était un accent agréable, chantant. Mme Maigret aussi était alsacienne et avait conservé à peu près la même taille, le même embonpoint.

— Il est devenu votre ami?

Elle se mouchait sans se soucier de son nez rouge.

— Il n'était pas toujours ici. Il passait rarement plus de deux ou trois semaines avec moi, puis il partait en voyage. Je me suis demandé,

au début, s'il n'avait pas une femme et des
enfants en province. Certains provinciaux re-
tirent leur alliance quand ils viennent à
Paris...

Elle semblait avoir connu d'autres hommes
avant Cuendet.

— Comment avez-vous su que ce n'était pas
son cas?

— Il n'était pas marié, n'est-ce pas?

— Non.

— J'en étais sûre. D'abord, j'ai compris
qu'il n'avait pas d'enfants à lui à la façon dont
il regardait les autres, dans la rue. On le sentait résigné à ne pas être père, mais il en
gardait la nostalgie. En outre, quand il vivait
ici, il ne se comportait pas en homme marié.
C'est difficile à expliquer. Il avait des pudeurs
qu'un homme marié n'a plus. La première fois,
par exemple, j'ai compris qu'il était gêné de
se trouver dans mon lit et il a été encore plus
gêné, le matin, en s'éveillant...

— Il ne vous a jamais parlé de sa profession?

— Non.

— Vous ne la lui avez jamais demandée?

— J'ai essayé de savoir, sans me montrer
indiscrète.

— Il vous disait qu'il voyageait?

— Qu'il était obligé de partir. Il ne préci-
sait ni où il allait, ni pourquoi. Un jour, je lui
ai demandé s'il avait encore sa mère et il a
rougi. Cela m'a donné à penser qu'il vivait

peut-être avec elle. En tout cas, il avait quelqu'un pour raccommoder son linge, ravauder ses chaussettes, et qui ne le faisait pas très soigneusement. Les boutons étaient toujours mal cousus, par exemple, et je le plaisantais.

— Quand vous a-t-il quittée pour la dernière fois?

— Il y a six semaines. Je pourrais retrouver la date...

Elle questionnait à son tour :

— Et quand est-ce que... que cela est arrivé?

— Vendredi.

— Il n'avait pourtant jamais beaucoup d'argent sur lui.

— Quand il venait passer un certain temps avec vous, apportait-il une valise?

— Non. Si vous ouvrez l'armoire, vous trouverez sa robe de chambre, ses pantoufles et, dans un tiroir, ses chemises, ses chaussettes et ses pyjamas.

Elle désignait la cheminée et Maigret apercevait trois pipes, dont une en écume. Ici aussi, il y avait un poêle à charbon, comme rue Mouffetard, un fauteuil près du poêle, le fauteuil d'Honoré Cuendet.

— Excusez mon indiscrétion. Je suis obligé de vous poser la question.

— Je la devine. Vous voulez parler d'argent?

— Oui. Il vous en donnait?

— Il a proposé de m'en donner. Je n'ai pas accepté, car je gagne assez bien ma vie. Tout ce que je lui ai permis, parce qu'il insistait et que cela le mettait mal à l'aise de vivre ici sans payer sa part, c'est de régler la moitié du loyer.

« Il m'offrait des cadeaux. C'est lui qui a acheté les meubles de cette pièce et fait arranger mon salon d'essayage. Vous pouvez le voir... »

Une pièce exiguë, meublée en Louis XVI, avec une profusion de miroirs.

— C'est lui aussi qui a repeint les murs, y compris ceux de la cuisine, et qui a tapissé le living-room, car il adorait bricoler.

— A quoi passait-il ses journées?

— Il se promenait un peu, pas beaucoup, toujours le même tour, dans le quartier, comme les gens qui font prendre l'air à leur chien. Puis, il s'asseyait dans son fauteuil et lisait. Vous trouverez des tas de livres dans l'armoire, presque tous des livres de voyage.

— Vous n'avez jamais voyagé avec lui?

— Nous avons passé quelques jours à Dieppe, la seconde année. Une autre fois, nous sommes allés en vacances en Savoie et il m'a montré les montagnes de Suisse, de loin, en me disant que c'était son pays. Une autre fois encore, nous avons fait Paris-Nice en autocar et visité la Côte d'Azur.

— Il dépensait largement?

— Cela dépend de ce que vous appelez largement. Il n'était pas pingre, mais n'aimait pas

qu'on essaie de le voler et il revoyait les notes
d'hôtel et de restaurant.

— Vous avez passé la quarantaine?

— J'ai quarante-quatre ans.

— Vous avez donc une certaine expérience
de la vie. Vous ne vous êtes jamais demandé
pourquoi il menait cette existence double? Ni
pourquoi il ne vous épousait pas?

— J'ai connu d'autres hommes qui ne m'ont
pas proposé le mariage.

— Du même genre que lui?

— Non, bien sûr.

Elle réfléchissait.

— Je me suis posé des questions, évidemment. Au début, je vous l'ai dit, j'ai cru qu'il
était marié en province et que ses affaires l'ap-
pelaient à Paris, plusieurs fois par an. Je ne
lui en aurais pas voulu. C'était tentant d'avoir,
ici, une femme pour l'accueillir, un intérieur.
Il détestait les hôtels, je l'ai bien vu quand
nous avons voyagé la première fois. Il ne s'y
sentait pas à son aise. Il semblait toujours
craindre quelque chose.

Parbleu!

— Puis, à cause de son caractère et des
reprises à ses chaussettes, j'ai conclu qu'il
vivait avec sa mère et que cela le gênait de me
l'avouer. Plus d'hommes qu'on ne le pense ne
se marient pas à cause de leur mère et, à cinquante ans, sont encore devant elle comme des
petits garçons. C'était peut-être son cas.

— Il fallait cependant qu'il gagne sa vie.

— Il pouvait avoir une petite affaire quelque part.

— Vous n'avez jamais soupçonné une autre sorte d'activité?

— Laquelle?

Elle était sincère. Il était impossible qu'elle joue la comédie.

— Que voulez-vous dire? Maintenant, je suis prête à tout. Qu'est-ce qu'il faisait?

— C'était un voleur, mademoiselle Schneider.

— Lui? Honoré?

Elle riait d'un rire nerveux.

— Ce n'est pas vrai, n'est-ce pas?

— Attendez! Il a volé toute sa vie, depuis l'âge de seize ans, alors qu'il était en apprentissage chez un serrurier de Lausanne. Il s'est enfui d'une maison de redressement, en Suisse, pour s'engager dans la Légion étrangère.

— Il m'a parlé de la Légion quand j'ai découvert son tatouage.

— Il n'a pas ajouté qu'il avait fait deux ans de prison?

Elle s'asseyait, les jambes coupées, écoutait comme si c'était d'un autre Cuendet, pas du sien, pas d'Honoré, qu'on l'entretenait.

De temps en temps, elle hochait la tête, encore incrédule.

— C'est moi-même, mademoiselle, qui l'ai arrêté autrefois et, depuis, il est passé plusieurs fois par mon bureau. Ce n'était pas un voleur ordinaire. Il n'avait pas de complices, ne fréquentait pas le milieu, menait une existence rangée. De temps en temps, il repérait un coup, en lisant les journaux ou les magazines et, pendant des semaines, il observait les allées et venues d'une maison...

« Jusqu'au moment où, sûr de lui, il y pénétrait pour s'emparer des bijoux et de l'argent. »

— Je ne peux pas, non! C'est trop incroyable!

— Je comprends votre réaction. Pourtant, vous ne vous êtes pas trompée au sujet de sa mère. Une partie du temps qu'il ne passait pas ici, il le passait chez elle, dans un logement de la rue Mouffetard où il avait aussi ses affaires.

— Elle sait?

— Oui.

— Elle a toujours su?

— Oui.

— Elle le laissait faire?

Elle n'était pas indignée, mais surprise.

— C'est à cause de ça qu'on l'a tué?

— Plus que probablement.

— La police?

Elle se durcissait, moins cordiale, moins confiante.

— Non.

— Ce sont les gens chez qui... chez qui il voulait voler qui l'ont abattu?

— Je le suppose. Ecoutez-moi bien. Ce n'est pas moi qui suis chargé de l'enquête, mais le

juge d'instruction Cajou. Il a confié un certain
nombre de tâches à l'inspecteur Fumel.

Celui-ci inclinait la tête.

— Ce matin, l'inspecteur est ici officieusement, sans mandat. Vous aviez le droit de ne
pas répondre à mes questions et aux siennes.
Vous pouviez nous empêcher d'entrer chez
vous. Et, s'il nous arrivait de fouiller votre appartement, nous commettrions un abus de pou-
voir. Vous me comprenez?

Non. Maigret sentait qu'elle ne mesurait pas
la portée de ses paroles.

— Je pense...

— Pour être plus précis, tout ce que vous
nous avez confié au sujet de Cuendet ne figu-
rera pas dans le rapport de l'inspecteur. Il est
à prévoir que, quand il découvrira votre existence et vos rapports avec Honoré, le juge
d'instruction vous enverra Fumel ou un autre
inspecteur muni d'un mandat en bonne et due
forme.

— Qu'est-ce que je devrai faire?

— A ce moment-là, vous pourrez réclamer
l'assistance d'un avocat.

— Pourquoi?

— Je dis que vous pourrez. Vous n'y êtes
pas tenue par la loi. Peut-être Cuendet, outre
ses vêtements, ses livres et ses pipes, a-t-il
laissé certaines choses dans votre appartement...

Le yeux bleus exprimaient enfin la compréhension. Trop tard, car Mlle Schneider murmurait déjà, comme pour elle-même :

— La valise...

— Il est normal que, vivant avec vous une partie de l'année, votre ami vous ait confié une valise contenant des effets personnels. Il est normal aussi, qu'il vous en ait laissé la clé en vous recommandant, par exemple, de l'ouvrir s'il lui arrivait quelque chose...

Maigret aurait préféré que Fumel ne soit pas là et, comme s'il s'en rendait compte, l'inspecteur prenait un air absent, maussade.

Quant à Eveline, elle secouait la tête.

— Je n'ai pas la clé... Mais...

— Peu importe, encore une fois. Il n'est pas impensable qu'un homme comme Cuendet ait pris la précaution de rédiger un testament par lequel il vous charge, après sa mort, de certaines missions, ne serait-ce que de prendre soin de sa mère...

— Elle est très âgée?

— Vous la verrez, puisqu'il semble que vous soyez les seules femmes dans sa vie.

— Vous croyez?

Elle en était contente, malgré tout, et ne pouvait s'empêcher de le laisser voir par son sourire. Quand elle souriait, elle avait des fossettes comme une toute jeune fille.

— Je ne sais plus que penser.

— Vous aurez le temps, quand nous serons partis, de penser à votre aise.

— Dites-moi, monsieur le commissaire...

Elle hésitait, soudain rouge jusqu'aux cheveux.

— Il n'a... il n'a jamais tué personne?

— Je peux vous l'affirmer.

— Remarquez que, si vous m'aviez dit oui, j'aurais refusé de vous croire.

— Je vais ajouter quelque chose de plus difficile à expliquer. Cuendet, c'est certain, vivait d'un partie du produit de ses vols.

— Il dépensait si peu!

— Justement. Qu'il ait éprouvé un besoin de sécurité, le besoin de savoir qu'il possédait un magot à sa disposition, c'est possible et même probable. Je ne serais pas surpris pourtant, que, dans son cas, un autre élément ait joué un rôle essentiel.

« Pendant des semaines, je vous l'ai dit, il observait la vie d'une maison... »

— Comment s'y prenait-il?

— En s'installant dans un bistrot, où il passait des heures près de la vitre, en louant une chambre dans un immeuble d'en face lorsqu'il en avait l'occasion...

L'idée que Maigret avait déjà eue venait à l'esprit de la femme.

— Vous croyez que quand j'ai fait sa connaissance, à La Régence...

— C'est vraisemblable. Il n'attendait pas que les appartements soient inoccupés, que les locataires soient sortis. Au contraire! Il attendait, lui, leur retour...

— Pourquoi?

— Un psychologue ou un psychiatre répondraient mieux que moi à cette question. Avait-il besoin de la sensation du danger? Je n'en suis pas si sûr. Voyez-vous, il ne s'introduisait pas seulement dans un appartement étranger mais, en quelque sorte, dans la vie des gens. Ceux-ci dormaient dans leur lit et il les frôlait. C'était un peu comme si, en plus de leur prendre leurs bijoux, il emportait une part de leur intimité...

— On dirait que vous ne lui en voulez pas.

Maigret sourit à son tour et se contenta de grogner :

— Je n'en veux à personne. Au revoir, mademoiselle. N'oubliez rien de ce que je vous ai dit, aucun mot. Pensez-y calmement.

Il lui serra la main, à la grande surprise d'Eveline, et Fumel imita le commissaire, d'une façon plus maladroite, comme s'il était troublé.

Dans l'escalier, déjà, l'inspecteur s'exclamait :

— C'est une femme extraordinaire!

Celui-là reviendrait rôder dans le quartier, même quand tout le monde aurait oublié Honoré Cuendet. C'était plus fort que lui. Il avait déjà sur les bras une maîtresse qui lui compliquait l'existence, et il allait s'ingénier à la compliquer davantage.

Dehors, sur les trottoirs, la neige commençait à tenir.

— Qu'est-ce que je fais, patron?

— Tu as sommeil, non? Entrons toujours prendre un verre.

Il y avait quelques clients, à présent, dans la brasserie où un voyageur de commerce copiait des adresses dans le bottin des professions.

— Vous l'avez trouvée?

— Oui.

— Gentille, hein? Qu'est-ce que je vous sers?

— Pour moi, un grog.

— Pour moi aussi.

— Deux grogs, deux!

— Cet après-midi, quand tu auras dormi, tu rédigeras ton rapport.

— Je parlerai de la rue Neuve-Saint-Pierre?

— Bien entendu, et de la Wilton qui habite en face de l'hôtel Lambert, Cajou te convoquera à son cabinet pour te réclamer des détails.

— Il m'enverra perquisitionner chez Mlle Schneider.

— Où, je l'espère, tu ne trouveras rien, que des vêtements dans une valise.

Malgré son admiration pour le commissaire, Fumel était mal à l'aise et fumait nerveusement sa cigarette.

— J'ai compris ce que vous lui disiez.

— La mère d'Honoré m'a dit : « *Je suis sûre que mon fils ne me laissera pas sans rien.* »

— Elle me l'a répété, à moi aussi.

— Tu verras que le juge n'aura aucune envie de voir cette affaire aller plus loin. Dès qu'il entendra parler des Wilton...

Maigret buvait son grog à petites gorgées, payait les consommations, décidait de prendre un taxi pour retourner à la P. J.

— Je te dépose quelque part?

— Non. J'ai un autobus direct.

Peut-être Fumel, craignant que la jeune femme n'ait pas bien compris, avait-il l'intention de remonter chez elle?

— Au fait! Cette histoire de couverture me tracassse. Continue donc à te renseigner...

Et, les mains dans les poches, Maigret se dirigea vers la station de taxis, place Constantin-Pecqueur, d'où il apercevait les fenêtres de l'inspecteur Lognon.

8

Q<small>UAI DES ORFEVRES,</small>
tout le monde était exténué, aussi bien du
côté des inspecteurs que de celui des hommes
arrêtés pendant la nuit. On était allé chercher les témoins à domicile et on en trouvait
dans tous les coins, certains mal éveillés, de
mauvaise humeur, qui harcelaient Joseph :

— Quand se décidera-t-on à nous entendre?

Qu'est-ce que le vieil appariteur pouvait
leur répondre? Il n'en savait pas plus long
qu'eux.

Le garçon de la brasserie Dauhine apportait une fois de plus un plateau de petits pains
et du café.

Le premier soin de Maigret, en s'installant
dans son bureau, fut d'appeler Moers, qui
n'était pas moins occupé, là-haut, à l'Identité
Judiciaire.

On avait fait sur les mains des quatre hommes le test de la paraffine; autrement dit, si l'un d'eux avait tiré avec une arme quelconque au cours des trois ou quatre jours précédents, on retrouverait, dans la peau, de la poudre incrustée, même s'il avait pris la précaution de se ganter.

— Tu as les résultats?

— Le laboratoire vient de me l'apporter.

— Lequel des quatre?

— Le numéro trois.

Maigret consulta la liste qui portait un numéro en regard de chaque nom. Le n° 3 était Roger Stieb, réfugié tchécoslovaque, qui avait travaillé un certain temps dans la même usine que Joseph Raison, quai de Javel.

— L'expert est formel?

— Absolument.

— Rien chez les trois autres?

— Rien.

Stieb était un grand garçon blond qui, pendant la nuit, s'était montré le plus docile de tous et qui, maintenant encore, en face de Torrence qui le harcelait, regardait l'inspecteur avec flegme comme s'il ne comprenait pas un mot de français.

C'était pourtant le tueur de la bande, chargé de protéger la fuite des assaillants.

L'autre, Loubières, un homme trapu, musclé et velu, originaire de Fécamp, tenait un garage à Puteaux. Il était marié, père de deux enfants, et toute un équipe de spécialistes était occupée à fouiller son établissement.

Chez René Lussac, la fouille n'avait rien donné, non plus que dans la villa de la belle Rosalie.

De tous, celle-ci était la plus bruyante et Maigret entendait ses glapissements, bien qu'elle fût enfermée deux bureaux plus loin en tête à tête avec Lucas.

On avait commencé les confrontations. Les deux garçons de café, impressionnés, n'osaient pas être trop catégoriques, mais croyaient reconnaître en Fernand le client qui se trouvait dans la brasserie au moment du hold-up.

— Vous êtes sûrs d'avoir toute la bande? avaient-ils demandé avant la confrontation.

On leur avait répondu que oui, encore que ce ne fût pas tout à fait vrai. Il manquait un complice, celui qui conduisait l'auto et sur lequel on ne possédait aucune indication.

Celui-ci, comme toujours, devait être un as du volant, mais n'était probablement qu'un comparse.

— Allô!.. Oui, monsieur le procureur... Cela progresse... Nous savons qui a tiré : le nommé Stieb... Il nie, oui... Il niera jusqu'au bout... Ils nieront tous...

Sauf la pauvre Mme Lussac qui, chez elle, s'occupant de son bébé en compagnie de l'Assistante sociale, restait effondrée.

Maigret avait de la peine à garder les paupières ouvertes et le grog de La Régence n'avait rien arrangé. Il lui arriva de saisir, dans son placard, la bouteille de fine qu'il y conservait pour les grandes occasions et, non sans hésiter, d'en avaler une gorgée.

— Allô!... Pas encore, monsieur le juge...

On l'appelait à deux appareils à la fois et il était dix heures vingt, quand il reçut enfin le bon coup de téléphone. Il provenait de Puteaux.

— On a trouvé, patron.

— Tout?

— Il ne manque pas un billet.

On avait laissé annoncer dans les journaux que la banque connaissait les numéros de série des billets volés. C'était faux. Le mensonge n'en avait pas moins empêché les gangsters de mettre l'argent en circulation. Ils attendaient l'occasion d'écouler les billets en province ou à l'étranger; Fernand était assez malin pour ne pas se presser et pour empêcher ses hommes de quitter la ville tant que l'enquête battait son plein.

— Où?

— Dans le capitonnage d'une vieille bagnole. La mère Loubières, qui est une maîtresse femme, ne nous lâchait pas d'un poil...

— Elle paraît être au courant?

— C'est mon avis. On a fouillé les voitures une à une. On les a même quelque peu démontées. Enfin! on tient le paquet!

— N'oublie pas de faire signer Mme Loubières.

— Elle refuse. J'ai essayé.

— Alors, prends des témoins.

— C'est ce que j'ai fait.

Pour Maigret, c'était la fin, ou presque. On n'avait pas besoin de lui pour questionner les témoins et procéder aux confrontations. Il y en avait pour des heures.

Après quoi, chacun des inspecteurs lui ferait son rapport. Et il aurait personnellement un rapport général à établir.

— Passez-moi le procureur Dupont d'Hastier, voulez-vous?

Et, l'instant d'après :

— On a retrouvé les billets.

— La mallette aussi?

Il en demandait trop. Pourquoi pas avec des empreintes digitales bien nettes?

— La mallette flotte quelque part dans la Seine ou a été brûlée dans un calorifère.

— Chez qui a-t-on découvert l'argent?

— Le garagiste.

— Qu'est-ce qu'il dit?

— Encore rien. On ne lui en a pas parlé.

— Veillez à ce que son avocat soit présent. Je ne veux pas de contestations ni, plus tard, d'incidents d'audience.

Quand les couloirs seraient enfin vides, on emmènerait les quatre hommes au Dépôt, la femme Rosalie aussi — pas dans la même pièce — et là, nus comme des vers, ils passeraient à l'anthropométrie. Pour deux d'entre eux au moins, ce n'était pas une expérience nouvelle.

Ils dormiraient vraisemblablement dans une cellule du rez-de-chaussée, car le juge d'instruction tiendrait à les voir le lendemain matin avant de les écrouer à la Santé.

L'affaire ne viendrait devant les assises que dans plusieurs mois et, d'ici là, d'autres bandes auraient le temps de se former, de la même manière, pour des raisons qui ne regardaient pas le commissaire.

Il poussa une porte, puis une seconde, trouva Lucas devant une machine à écrire, tapant à deux doigts, en face d'une Rosalie qui allait et venait, les poings aux hanches.

— Vous voilà, vous! Vous êtes content, hein? L'idée que Fernand était en liberté vous empêchait de dormir et vous vous êtes arrangé pour lui remettre le grappin dessus. Vous n'avez même pas honte de vous en prendre à une femme, oubliant que, jadis, il vous est arrivé de venir boire un verre à mon bar et que vous n'étiez pas fâché que je vous refile des tuyaux...

C'était la seule à n'avoir pas sommeil, à garder son énergie intacte.

— Et vous le faites exprès, pour m'humilier, de me mettre dans les mains du plus petit de vos inspecteurs... Un homme comme ça, moi, je n'en fais qu'une bouchée...

Il ne répondait pas, clignait de l'œil à l'adresse de Lucas.

— Je vais me coucher une heure ou deux. On a trouvé l'argent.

— Quoi? hurlait-elle.

— Ne la laisse pas seule. Appelle n'importe qui, pour lui tenir compagnie, un grand si elle y tient, et installe-toi dans mon bureau.

— Bien, patron.

Il se fit reconduire par une voiture-pie. Il y en avait plein la cour, car on vivait depuis la veille en état de mobilisation générale.

— J'espère que tu te couches? lui dit sa femme en préparant le lit. A quelle heure dois-je t'éveiller?

— Midi et demi.

— Si tôt?

— Il n'eut pas le courage de prendre un bain tout de suite. Il le ferait après avoir dormi. Il commençait à peine à s'assoupir, la tête chaude, quand la sonnerie du téléphone retentit.

Il déploya le bras, grogna :

— Maigret, oui...

— Ici, Fumel, monsieur le commissaire...

— Je te demande pardon. J'étais en train de m'endormir. Où es-tu?

— Rue Marbeuf.

— Je t'écoute.

— J'ai du nouveau. Au sujet de la couverture.

— Tu l'as retrouvée?

— Non. Je doute qu'on la retrouve un jour. Mais elle a existé. Le pompiste de la rue Mar-

beuf est catégorique. Il l'a encore remarquée
il y a une semaine environ.

— Pourquoi l'a-t-il remarquée?

— Parce que c'est rare de voir une couverture, surtout en fourrure, dans une auto de
grand sport...

— Quand l'a-t-il vue pour la dernière fois?

— Il ne peut pas préciser, mais il prétend
qu'il n'y a pas longtemps. Voilà deux ou trois
jours, quand le fils Wilton est venu faire le
plein d'essence, elle n'y était plus.

— Mets ça dans ton rapport.

— Qu'est-ce qui va se passer, selon vous?

Maigret, qui avait hâte d'en finir, se
contenta de laisser tomber :

— Rien!

Il raccrochait. Il avait besoin de sommeil. Il
était d'ailleurs presque sûr de ne pas se
tromper.

Il n'arriverait rien!

Il imaginait l'air pincé du juge d'instruction
si Maigret était allé lui dire :

— Honoré Cuendet, la nuit de vendredi à
samedi, vers une heure, a pénétré dans l'hôtel particulier de Florence Wilton, née Lenoir,
rue Neuve-Saint-Pierre.

— Comment le savez-vous?

— Parce qu'il surveillait la maison depuis
cinq semaines, d'une chambre de l'hôtel Lambert.

— Ainsi, parce qu'un homme prend une

chambre dans un hôtel douteux, vous en concluez...

— Il ne s'agit pas d'un homme quelconque, mais d'Honoré Cuendet qui, depuis bientôt trente ans...

Il décrirait la manière de Cuendet.

— Vous l'avez déjà pris sur le fait?

Maigret était bien obligé d'avouer que non.

— Il avait les clés de l'hôtel particulier?

— Non.

— Des intelligences dans la place?

— C'est peu vraisemblable.

— Et Mme Wilton était chez elle, ainsi que ses domestiques?

— Cuendet ne s'introduisait jamais dans des maisons inoccupées.

— Vous prétendez que cette femme...

— Pas elle. Son amant.

— Comment savez-vous qu'elle a un amant?

— Par une prostituée nommée Olga, qui, elle aussi, habite en face.

— Elle les a vus ensemble dans un lit?

— Elle a vu la voiture.

— Et qui est cet amant?

— Le fils Wilton.

Les images devenaient un peu incohérentes, puisque Maigret voyait le juge ricaner, ce qui seyait mal à son caractère.

— Vous insinuez que cette femme et son beau-fils...

— Le père et la belle-fille ont bien...

— Comment?

Il raconterait l'histoire de Lida, qui avait été la maîtresse du père après avoir épousé le fils.

Voyons! Est-ce que ces choses-là sont possibles? Est-ce qu'un magistrat sérieux, appartenant à la meilleure bourgeoisie de Paris, peut un seul instant admettre...

— J'espère que vous avez d'autres preuves?

— Oui, monsieur le juge...

Il devait dormir, rêver, car il se voyait lui-même, tirant de sa poche un petit sachet dans lequel se trouvaient deux fils à peine visibles.

— Qu'est-ce que c'est que ça?

— Des poils, monsieur le juge.

Encore une indication que c'était un rêve, que ça ne pouvait être qu'un rêve : le magistrat prononçait, cette fois :

— Des poils de qui?

— De chat sauvage?

— Pourquoi sauvage?

— Parce que la couverture, dans l'auto, était en chat sauvage. Cuendet, pour une fois, après une si longue carrière, à dû faire du bruit, renverser un objet, donner l'alarme, et on l'a assommé.

« Les amants ne pouvaient pas appeler la police sans que...

Sans que quoi? Ses idées n'étaient plus très claires. Sans que Stuart Wilton apprenne ce qui se passait, évidemment. Et Stuart Wilton, c'était l'argent...

Ni Florence, ni son amant ne connaissaient cet inconnu qui avait fait irruption dans leur chambre. N'était-ce pas une sage précaution que de le défigurer?

Il avait beaucoup saigné, obligeant le couple à tout nettoyer...

Puis l'auto...

Et là, il avait encore sali la couverture...

— Vous comprenez, monsieur le juge...

Il était là, penaud, avec ses deux poils.

— Et d'abord, qui vous dit que ce sont des poils de chat sauvage?

— Un expert.

— Et un autre expert viendra se moquer de lui à la barre en affirmant que ce sont des poils de je ne sais quel animal...

Le juge avait raison. Cela se passerait ainsi. Il y aurait des éclats de rire.

Et l'avocat, dans un envol de manches :

— Voyons, messieurs, soyons sérieux... Qu'apporte-t-on pour nous accuser... Deux poils...

Cela pourrait se dérouler autrement, bien sûr. Maigret irait par exemple sonner chez Florence Wilton. Il lui poserait des questions, furèterait dans la maison, interrogerait les domestiques.

Il aurait aussi, dans le silence de son bureau, une longue conversation avec le jeune Wilton.

Seulement, tout cela n'était pas réglementaire.

— En voilà assez, Maigret. Oubliez ces fantaisies et emportez ces poils...

Il s'en fichait, d'ailleurs. Est-ce que, tout à l'heure, il n'avait pas adressé un clin d'œil à Fumel?

L'inspecteur aux amours malheureuses, réussirait-il mieux avec Eveline qu'avec les autres femmes?

En tout cas, la vieille, rue Mouffetard, ne s'était pas trompée.

— *Je connais mon fils... Je suis sûre qu'il ne me laissera pas sans rien...*

Combien d'argent y avait-il dans la...?

Maigret dormait profondément.

On ne le saurait jamais.

FIN

Noland, le 23 janvier 1961.

Achevé d'imprimer le 2 mars 1982
sur les presses de l'Imprimerie Bussière
à Saint-Amand (Cher)

— Nº d'édit. 1492. — Nº d'imp. 355. —
Dépôt légal : 2ᵉ trimestre 1967.
Imprimé en France